Israel Galindo

The Hidden Lives of Congregations

Understanding Congregational Dynamics

THE ALBAN INSTITUTE

Herndon, Virginia
www.alban.org

Scripture quotations, unless otherwise noted, are from the New Revised Standard Version of the Bible, copyright © 1989, Division of Christian Education of the National Council of the Churches of Christ in the United States of American and are used by permission.

Scripture quotations from the Good News Bible—Today's English Version (TEV) are copyright © 1992 by the American Bible Society and used by permission.

Scripture quotations from the Holy Bible—Contemporary English Version (CEV) are copyright © 1995 by the American Bible Society and used by permission.

Scripture quotations from the Holy Bible—King James Version (KJV) are copyright © 1999 by the American Bible Society and used by permission.

Cover design: Adele Robey, Phoenix Graphics

Library of Congress Cataloging-in-Publication Data

Galindo, Israel.
    The hidden lives of congregations : understanding church dynamics / Israel Galindo.
        p.   cm.
    Includes bibliographical references.
    ISBN 1-56699-307-5
    1. Pastoral care. 2. Pastoral psychology. 3. Systemic therapy (Family therapy)
I. Title.

    BV4011.3.G34 2004
    250—dc22

                                        2004018051

    08   07   06   05   VG   2   3   4   5   6   7   8   9   10

Contents

*To Lawrence E. Matthews, with appreciation and affection,
and to Bruce Merkle, who keeps me informed.*

Foreword

WHEN I GRADUATED FROM SEMINARY MORE THAN 38 YEARS AGO, I thought I knew what my work in the church would be and how I would do it. It took only a few board meetings and worship services for me to question, "What am I doing here? How am I ever going to get a handle on this place?" I was overwhelmed and uncertain about how to proceed. It would have been a tremendous gift to have had this book by Israel Galindo, on *The Hidden Lives of Congregations.*

It is easy for us as pastors and church leaders to get caught up in the immediate issues and daily challenges of congregational life which, one shot at a time, can build the level of anxiety in us and in our congregations. Dr. Galindo puts these issues into the context of "the bigger picture." The last twenty years have seen the publication of several useful congregational studies. He has assimilated many of them, given them his own slant, and integrated them into one very helpful volume. He gives us a wide-angle view of church life that brings these specific, daily issues into better focus.

Dr. Galindo, a professor at Baptist Theological Seminary at Richmond, brings into the daylight "hidden" aspects of congregational life that affect the message and mission of the church. These hidden elements are powerful dynamics that range from the stage in the organizational life cycle of a congregation, to its stage of faith, to the emotional forces described by family systems theory. Each chapter helps to build an assessment of the local congregation and gives specific implications for leadership.

Dr. Galindo's approach centers on congregations as "living organisms" that grow and develop. Throughout the book, he contrasts this organic view of congregational life, consistent with thinking about the church as the Body of Christ, with the business-oriented models of corporate life that have recently influenced thinking about church ministry and our standards for measuring success. His organic approach is more biblically based, theologically sound, and appropriate to what the church is about.

Dr. Galindo thinks about congregations as emotional relationship systems. He shows how the hidden processes of "homeostasis and differentiation," along with the separateness and togetherness forces, affect congregational life. His work does not focus on individual members, or pastors as "stars," but he sees the overall interdependent mix of members and pastors, within their unique setting, as establishing the character of the local church.

Starting with the earliest churches, those "called out" (the *ekklesia*) from their Jewish and Greek communities, Dr. Galindo shows how cultural and natural human life forces began to affect the church early in its development and how these forces have continued to shape congregational life today. Our faith will become secondary to these hidden forces unless we intentionally create a formation process that goes counter to our cultural setting.

Dr. Galindo's concluding chapters on leadership are worth the price of the book by themselves. A believer in longer pastoral tenures, he suggests that it may take about five years to get to know a congregation well enough to articulate a vision of ministry. This seems exactly right to me. During that time, the pastor can become an accurate observer of the congregation, get to know the subterranean forces at work, and make a solid connection with the leaders and members, finding out what "church" means to them. It is also critical that the pastor find ways to honor and respect the members of this church and what they have created over time. Within this context, the pastor then courageously upholds a vision for mission and ministry that fits that specific congregation.

Dr. Galindo identifies some of the personality-centered myths of leadership and challenges the expert "I know what you need to do" stance that some clergy assume. He offers a view of leadership that starts with his understanding of the book of Proverbs. He sees the leader as a person with God-given strengths of character and virtue who guards against the cultural erosion of the church's faith and values.

Stemming from his understanding of family systems theory, Dr. Galindo mentions a number of personal skills pastors need to cultivate; for example, developing greater tolerance for the pain and anxiety of church members so we do not inappropriately rush in to rescue them. The members' own anxiety can lead them to discover their ministry, and the consultant/coach pastor can simply be with them as they work through their struggle. This means "pastoral care" extends to the larger system of the church and not just to individual members.

Since power is about the ability to "influence" others, not the ability to control them, Dr. Galindo suggests the teaching role of the pastor is critical to being a good leader. Too many pastors have backed away from doing much teaching. (Incidentally, Dr. Galindo has a reputation as an outstanding Christian educator. Larry Matthews, founder of the Leadership in Ministry program, says Israel Galindo "is the best Christian educator I know.")

This book is full of provocative ideas about the nature of the church, the way it really functions, and how to lead it out of its cultural captivity. It gives us the fundamental questions we must address if we want to live as the Body of Christ in the world. It will be valuable to pastors and churches across the theological spectrum from Evangelical to Unitarian.

The Hidden Lives of Congregations is an antidote to the malaise that has infected many church leaders and pastors. It is stimulating to have so much valuable material gathered together to help focus our ministry in the church. The Alban Institute has given us many useful books that further our understanding of ministry in the local congregation and this is one of their best. It will be a valuable tool for many years to come.

Ronald W. Richardson

Acknowledgments

SPECIAL THANKS TO THE FOLLOWING FRIENDS AND COLLEAGUES for helping make this a better book: Steve Booth, Marty Canaday, Patricia Clement, Alex Gonzalez, Terry Maples, Jonathan Messer, Dave McNeely, Burdette Robinson, and, always, Barbara. A special acknowledgement to my editor on this book, David Lott, whose editorial eagle eye and sharp thinking made this a better work. Thanks also to the members of G.R.A.C.E., for their encouragement and collegiality.

Introduction

DURING A CONSULTATION WITH A CHURCH STAFF AND DIACONATE, I attempted to guide that leadership group in getting "unstuck" about a conflict with which they had been dealing for some months. In this process, I was struck once again at how difficult it is for congregational leaders, whether they are clergy or laypersons, to "see below the surface" in order to understand what really is going on in the life of their congregation. Over the course of two hours, however, this motivated group (pain is a big motivator!) was able to work past surface issues and symptoms and begin to come to grips with the dynamics that were at play in their church. Once they understood the relational dynamics that informed the conflict that had gripped their congregation, they were quickly able to get clear about their appropriate responses and to plot a course of action.

At the heart of much of what troubles congregations today is a continued failure to understand the corporate nature of congregational relationships and the underlying, often invisible, dynamics at play therein. In the press of day-to-day ministry and periodic conflict, clergy and congregational leaders tend to deal only with surface issues and symptoms. This leads to a reactive, rather than a proactive, approach to ministry and congregational leadership. Lacking awareness of the underlying dynamics of congregational life, leaders cannot provide vision, manage crises, or move a congregation from being stuck to moving forward. Instead, clergy and lay leaders can only hope to ride the wave of momentum in good times or weather the fickle ill winds of occasional and recurring crises.

The thesis of *The Hidden Lives of Congregations* is that congregations are living organisms that follow universal principles of systemic relationships. Understanding these principles and the processes that operate in congregations will help clergy and lay leaders to better understand two things. First, leaders will discover how a congregation works and why it sometimes doesn't work. Second, leaders will have a clearer understanding of their leadership roles within the congregation. Being able to see below the surface and identify the hidden lives of their congregations, leaders can be more discerning about the dynamics at play in congregational relationships and about how to respond effectively.

Despite decades of gloomy predictions about the decline and demise of churches—particularly mainline Protestant churches—reality contradicts the ecclesiastical dystopia that seems popular among critics of the organized church. Currently, in our so-called post-denominational and secularized society, just under half of the American population gathers weekly in over 350,000 congregations to worship, learn, fellowship, participate in ministries and mission, and to give over $10 billion a year to their churches and to church-related charitable causes.[1] And while it remains true that congregations—as a form of the institutionalized church—have never fully realized the full expression of what they "should" be, it is true also that the local church is where the theology of the Body of Christ is most incarnate today. Persons attend congregations because there, through their membership and participation, they find a sustaining community of faith, receive affirmation and care, and experience love as well as challenge. Congregations perpetuate enduring values and beliefs that people need to help inform their lives and provide a sanctuary for healing and restoration in response to the brokenness and fragmentation that come from the hard edges of the world.

A key to understanding a congregation is to appreciate that although it is made up of individuals, it is, in essence, a corporate entity. A congregation is a true expression of Church, grounded in the nature of the Christian faith, which in itself is a corporate phenomenon, not an individual one. As theological educator C. Ellis Nelson put it, "The individual is the basic reality of our conscious life, but . . . the Christian faith is rooted in a local community where people share the meaning of faith and organize to do God's will in the world."[2]

This book carries some defining assumptions about congregations. First, it is grounded in an understanding of a congregation as a particular kind of social, relational, and religious institution—a localized, unique, and institutionalized religious expression of the Church. While a congregation is a legitimate and authentic expression of Church, at the same time, it is not equivalent to it. The local congregation is subject to hidden life forces that affect its temporal and contextual setting. As such, it is both a limited and self-limiting relationship organism rather than an eternal organization. Congregations are particular in that they are unique social institutions. They are gathering places for people who share particular faith stances and beliefs shaped by the cultural circumstances of their life patterns—some of which are more overtly "Christian" than others.

Second, congregations have a corporate identity that is the result of their context: the history of the congregation, its locale, the size and style of the congregation, and its leadership—both clergy and laypersons. In addition, the congregation's corporate identity finds its source in dynamic relational forces, rather than static objects or conditions. Therefore, this book's emphasis is on the corporate nature of congregations and congregational leadership, rather than on how congregations affect the individual players in the congregation. This is because of the not so self-evident reality that a congregation is primarily a corporate relationship organism rather than an organization merely made up of individual members.

The third assumption is that congregations are complex, multilayered, intergenerational, and multigenerational institutional relationship systems. These dynamics, which I call the "hidden lives of congregations," generate a congregation's corporate identity. In turn, the identity informs the nature of a congregation's corporate relationships, and relationship is what shapes faith.

Congregational leaders ignore the hidden life of the congregation to their own peril, and to the detriment of the congregation. Leaders too often make ministry and mission decisions with little attention to the way these hidden life forces both potentially and actually impact those decisions. In doing so, they fail to tap into the very forces that can inform appropriate, healthy, and authentic practices of the congregation.

Part one of the book provides foundational issues about the congregation as Church, including its mandate and an understanding of the nature of a congregation. Part two focuses on the hidden life of congregations. The four chapters that make up this section identify and examine the hidden lives of congregations and explicate how they impact the members and leaders of the local church. The final part of the book focuses on the leaders in the congregation. These final chapters will highlight how congregational leaders, the pastors and the lay leaders, need to understand and focus their leadership functions in light of the hidden lives of congregations.

PART ONE

Understanding the Congregation

THIS FIRST PART OF THE BOOK IS INTENDED TO BE FOUNDATIONAL. That is, it will provide an orientation for how to understand the congregational dynamics explored in the rest of the book. As an educator, I stress to my students that in order for "deep understanding" to take place, in whatever enterprise, one needs to be informed by theory. In order to have a "deep understanding" of congregations (a very complex enterprise), for example, one needs to be informed by theology, a theory of organizations, and a theory of relationships. In this book I'll strive for a biblical theology of Church, though I'll confess that theology has a bias toward a Protestant understanding.

In terms of a theory of organization and relationships, I am informed by Bowen family systems theory (BFST). Those who are familiar with Bowen systems' application to congregations in the works of Edwin Friedman, Peter Steinke, Ronald Richardson, Roberta Gilbert, and others will recognize it. This is not a book *about* family systems theory, but it may be a good example of how theory can inform how one interprets the object under consideration—in this case, the congregation. For example, Bowen family systems theory challenges our understanding of congregational dynamics because it redefines one's understanding of the nature of leadership, and therefore of what it means to be a leader in the congregational setting. In terms of relationships, it provides an understanding of what really is going on in the emotional processes of being a congregation and living out what that means.

Simply put, family systems theory informs my understanding of a congregation as an emotional relationship system—which is, after all, what a faith community is. This is why a congregation is best understood as a system of relationships, much like a family, despite its corporate organization. Rabbi and therapist Edwin H. Friedman highlighted this fact in his now classic book, *Generation to Generation*, in which he applied the family dynamics concepts of Bowen family systems theory to congregations.[1] The emotional processes in a congregation, which in

7

great part impact all of the components of the hidden lives of congregations that we will explore, parallel those of a nuclear family system. This
is, in part, because the rules that govern emotional processes are universal in relationship systems. Bowen family systems theory strives to be
"scientific" and as such, concerns itself with "observable facts," so it
does not delve into theological, ecclesiological, philosophical, or moral
issues per se. That does not mean, however, that family systems theory
cannot inform, or be useful to, congregational leaders who do claim a
faith stance.

For example, clinical psychology as a discipline does not concern
itself with "sin," either theologically or morally. But its discipline has in
one sense redefined and helped us understand better some aspects of
human behavior. The result is that certain human behaviors that we
once categorized or understood as "sin" or as a "moral deficit" we now
understand, from a religious orientation, to be disassociated from a moral
framework. We still attempt to help people deal with those behaviors,
but do not condemn the person for it, and are now better able to "condemn the sin but love the person."

Theories, by definition and nature, are not "about" creating or undo-
ing anything, and Bowen family systems theory applied to congregations is not about getting people to do things or to make things happen.
Neither is it about "making the system less anxious," though that tends
to be a common misunderstanding. Unfortunately, I still hear that misconception often, even from "experts" in systems theory—stated usually
along the line that the leader's job in the system is to "lower the anxiety."
It isn't. So, this will not be a "how-to" book. Theories are schemas that
help us understand the world more accurately by getting to the essential ways that "things actually are." However, theories are applied in various forums—in the case of Bowen family systems theory, for example, it
has found application in therapy, counseling, organizations, leadership,
and more specific to our concern, in congregational relationships and
systems.

Choosing the specific context of a congregation for our focus will
help us more accurately see the benefits of "applied theory." We will do
this by giving attention to the fundamental and universal principles that
the theory provides. For example, the theory helps us understand that as
the church finds its communal expression in a congregational form, it
provides intimacy in relationship (the church as a "family"), but it also
requires structures that make it more permeable than a biological nuclear
family allows. For one thing, congregations need to be forward-looking
in their perspective, which entails being willing, at times, to leave the
past—including values, property, and relationships—in order to realize

a vision and to fulfill its mission, in ways a family cannot. A family that does that disintegrates, but a congregation that does not do that stagnates. The hidden life force of institutional organization (described in part two), for example, provides the rationality for the congregational structures beyond the primary emotional dynamics that lie at the heart of it. It is through this organizational dynamic that a congregation can be future-oriented and make courageous decisions. The organizing force is what can facilitate those management processes that both respect and celebrate traditions and practices and can foster intimacy, while helping the congregation remain resilient enough to weather challenges and changes in the course of its institutional and communal development.

I need to make one other important clarification about nomenclature at the outset of this discussion. Throughout the book I intentionally use the terms "Church," "church," and "congregation" to designate aspects of the subject at hand. When referring to the ideal, the cosmic reality, the "mystery" (as Paul called it), and the theological concept of God's intent, I use the capitalized "Church," (or, "church with a big 'C,'" as my students wind up saying). "Church" with a capital "C" may be thought of, for example, as equivalent to the theological concept of the Kingdom of God. When referring to a local church, either ideally or particularly, then I use the term "church" (or, as my students say, "church with a little 'c'"). Mostly, however, I will reference the "congregation," which is, as I will explain, a local, organized, institutionalized, and authentic expression of Church, but not equivalent to it. At some points the distinction between Church and congregation will be critical to one's understanding. At other times, there will be a more subtle distinction between church and congregation. The primary focus in this book, however, will be on the congregation—what it is, how it works, and how to understand it.

Chapter 1

The Ideal and the Reality

I ARRIVED AT MY OFFICE AT THE SEMINARY CAMPUS AFTER THREE days of travel and conferences. Reluctantly, I looked at the phone, knowing that I'd have to cull through a number of messages in my voice mail before I'd be able to begin clearing the pile of mail on my desk. After getting a cup of coffee from the faculty lounge—more as a gesture of procrastination than a desire for the desultory effects of caffeine—I settled down to listen to the string of voice mails.

The third voice message caught my attention immediately. It was a cryptic message from Allen, a former student, asking that I call him back as soon as I was able. The tone of his voice suggested that what he had to share was bad news. Despite his attempt at sounding calm, the pain in his voice was impossible to hide. Given what I knew of his church situation, I could guess at what that bad news must be. This was Allen's first church right out of seminary. Typical of so many "first church" opportunities for young, inexperienced pastors, this was a small, rural church still made up primarily of three or four key extended families—some of which were "founding families" of the congregation. Like many rural churches they were facing the challenge of encroachment from an explosion of suburban development. Their once tight-knit community was now becoming the far-end bedroom community for professionals with a daily thirty-mile commute into the city. Add into that mix a young, inexperienced, but enthusiastic pastor still running on the idealism of an affirmative seminary experience, and you've got a potential train wreck.

I pressed the cancel button on the voice messages and immediately called my former student. He soon confirmed what I suspected. At the end of a Wednesday evening Bible study, the deacons presented him with a list of grievances and asked for his resignation. Allen was taken completely by surprise. There had been little warning that anything like this would happen during what he thought was a routine church Bible study. Allen had been pastor at that congregation less than two years. We talked for about 20 minutes—or rather, he talked and I commiserated.

A week later, Allen was feeling a bit better than when he first called and left another message on my voice mail. The passing of time and some supportive conversations with colleagues had buffered the initial shock of that evening when he'd felt like he'd been "kicked in the stomach." I called him back, and we agreed to meet for lunch in a few days.

After I hung up the phone I remembered his installation service at that church. It was an occasion marked by joy, hope, and great expectations. The upbeat service was followed by a church dinner. Visiting with the friendly and down-to-earth folks of Allen's new congregation I could not help but feel envious at the palpable sense of family and community as we talked and enjoyed the covered-dish meal on the church grounds. A Hollywood director wanting to capture the American icon of "church" could not have scripted a better afternoon.

So what went wrong? What could Allen have done to cause the church to go from hopeful enthusiasm to such a level of frustration so as to call for his resignation in less than two years? The sad truth is that, aside from suffering the sin of the naïveté of a young and inexperienced minister, Allen had not done anything wrong. He was just a victim of what I call the hidden lives of congregations.

The Church as Congregation

The fact is, despite notions to the contrary, there's nothing sacred about the way we've chosen to do church. What we call a "congregation" is just one culturally scripted expression of Church (with a capital "C"). And while a congregation is an authentic institutional *expression* of Church, it is not *equivalent* to Church. In other words, a congregation is a created, localized form of a more essential and universal entity, namely, the religious community. As researcher Penny Edgell Becker puts it, "Congregational models are a specific example within the institutional field of American religion, of a more general phenomenon. . . , the *institutional model* of the group or organization."[1]

Because congregations are organic relationship systems, they have "hidden lives" comprised of forces and dynamics that operate below the surface. These dynamics are "hidden" in the sense that they are not directly observable, even to those who are part of the congregational relationship system. In fact, it may be argued that these hidden lives are *especially* invisible to those who are in the system. While we cannot directly see these dynamics and forces, we can recognize their effects. If we know what to look for, we can see how these forces get played out in the way the congregational members make decisions, get stuck on issues, and relate to one another and to those outside of the congregation.

These hidden lives of congregations also impact how a congregation relates to the pastor and other congregational leaders. The hidden life forces can help or hinder a minister's ability to lead a congregation if she or he is not aware of "what's really going on" under the surface. As far as my former student, Allen, was concerned, everything looked great on the surface. Allen was doing all the things he knew to do based on his seminary training and on his experience in the business world. No slacker, if Allen had a fault it was one common to many in the pastorate— overfunctioning. If he failed it wasn't because he was not doing enough, but more likely because he was taking too much of the responsibility that belonged to the church members. Further, it wasn't that he wasn't doing the right things. Compounding Allen's pain at being asked to resign from his first church was the confusion he felt when, upon reviewing what he had done and how he had gone about providing pastoral care during his short tenure, he realized that he'd done nothing wrong. Aside from a few minor and benign "mistakes" and blunders, there was nothing he would do different.

The Ideal

The picture of what a congregation as Church *should* be seems to be a commonly shared ideal. We want a congregation to be a loving community with a feeling of family, where everyone is welcomed and strangers can find a home. It's a place where, to paraphrase a popular TV theme song, "everybody knows your name and everybody's glad you came."

The ideal we hold dear for a congregation is that it is engaged in transformative mission in its immediate neighborhood, a place that is well regarded and influential in the civic environment, whose opinion in the public square is weighty, respected, and counts for something. We want congregations to be places where a pastor and his or her family find immediate acceptance and enjoy a supportive community. We want congregational members to be courageous people who respond to their leader's prophetic challenges to be the authentic people of God at church, at home, and in the world. We think of congregations as being one of the few places in our society where concerns about mission win over concerns about money or convenience. In our most optimistic days, we think of congregations as places where (with apologies to Garrison Keillor), "all the members are faithful, all the deacons are good looking, and all the tithes are above average."

But this is wishful thinking. The fact of the matter is that the church has never realized its ideal in whatever epoch it has existed or in whatever forms it has taken. The high calling of congregations is to model a religious life as alternative, countercultural communities in the face of their prevailing cultural settings—a calling they continually fail to realize.[2] The hidden life forces we will examine in this book are evident as early as the first recorded biblical episodes of the church. From the crises that led to the Jerusalem Council in the book of Acts, to the accounts of less than harmonious church relationships in Paul's epistles, we see evidence that the hidden life forces affect the way churches work and live (I'll discuss this historical evidence more in chapter 2).

In the case of Allen's congregation, these perennial dynamics that Allen was not able to see meant that he was powerless to address them, and eventually, they led to his shocked realization that his leadership was not being accepted by the members. Allen's enthusiastic, future-oriented vision for change, for example, caused anxiety surrounding change, and was felt as a threat and perceived as a lack of appreciation for the church's traditions. His reaching out to newcomers, while in response to what the church said it wanted, caused a fear of a loss of identity and intimacy. His confidence in his calling as pastor was often perceived as a lack of appreciation for the matriarchs and patriarchs in the church.

The Reality

In a very real sense, every congregation shares the same mission: to be the living manifestation of the Body of Christ, to engage in religious practices (worship, prayer, ministry to others, and so forth), to perpetuate the faith through educational enterprises, and to be a redeeming presence for its members and for its surrounding community and the world. Congregational members can be very clear about this. When asked, almost all church members, no matter what their tenure—recent convert or lifelong member—will be able to articulate what a congregation "should" be about. Pressed beyond personal perspectives, causes, and needs for intimacy from their church, most members can articulate a surprisingly sophisticated theological understanding of the Church's redemptive mission in the world. At the same time, however, the church faces some challenges that highlight the disparity between what the church "should" be and what it actually is.

Alarming indicators of the actual state of affairs with congregations continue to challenge clergy and denominational leaders. According to the Barna researchers, only 43 percent of American adults attended church in a typical weekend in 2002. The median adult attendance per church service continues to drop; from 1998 to 1999, the average number of adult attendees fell from 95 to 90.[3] Additionally, the church continues to be affected by longstanding, unresolved challenges that translate into a crisis of relevance. Among the more prevalent, are those identified below:

The Church has all but lost its voice in the public square. The metaphorical wall of separation between church and state continues to grow higher and less porous—so much so that genuine dialogue between civic and ecclesial bodies has all but ceased. Additionally, where once the voice of the church and of her clergy were a *de facto* and welcomed presence in the public square, in some areas the role of the church in the life of civic communities has gone from being impatiently tolerated to being resisted with a level of antagonism never before seen in a country whose founding influences were decidedly religious. Ministering in the insular world of congregational ministry, most local church pastors may not experience this reality until the day they attempt to present building plans or request expansion permits to their local community zoning boards. Suddenly, formerly quiet and unseen neighbors become vehemently vocal about the undesirability of having a church presence in their neighborhood. Formerly a center of the community, the local congregation and its campus is now perceived as an unwelcome neighbor that potentially threatens to lower property values rather than contribute to the health and welfare of the community.

Conversely, the community's influence on the local congregation is tremendous. The destiny of most congregations is in great part determined by the fortunes and conditions of its immediate environment, including the population's quality of life, cultural values, and the changes that affect them. Most congregational leaders and members seem oblivious to this truth, perhaps because a congregation ultimately can do little to impact its civic environment financially and socially. The loss of the church's prophetic voice and its inability to address the needs of a declining neighborhood in concrete ways makes it vulnerable to its immediate context.

Congregations continue to adopt a business model for measuring success. During a tour of megachurches and megachurch wannabes a couple of years ago, I witnessed what seems to be a trend in that model of congregation. The majority of the full-time pastoral staff members of all of the churches I visited did not have formal theological education. Most were called out of their church membership and hired not for their theological training but for their business experience and managerial expertise.

Marketing and resource management are the new "pastoral skills" in demand as some congregations adopt a niche-market approach to ministry. Denominations and independent churches now embrace wholeheartedly and uncritically the corporation structure that was resisted by theological purists. And yet, despite the resource management and development approach to congregational development, any talk of the importance of tithing as a spiritual discipline for the average congregational member remains little more than myth. The average giving remains at or below 3 percent of income.[4] Even when adopting a business model for development, churches are playing a losing game—they seem unable to develop the giving potential of their clientele. But even more theologically tragic, the current use of business approaches like a niche-market approach to "outreach" and congregational development too often denies community and leaves out the poor, needy, and disenfranchised, purportedly because the people we do things *for* are never a part of the church. We seem to be willing to minister to the dependent and disenfranchised, but show a great reluctance in welcoming them into our churches to be a part of us.

Congregations resist embracing the countercultural mandate of the gospel. Hand in hand with the success model of congregational development comes a resistance to the perception of the church as being countercultural. The name of the game is accommodation. As congregations try to reach new members, their worship formats, preaching styles, programming, and facilities are shaped and crafted so as to feel "familiar" and "nonthreatening" to prospective church members. Churches fear that if they appear to be out of touch with the surrounding popular culture they will be seen as irrelevant. Few church leaders seem able to grasp the inherent paradox in this perpetual attempt to attract those outside the church by appearing to be "just like you." Those who are who are on the outside looking in, needing what the Church has to offer a hurting world, might well ask, "What's the difference?"

Congregations spend more money on institutional maintenance than on missional endeavors. I often tell my seminary students that a congregation has two primary, operational theological documents: the worship bulletin and the church budget. When you look at these two documents you can pretty much assess what the functional theology of a local congregation is. Regardless of what the mission or vision statement hanging in the church foyer may say, what a church actually believes and practices is summed up accurately in those two living documents. In the typical congregation, after staff salaries and personnel expenses, the biggest chunk of the budget is spent on property and institutional maintenance. The amount of budget resources available for educational and missional programming leaves staff and lay leaders with just enough to get by, and little, if anything, for "development." A committed church may maintain a "tithe" for missions, but even that will be dependent on giving trends—and in times of hardship, missions giving often is deferred as paying the bills becomes an issue.

The level of energy and attention required for institutional maintenance in most congregations means that even the most fundamental mission of the church often takes a back seat. This is understandable, since people's sense of ownership in their faith community and their level of commitment—in participation and in financial giving—are closely tied. People who find community in their congregation are deeply attached to it, and they will invest first in what they know best and in what they perceive meets their spiritual and personal needs.[5]

Because congregations are institutional, they fall prey to the hidden life forces inherent to organizations. One of the most powerful of the hidden life forces is the congealing effect of settling into a maintenance mentality more focused on self-preservation than on mission. Author and denominational leader Eddie Hammett, in *Making the Church Work*, lists some indicators that give evidence of a church's drift into a maintenance posture:

- When committee meetings focus on institutional concerns (budgets, maintenance, and relationships) rather than on mission concerns (reaching new people groups, reconciling relationships,rallying to change the injustices in the community and/or world);
- When budget planning begins with what we have to work with rather than what God has in mind for us;
- When annual planning consists of doing what we did last year, just on another calendar date (or maybe even on the same date one year later);
- When most conversations revolve around meeting the needs of those in attendance rather than reaching those who are not in attendance;
- When planning, budgeting, and calendaring revolve around institutional buildings and schedules rather than around the needs, conveniences, and comfort zones of those outside the organization;
- When preserving programs, traditions, and rituals get more meeting time, dialogue time, and budget than creating and resourcing new strategies to reach the unchurched, lost, and broken world;

- When people's intent and energy focus more on humoring those in the pew than on penetrating their communities, families, and workplaces for the cause of Christ.[6]

There is a crisis of ministerial leadership in the church. Aside from the much-discussed issue of the "clergy shortage" that denominations anticipate (and which some are currently experiencing), a more immediate crisis of leadership in congregations has to do with effectiveness. Symptomatic of this is the chilling reality that the average tenure of a pastor in a congregation continues to decline. Two decades ago the average pastor's tenure was about seven years. Today, it's less than five years.[7] This is sobering, given that most pastors will not even begin to be able to lead a congregation in making essential changes in structure, vision, and processes until well into their tenth year of ministry in one place.[8]

One common misunderstanding that plays into the hidden lives dynamics is the idea that pastoral *competence* is synonymous with pastoral *effectiveness*. Ministers can be very competent at what they do—preaching, counseling, administering, teaching, and so forth. But performing those typical ministerial tasks well does not necessarily translate into being effective in providing congregational leadership.

Another challenge faced by congregations—related to the hidden life of congregations we will examine in part two—is the need to attain and maintain a homeostatic state of affairs. Such is the power of homeostasis that congregational leaders who are charged with bringing about healthy change by prodding the church toward prophetic relevance soon find themselves in collusion with the system to maintain order and ensure the status quo. In many congregations, this resistance to change is overt. In most congregations, however, this reality is communicated more subtly, often through sabotage, resistance, or lack of cooperation and support for any effort on the part of leadership to challenge the members toward fulfilling their mission mandate. It does not take long for a pastor to understand the unspoken contract that exists between the leaders and the congregation. Author and pastor C. John Miller puts it bluntly when he says that this contract between the clergy and the congregation "states that the congregation will support, honor, and pay the pastor and [spouse] as long as they are inspiring yet dignified, sweet but saltless. In return the pastor . . . is expected to do all the real work of the local church—that is, he [or she] is expected to do his [or her] own work and everyone else's too."[9]

We may not want to admit that there exists such a disparity between the ideal and the reality in our congregations, but confession is the first step toward bridging the gap between the ideal and the reality. So let's confess that the reality is that congregations may not be representing the Church well.

The Fundamental Misunderstanding: Organization vs. Organism

The fundamental trap that hinders our being able to realize the power and reality of the Church in congregations is the continuing tension of the very real and fundamental dichotomy between the Church needing to exist as an *organism* and the congregation trying to be Church as an *organization*. I believe that congregational leaders who continually fail to discern this fundamental distinction will also be unable to recognize the impact that the hidden dynamics of congregational life have on their leadership effectiveness. Such congregational leaders fall into the common trap of trying to fix organic relational problems through administrative means. The corollary is the beginning teacher's naïve attempt to correct a class-management problem by using an instructional technique. It just doesn't work, because using a novel teaching method cannot address the systemic relational causes of a class-management problem. Likewise, attempting to fix a budget problem by administering a stewardship campaign while ignoring the reality that stewardship is a spiritual issue related to the members' relationships with God and with each other is doomed to failure.

The problem is not that we don't know better, of course. We regularly teach children that the Church is the people and not the building. And we periodically preach sermons on the theology of the Body of Christ. And yet the tension between the Church as organism and the congregation as institution continues to challenge our ability to be effective in realizing the Church's mission and purpose. While we may embrace a community of faith metaphor for our shared identity, when it comes to decision making we organize ourselves more like a company with a CEO and board of directors. The more theological concept of corporate "discernment" hardly even comes into play in most congregations when there is a problem to solve or a decision to be made. *Robert's Rules of Order* and by-laws usually dictate how congregations "do business." This bears little semblance to a community process where discernment is the patient process of discerning the corporate will of the people and the will of God, and where the dissenting voices are encouraged and listened to because of the realization that such voices, however unpleasant to hear, often are prophetic.

The hidden lives of congregations has to do with the reality that a congregation is an organism—despite our best efforts to unwittingly organize the life out of a living thing, or to program the messiness out of a very human enterprise. Until our thinking about being the Church changes from an institutional organization that we grow and manage, to a relationship system that we need to nurture and develop, we will fail to appreciate the power of the unseen dynamics at work in the congregation. In the next chapter we'll examine the nature of congregations as Church as a prelude to examining the hidden lives of congregations.

Chapter 2

The Congregation as Church

WHAT IS A CONGREGATION? ONE ACCURATE DEFINITION—THOUGH unsatisfactory and nontheological—is: *A congregation is a specific type of institution located in a specific context that does particular things for particular ends.* To be more specific, but still nontheological, we can say that *a congregation is an organized and institutionalized religious relationship system framed by a matrix of cultural norms and religious goals, including worship and religious education, proclamation, mission, and community development.* Congregational researcher Jackson Carroll described congregations as "open systems," by which he meant that they are "an organization of identifiable, semi-autonomous but interdependent parts that interact with one another as the congregation pursues its mission. . . ."[1] Again, accurate, but unsatisfying. It is unlikely that any person joins a church with a view to participating in a sociological phenomenon. For most members, a congregation is a *church*—an extended family, a community of faith, a place to find comfort and meaning, a place to worship and to find friendship and purpose. For some people, their congregation is also a place to learn about religious belief and to work at the questions around the meaning of life and purpose (and, on occasion, to discuss deep theological matters). But if pastoral leaders are to lead a congregation effectively, they must understand it for what it is beneath the surface. Unless we understand the nature of what a congregation is, we risk being unable to provide the kind of leadership it needs. Additionally, congregational leaders, whether pastor, staff, or laypersons, need to understand the hidden lives of congregations—those forces and dynamics that shape the congregation as a relationship system and affect the lives of its members.

Every local congregation creates a specific matrix of understandings about its identity, about what it means to be "us" as opposed to another congregation whose mission is the same and whose theology may be the same.[2] Worship and religious education are the most central tasks common to all congregations (although, according to congregational

researcher Nancy Ammerman, eating together is nearly tied with education—and sometimes, more valued than the educational enterprises of
the church).[3] These two practices represent the *sine qua non* ("that without which it is not") of what it means to be a church. Other organizations
provide similar programs and functions as congregations, including
prayer and support groups, ministry services, community service, outreach, spaces for gathering, even corporate singing and proclamation of
religious confessions. But what makes a congregation a church is the
corporate act of confessional worship and a religious education designed
to perpetuate the faith. How a church organizes itself into a matrix of
practices—including worship and religious education—is a clue as to
its nature as a system of relationships that works a certain way and shapes
the lives of its members as a consequence.

The Rise of the Corporation Church

The Church's self-understanding is that of being *ekklesia. Ekklesia* is a
corporate term, meaning "called out" to come together. There is no historical record for when the Church first understood itself this way or of
the first use of the term, but it seems to have happened very early. The
earliest book in the New Testament, Paul's Epistle to the Thessalonians
(c. 50 c.e.) contains the term. Congregational researcher Carl Dudley and
New Testament scholar Earle Hilgert suggest that "the fact that Paul
makes no attempt to explain its meaning in a Christian context tells us
that the word was already significantly alive in Christian community
experience."[4] The early believers seem to have chosen a common contemporary term familiar to both of the significant groups making up the
early church, Jews and Gentiles, which carried with it the understanding
of a higher power calling out citizens to come together. "Thus the term
ekklesia could work dynamically to bring Jews and Gentiles together
into a new sense of common identity," say Dudley and Hilgert.[5]
Evidence exists suggesting that the Church as a movement gave way
to an organized and structured institution by the end of the first century.
The movement, or "the Way," as Paul called it, gave rise to a widely scat-
tered group of organized congregations with a clear structure that included officers and a way of worship and education based primarily on
Jewish, but also on Roman and Greek, traditions. While it is true that
relationship systems cannot help but organize—it is the nature of living
things to do so—there is no determinative reason or particular logic for
this progression from a movement to a congregational institutional system. Given a different set of circumstances, it is possible the Church

would have chosen to organize as something other than the congregational form we are familiar with today. In other words, there is nothing biblically prescriptive about the congregational expression of Church—we've just chosen to do it this way. In times of frustration many people call for a "return to the New Testament Church." Of course, this assumes that the early organized churches are the ideal—a naïve assumption at best and a misinterpretation of the evidence by any means. There was never such a thing as a singular New Testament Church. It is more accurate to say that there were many New Testament churches—most were small familial or community groups that, for a time, remained indistinct from their culture.

Rather than too quickly emulating the idealized model of the early church as a template for congregations, we need to at least entertain the notion that perhaps that model was a sign of failure, not of a success. Jesus challenged the disciples to resist putting new wine into old wineskins (Luke 5:37-38). Very early after the formation of the Church, Jesus' followers seemed to succeed in maintaining the spirit of a movement. But left with only the command to "go and make disciples," and lacking instructions about how to go about doing that, the early disciples failed to follow Jesus' challenge about wineskins. Rather than create a new thing suitable to contain the new creation that was the Church, they used an existing congregational form—the synagogue—and shoehorned the new movement into it, even borrowing its liturgy in the practice of corporate worship. So perhaps the early church congregational model was more an unfortunate error than a template meant to be followed.

Only as the movement developed a new theology to contain its unique epistemology about the world order—a new relationship between the world and God based on the mediating work of Jesus Christ—did the Church find the need to differentiate itself from the culture around it. This led to the need to organize itself in a way radically different from the dictates of the contemporary Greek and Roman cultural mores. Taking a cue from its Jewish roots, the Church understood its self-identity to be that of a people set apart. For a time, this led to a radically countercultural expression of Church. Biblical scholar Bruce Birch describes the extent of this countercultural stance: "The earliest Christians forsook ownership of goods and shared economic resources on the basis of need. They ignored political boundaries of their world and converted women and slaves and persons of all economic and social classes or nationalities. The politics of the early church were based on servanthood and not power, on community and not status."[6]

The formation of the congregation as an expression of Church happened before the close of the New Testament era in the first century.

Jesus' followers progressed from being a movement ("the Way") to a variety of countercultural groups—both Jewish and Gentile—and then to a network of congregations that patterned themselves in similar organizations and structures (Acts 2:43-47; 4:32-37). Early on, these varied groups followed the social and organizational patterns of the communities in which they were localized. But with the distinctive identity of "Christian" and through a network of visiting apostles and other spiritual leaders, a set pattern for worship and structure took hold. In the Pastoral Epistles, like 1 Timothy and Titus, we see evidence of a desire for organization and structure in congregations. Furthermore, in the first-century Epistle of Clement we see the beginnings of organized offices for congregational leadership in the specific mention of the offices of bishop and deacon. A clear apostolic hierarchy is evident by the second century in the writings of Ignatius, bishop of Antioch. In his letters to the churches in Asia Minor and Rome, he not only mentions specific church offices, but also stresses the necessity of hierarchical obedience to bishops.[7]

The effects of culture, modernity, and modernization continue to reshape the congregation as an expression of Church. The much-bemoaned decline of denominationalism and slipping loyalty to religious authorities of position and office continues to shift the focus to local congregations. Furthermore, the continuing influence of parachurch groups and religious organizations that compete with both local churches and denominations for resources and member loyalty is yet another development that continues to challenge former assumptions of everything from what a congregation is supposed to provide to what it means to be a loyal believer and a "member."

The ideal of what the contemporary congregation should be is an expression of a religious stance driven by cultural values and mores—so much so that it may be more accurate to think of a congregation as a bounded relationship system shaped more by culture than by theology. What constitutes a congregation may be found more in the attachment or affiliation style that individual members have than in belief, doctrine, theology, or even tradition. Such churches all exhibit a propensity toward an individual-expressive style of religious attachment. This style of affiliation is what Penny Becker called "the paradigmatic mode of religious commitment for white, middle-class Americans."[8] Consistent with America's efficient tendency to export products and ideas, Becker believes that this style of affiliation is not only becoming more evident outside of middle-class America, but may become more prominent across the religious landscape.[9]

How Congregations Organize Themselves

Our cursory review of the progression from Church as movement to Church as congregation serves to illustrate that relationship systems cannot help but organize. No matter how small or intimate the group, relationship systems seek to organize themselves. Some relationship systems favor a more intimate, familial, high-touch way of being together and going about their work. Congregations like that will tend to resist efforts to organize (or, at least, to be organized for efficiency), fearing a loss of the feelings of intimacy and freedom they value. Other relationship systems feel and function better when organization and structures are put in place to help frame or to "bound" the relationship network. High-organization congregations, for example, can tolerate a high level of emotional distance from leadership, which persons in the high-touch relationship systems would likely perceive as aloofness.

High-touch congregations seek to maintain an intimate feeling among their members. Often, there are strong familial ties in the relationship network and makeup of the congregation, such as with a Family-Size church (see chapter 5). Communal sharing and sacred places are important, as are traditions and a sense of continuity with the past. This congregational system needs both to love its pastor and to feel loved by the pastor in return. High-organization congregational systems, in contrast, function on a more contractual relationship with both members and pastoral leadership. They value and respect organizationally designated positions, individual effort, competence, and professionalism. They are more open to change, since they tend to be more goal- and future-oriented than the high-touch congregational systems. Staying on task and accomplishing things is more important than just being together.

These two distinct congregational styles—high-touch (intimacy, relationships, togetherness) and high-organization (distance, effectiveness, boundaries)—may be points on a spectrum along which a particular congregation moves during its development. Conversely, one or another of these points may become the set emotional tone of the congregation that will characterize who the members are and how they relate to each other and to outsiders. Settling in at any given point along the togetherness–separateness spectrum will enable some things to happen but may limit the congregation's ability to achieve other things. For example, the high value placed on intimacy that tends to characterize a small, Shepherding-Size congregation (see chapter 5) will ensure a sense of family, but will tend to hinder a congregation's ability to be "professional" in its procedures and operational practices. One pastor who went from a large, multistaff, Corporation-Size church (see chapter 5) to a smaller congregation became puzzled by the resistance to the regular memos he used as a communication tool. People would not respond to that form of communication, preferring face-to-face meetings or casual communications like phone calls or visits during which "business" was the last thing discussed.

Congregational leaders need to be able to discern this perpetual tension between togetherness and separateness and to know how and when to push one way or the other. The natural tendency will be for the leader to push a congregation toward what it resists. Perceiving a system that values freedom and intimacy as too "loose" and unfocused, the leader may try to impose order through structure. In turn, the members of the relationship system will resist this structure, seeing it as a heavy-handed attempt at control. Conversely, the congregational leader who finds him or herself in a highly structured and organized system may attempt to help the congregation "relax" by being playful, adopting a *laissez-faire* leadership style, or even attempting to dismantle unwieldy structures and processes. The congregation, in turn, may perceive this as a move toward disorganization, chaos, and disorder.

What Makes a Congregation a Real Faith Community

Regardless of the style that a congregation adopts, it is important to remember that all congregations are by definition local communities of faith. And they are *genuine* communities, with all of the relationship dynamics, and structures universally found in communities. Life and practice in a congregation center on communal events that shape the lives of its members. Historian Donald Livingstone wrote that the marks of a genuine community are the temple, the graveyard, and the wedding ceremony.[10] This reality is why I believe the members of a congregation form a genuine community. A congregation is a faith community when its members center their corporate lives around the rituals universal to all communities. Members of a congregation share a relationship with the larger corporate body that goes beyond function—what they do in and for the community—to issues of identity. In communities, people not only share values, they share self and identity. That identity is shaped by a shared life structure and a shared corporate memory that is dynamic, ever-evolving, and mutual. This shared corporate memory, the ability to speak in terms of "our story," is itself created through the rituals of shared structured living. The activities of church community life—worship, gatherings, meals, doing business, observing and participating in rites and rituals—center around mutual confession about the fragility and temporal nature of life and living and the unspoken confession that we need each other deeply to navigate this precious and harsh thing called life. Congregational members become a faith community when they celebrate and acknowledge both birth and death; not just that these events happened—other institutions do that too—but in speaking to what these events *mean*. A hospital birthing ward acknowledges a birth that occurs in our families, but it cannot speak to what it means—only the community that claims us as one of its own can do that. Funeral homes serve us well and acknowledge that a death has occurred—but they cannot speak to what that death means, or to what that life meant—only the community to which we belong can do that.

Congregational leaders must approach their ministry, decision-making process, and institutional management with the understanding that a congregation is, at heart, more *community* than *organization* in nature. Communities of faith go about their mission in qualitatively different ways than service organizations do. The congregation's primary enterprise is the shaping of the faith of its members and of those whom it reaches out to in witness and ministry; the ways that congregations do that is primarily through communal, not administrative or programmatic, means.

Because members of a congregation center their life together on rituals of meaning and confession, they are not just communities, but communities *of faith*. Like in all communities, practices and values in congregations are negotiated, shared, modified over time, and inculcated into the life structure of the participants. The reasons why individuals join a congregation are varied, but common, having everything to do with meeting the needs—actual or perceived—people believe can be provided only through the shared, grounding religious experiences that a congregation as a faith community offers. Congregations are genuine faith communities because they are places where people come together to participate in and practice their shared religious values that inform both corporate and individual identity.

Like in all communities, a large part of the members' shared experience is informed by the cultural context in which a congregation exists. The cultural context of a congregation includes a shared worldview, beliefs (the content of faith), practices, customs, and artifacts (like symbols and objects). These cultural components are what make intimate interaction possible among congregational members and also provide the boundaries of a particular congregation—that is, they help identify who is a part of the community and who is not. Those who are a part of the community know the peculiar idiom of the group, know how to behave (and how *not* to behave), know the community's stories and symbols and what these represent, and understand how to use the artifacts of the community. What makes congregations so appealing in our culture is that, in most places, they are the closest thing to an intimate community that is available to people—and being part of a community is a powerful basic human need. The appeal of intimate communities is their ability to bind individuals in a group while shaping the values and structure of their lives, say Dudley and Hilgert. And they rightly point out that the hidden life forces that hold a community together are emotional, not rational beliefs or agreements in doctrine, theology, or concepts.[11]

Congregations as faith communities are shaped by the dynamics of how people find ways to become a group. These ways include how people enter into a group and how they move toward the center of community life. Many complex factors facilitate those dynamics. For our purposes I will focus on three critical factors that congregational leaders must be aware of and can address through their influence. The three factors I will examine are (1) a congregation's shared language, (2) how it finds ways for its members to be together, and (3) the importance of a congregation's culture in the formation of its members (because the issue of culture is so important, and complex, I will deal with it in more detail later in the chapter).

Shared Language

In all communities, language serves a particular function (or, as my high school English teacher said, "Words don't have meaning, they have usage"). In a faith community, language serves a formative function and is one indicator that a congregation is a genuine community of faith. That is, the community's idiom—consisting of its vocabulary, patterns of speech, spoken rituals and rites (like blessings and prayers)—functions in ways that shape the faith of its members. For idiom to be formative, the language that is used by a local congregation must have two components: (1) it must be grounded in shared experiences; and (2) it must remain sufficiently religiously distinctive as to express the community's peculiar identity.

The *shared experiences* of the congregation may include part of the language of a larger denomination or faith tradition; more importantly, however, they must include the localized story of the particular faith tradition. The local stories that arise out of the members' shared experiences are what carry their interpretation of the meaning of God's activity

in the life of the community and of its members. Furthermore, these stories are localized in part because they are told in the idiom of the local
congregation. This is why seminary professors tell seminarians who aspire to be preachers that, while a responsible hermeneutical and ex-
egetical study of the biblical text to be preached is necessary, when it
comes to using the academic and ecclesiastical tools of the trade they
must "leave them in the study" and not carry them into the pulpit. The
congregational leader must use the language of the functional theology of the community that is grounded in the contextual shared experiences.

Paying attention to the cultural language of a congregation is one of
the things I've found to be very helpful in my visits to many churches in
my consultation work. Being able to "speak the language" of the
congregation's culture facilitates my ability to communicate in a way
that connects with the members. For example, some churches are "Jesus"
churches, while others are "God" churches. Congregations with a "God
language" tend toward a more transcendent spirituality (see chapter 6).
References to religious experience tend to be poetic, abstract, corporate, and lean toward an appreciation for *gravitas* in the decorum of
corporate worship. For instance, prayers in corporate worship are addressed to God (not to Jesus), using the plural to designate the prayer of
the people ("Almighty God, we confess today . . . "). In contrast, congregations whose culture favors "Jesus language" tend toward a more immi-
nent, christocentric spirituality. The language of faith is expressed in
terms of Jesus as Lord, or conversely, in a more intimate Jesus as friend,
or Jesus as Savior, orientation. Addressing Jesus in the first person during personal or corporate prayers is common, and the language of faith
tends to be personal, devotional, and intimate.

The late James Hopewell, in his groundbreaking book *Congregation*,
found that congregations adopt language closely in ways that parallel
literary categories. He identified congregations who, for example, use
the comic worldview with its accompanying optimism ("possibility thinking" language). Other congregations use the language of the tragedy,
which includes beliefs about the plight of the flawed and fallen state of
humanity. The fallen state of humanity finds its answer in the tragic yet
triumphant death on the cross. In contrast, in those congregations that
use the language of romance, an embrace of reality with its imperfec-
tions is common. They have no illusions about the nature of the world,
and the experience of pain is not something to be easily remedied, for it
is part of the human experience. Each language type facilitates the use
of symbols, metaphors, and imagery that shape the congregation's
worldview and identity.[12]

Giving attention to and shaping its own language is one of the primary ways that a congregation acquires an identity. Creating opportunities for congregational members to do this by "telling our story" must be both valued and implemented as a critical educational function, which means that congregational leaders must program and schedule regular and frequent opportunities for the community members to hear and tell their stories of interpretive meaning.

The *distinctiveness of the congregational language* is also essential for faith formation. Uncritical attempts to borrow language from popular culture or from another tradition, ungrounded in shared unique religious experiences, in an attempt to "accommodate" seekers or potential members may prove to have the opposite effect. Imposing such language on the faith community serves only to deny the distinctive identity of the congregation. Further, the power of language leaves open the temptation to adopt the values that the borrowed language conveys—some of which may be foreign or even antagonistic to the congregation's values.

Being Together

A second indication that a congregation is a real community is that it facilitates ways for its members to be together. Congregations provide spaces and places to gather around activities, programs, and events that allow people to spend time together doing things they find meaningful. The huge investments that congregations make in buildings and campuses are not just institutional symbols of power or affluence; they also shape how people live out their faith and relate to each other. In the same way, congregational programs, regardless of their overtly announced agenda (for instance, worship, learning, mission activities, administration or business), taps into the congregation's hidden need for spending time together in mutually shared experiences.

The dilemma faced by contemporary American congregations, however, is the tension between the separateness and togetherness forces so prevalent in the culture. America is the quintessential individualistic nation. The cultural American icon is that of community and community values—mom, apple pie, and baseball. Norman Rockwell's Americana—the small town with its civic downtown square with city hall at one end and a white clapboard steepled church at the other—is the perennial image found everywhere, in advertisements, movies, and even on church Sunday bulletin covers. People yearn after and seek out groups that will make them feel at home in a complex and confusing world. At the same time, they resist any group that makes demands or attempts to impose group ethical norms or makes prophetic calls to accountability. Congregations live in this cultural tension and spend a lot of time attempting to be genuine communities of faith while juggling these contradictory forces of togetherness and separateness.

As a result, congregations are tempted to "define community down" as they organize themselves as religious institutions. Some narrow the scope of who belongs in the community by overtly inviting members who are alike in some way, like those of a particular ethnicity, or socio-economic level, or similar educational background. Other congregations stress a "community-as-support-group" approach, expecting their members to develop close interpersonal relationships in an atmosphere of emotional support and mutual encouragement. In these congregations the educational enterprises tend toward the therapeutic, like support groups or self-help classes framed in the language of a faith orientation. Education tends to be more supportive and affirming, rather than challenging, of beliefs. The worship experiences will tend to have predictable themes of healing, wholeness, recovery, and restoration.

But being together in community involves more than a focus on people's needs. Community implies mutuality. It is in this sense that faith communities with their religious traditions offer a truer image: community as a gathering that enlarges, challenges, and completes the individual's personal vision by providing a place where both their strengths and their needs are welcomed. A community is more than another name for intimate self-disclosure and emotional support. A community creates opportunities for being together where the possibilities of shared values can move members to action in the public square, undertaken in a context of mutual concern and inspired by a corporate vision of the Church's mission in the world.

Creating a shared life together requires that congregational leaders address some fundamental questions about the congregation as community. During the course of a congregation's lifespan (see chapter 4) and of its development (see chapter 5), these fundamental questions need to be revisited:

- What is the major purpose of this group? What is its mission and vision?
- How fully are members involved in the life of the church community?
- Is intimacy encouraged?
- Is the leadership function shared or is it delegated to one person or position?
- How effective is the community in teaching, sharing, and perpetuating its values and beliefs?
- How are group behavior and norms regulated?

- How obligated do members feel to each other and to the group?
- How are group members evaluated as to their Christian disciple-ship, growth, and participation?
- How effective is the community in inviting and assimilating new members?
- What does it mean to belong to this community? How does it hap-pen and what is assumed and expected?

These fundamental questions are too important to merely assume that all members understand them. The answers to these questions hint at the ways that the hidden lives of congregations are actively operating under the surface. Therefore, if congregational leaders fail to understand how these questions are manifested in the congregation, they will also lack understanding as to how well their congregation is functioning as an authentic Christian community.

The congregation as a church is a local body of believers whose religious hope is expressed in their life together and in their ministries of service and worship. Because the mission of a congregation includes both internal and external ends (a movement inward and a movement outward), the church must organize and develop the social forms of a faith community. Faith communities, congregations included, must nour-ish and express the communion that exists among its members: from the shared meaning and identity that make them a distinctive group, to participation in the common mission that moves their members into the world. Ultimately, the congregation's mission is that of the Church: to witness to the world the saving presence of God among us. There is no greater vehicle for that than a community.

Christian Formation in Community

Faith communities go about the formation of their members in three primary ways: through the matrix of (a) their use of language, (b) their ways of being together, and (c) their culture. In a congregational faith community, those three elements that facilitate formation must be dis-tinctively Christian if they are to be authentic. Christian formation in a congregation requires that the members support with their lives and resources a close-knit cohesive community of faith whose culture is sharply distinguished from society at large. The formation process re-quires also a commitment to developing and preserving the community's distinctive Christian identity and way of life while still participating in the wider culture to which its members belong.

This Christian formation is facilitated to a great extent by the educational enterprise in which the members participate. Coming together to participate in educational experiences must serve to help the members reflect critically on the Church as they know it, bounded as it is in the institutionalized congregation, and the experiences they share within it. The educational enterprise of a congregation must be overtly and intentionally Christian, because the Christian faith cannot be inherited or simply passed on. At some point education needs to provide a context for persons to make a decision for or against the faith that is confessed by the community at a corporate level. In other words, the Christian educational enterprises of the faith community must be aimed at facilitating the *conversion* of the individual—being that point in time when the individual, as a member or part of the community, chooses to accept and incorporate being Christian on a personal level, both as one who is part of the community of faith, but who is also an individual within it. Congregations of various faiths do this in many different ways, of course. In some evangelical congregations, infant dedications—or more commonly these days, "family dedications"—are rites of covenant in which parents and community are charged with leading the individual toward a future personal commitment to faith and membership. In other traditions, the practices range from infant baptism, to adult and adolescent rites of passages that call for a personal commitment to membership into, and loyalty to, the community of faith. In all these, congregations find ways to educate individuals in the faith and to provide the means to make personal decisions overt.

Congregational Culture and the Formational Process

Christian formation requires intentional communal life, and therefore, participation in a community of faith remains key. Quite simply, the process of Christian formation is the experience of being changed by the relationships of a Christian community of faith. This is why it is critical to understand the hidden lives of congregations and how they work in a congregation's culture. The experiences and relationships that a congregation fosters through its culture as a community of faith shapes people's Christian faith.

Congregations that seek to be authentic faith communities need to give attention to some key components of a formation community. The first component is the *congregation's ritual life*. One of the most powerful formative ways a congregation shapes the faith of its members is by their participation in the repetitive symbolic actions that are expressive of the community's sacred narrative. This sacred narrative both informs and is manifested in the congregation's common life. The sacred narrative of the congregation includes a set of personal and communal rites by which the community is bound together over time. A congregation uses this sacred narrative to identify itself as a distinctive community of faith, with a set of beliefs, a particular character, consciousness, and identity. The ritual life of a congregation includes how the community uses language—its attention to naming things (Does the congregation gather in a "sanctuary," an "auditorium," or a "worship room"?) and to theological language (Is God always referred to as "Father"? Are prayers expressed in "we" language as the corporate prayers of the people or in individualistic "I" language?)

Another important component of the formation process is the *role models* that the community holds up as examples for its members. Role models include heroes, prophets, and leaders, those whose lives are celebrated and whose teachings and ways of living are witnessed and affirmed. A community's role models include the persons it chooses to occupy the places of common authority—those positions that it establishes and uses to govern its life and to discern its vision and how the Church should live out its mission.

The congregation's choice of heroes and leaders directly influences another critical component of the formation process, namely, the *interpersonal relations and interactions with members of the community* who prescribe and reinforce appropriate identity and behavior. The nature of relationships in congregations dictates that it needs a common life together that is more like a family than an institution. Just like in an intimate family relationship system this requires members to be willing to be influenced by others, to modify themselves in response to new and different interpersonal situations. Life together calls for members' patience, in order to tolerate the inevitable strain of personal accommodation and compromise. Community is not free; members who choose to be a part of a community pay for the benefits of belonging by giving up areas of personal accommodation and through compromise. This includes developing a capacity to be aware of other people's needs and the capacity to see things from their point of view. Most significantly, however, the cost of being a part of a community requires appropriately sharing part of one's self and the willingness to incorporate personal change in ways that strengthen rather than diminish the community.

Another important, and often overlooked, formation component are the *artifacts that support the particular culture* and the "habits of the heart" of the community members. These artifacts—symbols and objects, but also the practices associated with them—mediate meaning and corporate experiences of the members in the congregation. As such, a congregation's artifacts partly reflect the underlying cultural values of its members. Artifacts are objects that members use in their common life together and are always community-owned property.

Artifacts have function and significance. In a congregation with a divided chancel, for example, the locations serve the function of providing a focal point from which information comes. But it also means something that the Word of God comes from one point of focus while the word of man (the interpretation of the Word) from another. One function of artifacts is that they create sacred space. Even the placing of an ugly vase that belonged to long-deceased matriarch aunt Edith can create a sacred space in a sanctuary or parlor—one that the wise pastor knows not to remove casually regardless of its clash with the décor.

Other artifacts, however, tend to have their meaning and function much more universally securely fixed. Artifacts like the iconostasis, the altar, or a shrine create a clearly bounded sacred space within the congregational building. In this sense specific rooms can become artifacts, like a prayer room, for example. (That a room can be an artifact which serves a function does not mean that it will be "used" in actuality. Sometimes the function is symbolic, as in the case of a church I know that has a prayer room—with a kneeling stand, aesthetic and meditative décor, an open Bible on a stand, and a journal in which people can write thoughts and prayer requests. Upon opening the journal, I note that the last entry was over twenty years ago. Yet, the room remains an important artifact for that church—one that is pointed out to every visitor or potential member).

The artifacts of a congregation have a special aura that is generated by their direct association with the daily lives of people from another time—those who lived before us, but who shared our values, our beliefs, and our stories. This connection is the point at which the bridge between authentic artifacts and the imagination is fully realized. Symbolic artifacts provide a fetishistic contact with a meaning that lies beyond their physical existence. The meaning that the faith community ascribes to these symbolic artifacts forges a link through which to apprehend a transcendent existence and truth manifestly different from the temporal experience. Authentic artifacts, in other words, offer the members access to a spark of "reality" that may propel members to greater awareness of what binds them together—the mysteries of faith that Jesus hinted at in his High Priestly Prayer, for example (John 17). This is why the local artifact symbols of a congregation cannot be easily dismissed—no matter how garish or incomprehensible they may be to a new minister or member. And it is why genuine artifacts are not the same as "props." There is no such thing as an instant artifact, no matter how well explained or aesthetic, because artifacts belong to the communal experience and are developed over time.

In one congregation, the new young pastor, who considered herself to have a flair for worship and liturgy, wanted to be creative during Pentecost in her new church. She placed on the communion table a prop electric "cauldron" with artificial flames—to be sure, a nifty and clever prop that provided a dramatic light show. However, what she failed to appreciate was that the communion table in this church was set under a large beautiful stained-glass ceiling called by its members, "the Holy Spirit window," which depicted, among other things, flames of fire. One delightful phenomenon that was part of the aesthetics of the worship room was that when members observed communion, the entire window was reflected in each individual communion cup, floating on the top of the liquid. The window was a powerful and dynamic artifact that for the members symbolized the Holy Spirit coming from above and indwelling each individual member, making them one. It is no surprise then, that many members took offense at what they considered a cheap and misinformed "prop" and stunt that served only to highlight the new pastor's lack of understanding of their culture. What should not have been a big deal became one because artifacts mediate meaning and shared corporate experience.

Finally, *the social organization of the congregation* is an important component of formation. The hierarchy that is put in place in the common life—the roles assigned and the status ascribed—of the various social units that comprise a congregation form people's understanding of their place and worth in the community. Often, church polity informs this social organization, but sometimes, congregational culture determines it. The social organization includes how time is structured and programmed for the community, as well as the behaviors and practices that are affirmed and encouraged through life in the community.

Conclusion

In order to understand the hidden lives of congregations, we must first appreciate that the congregation is an institutionalized religious organization. But that does not diminish the reality that congregations are both genuine communities of faith or a genuine expression of Church. While the organizational nature of congregations provides real challenges to their ever achieving the ideal of what they aspire to be—that is, an ideal, local expression of what the Church is intended to be—nevertheless, congregations can be authentic and fully realized communities of faith that shape the lives and faiths of its members. Furthermore, to the extent that congregations can provide the critical components of a genuine formation community, they can both impact positively the lives of their members and be the redemptive force in the world that is God's intent for the Church.

All congregations provide two universal and core communal functions, regardless of their locale, tradition, theology, the style they choose, or the model of structure and processes they manifest: worship and religious education. Worship provides the members with a communal religious expression of their connection with the sacred dimension in their lives. Corporate worship ritualizes these into practices, rites, symbols, and language. The religious education enterprises serve to perpetuate belief through a variety of teaching approaches, from indoctrination and instruction to more humanistic educational modalities like support groups, spiritual direction, and personal development and enrichment programs. Additionally, religious education is what moves a congregation from belief to action by providing ways to put faith into practice.

Chapter 3

The Mandate, Mission, and Models
of Congregations

IN THIS FINAL CHAPTER OF PART ONE WE WILL EXAMINE THE BIBLICAL
and theological mandate for the ministry of the Church. Identifying these
mandates in conjunction with the functions of congregation as Church
will allow us to discern why things like mission and vision statements
can either help or hinder a congregation's viability as a community of
faith and as an authentic expression of God's intent. Function leads to
form, as they say, and so we will conclude this chapter by exploring how
models of congregations fit their mission and function. Identifying
schemas and models of churches is a helpful way of getting an understanding of what a congregation is and how it works. Models like those
of sociologist Penny Edgell Becker and others help us see the hidden
lives of congregations beyond the varied structural expressions that
they take in local contexts. Models help reveal how the hidden lives of
congregations—those dynamics that lie at the heart of the nature of
what a congregation is—get organized and institutionalized in patterns
of relationships and group processes. Models of congregations also help
identify at the local level the broader cultural and theological realities
of the Church, its tradition, history, ideologies, and mandated interaction with the world.

The Mandate

The nature of the Church is defined by its being the unique creation and
possession of God (1 Peter 2:9-10). God's purpose for the Church is two-
fold: (1) to confess the nature and being of God through worship and (2)
to proclaim the good news of redemption. Congregations do well to remind themselves regularly that the purpose of the Church is not to serve
itself or its own. When the Church practices its primary task of gathering

for corporate worship, the Church leads its members in confessing that "God is God and we are God's people." Neither is it the purpose of the Church to "serve others," as so often is believed. While congregations do engage in ministries and actions that are for the benefit of others, the primary purpose of the Church is to serve God. This is a fine distinction, but a meaningful one that helps clarify the Church's ethical purpose and reason for existence.

Three key New Testament passages sum up God's mandate to the Church and God's intent for it. The first is the passage commonly referred to as the Great Commission of the Church. In this passage there is an emphasis on the decidedly ethical dimension of the Church's educational function. Speaking from his own rightful authority, Jesus Christ commands his disciples, "Go, then, to all peoples everywhere and make them my disciples: baptize them in the name of the Father, the Son, and the Holy Spirit, and teach them to obey everything I have commanded you. And I will be with you always, to the end of the age" (Matthew 28:18-20 TEV).

In the second passage God's message to the apostle Paul echoes the Church's task of working with unbelievers, leading them to conversion to a new way of living and a new status: "I want you to open their eyes, so that they will turn from darkness to light and from the power of Satan to God. Then their sins will be forgiven, and by faith in me they will become part of God's holy people," (Acts 26:18 CEV).

The third passage is one of the clearest writings in the New Testament as to the nature of the Church and its purpose. Starting with a confessional statement that informs the unifying nature of the call to discipleship ("There is one body and one Spirit—just as you were called to one hope when you were called—one Lord, one faith, one baptism," Ephesians 4:4-5), Paul outlines the purpose of the Church for the people of God: "to prepare all God's people for the work of Christian service, in order to build up the body of Christ. And so we shall all come together to that oneness in our faith and in our knowledge of the Son of God; we shall become mature people, reaching to the very height of Christ's full stature . . . ; by speaking the truth in a spirit of love, we must grow up in every way to Christ, who is the head. Under his control all the different parts of the body fit together, and the whole body is held together by every joint with which it is provided. So when each separate part works as it should, the whole body grows and builds itself up through love." (Ephesians 4:12-13; 15-16 TEV).

The local church's mandate, then, comprises at least three actions: (*a*) educating in faith for obedience in discipleship; (*b*) leading unbelievers to conversion and into the life of faith in the Body of Christ; and (*c*) living and working together in unity to achieve maturity into the likeness of Christ. The primary mandate of the church is to be a transforming influence in the world. This is how the church becomes relevant in people's lives. The institutional tendency of organizations, however, is to focus primarily on self-preservation and on the comfort and benefit of their own members. And while a congregation is an institutionalized expression of the Church, it is wrong, and against its nature, when self-preservation and comfort become the primary reasons for its existence. When that happens, says pastor and author C. John Miller, the local congregation ceases to be the incarnate Body of Christ or a fellowship of disciples, and has become more like a retreat center where anxious members come to draw resources to help them cope with their own lives.[1]

Biblical scholar Paul S. Minear's classic study of biblical metaphors of the Church highlights the communal nature of the Church as "the body of Christ." This nature is theologically connected with the idea of a people of God in the Old Testament. Both Israel, as the people of God in the Old Testament, and the images of the Church in the New Testament suggest that God has a driving mandate for their presence in the world. This mandate, which permeates the images and metaphors of the Church, is what provides the energy of commitment for the particular activities in the life of the Church.[2]

Congregations are perhaps the primary places today where the Christian faith is communicated from and through one generation to the next. They are the primary places where the faith of the past is interpreted for the needs of today, and where the Christian faith of those called to be the people of God grows stronger through living life together and responding to God's threefold mandate (a) to educate in faith for obedience in discipleship, (b) to lead unbelievers to conversion and into the life of faith in the Body of Christ, and (c) to work toward maturity into the likeness of Christ. Furthermore, the corporate nature of congregations helps provide a corrective to the popular culture's overemphasis on individuality and accompanying stress on "personal spirituality." The mandate of God is to the *corporate* body of the Church—not to individuals. God's calling is primarily a corporate calling to which there are individual responses from within the corporate body of the Church. The corporate nature of congregations—a people of God called out and gathered—is a theological outworking of this critical truth about the corporate nature of faith.

Congregations are corporate expressions of the Body of Christ formed in response to God's initiative of grace and as a response to God's calling. As Minear's work on biblical metaphors suggests, this was true in the Old

Testament for the people of God and it remains true in the New Testament for the Church of God. In the Old Testament, God called out a tribal people to become the people of God (Exodus 14–15). In the New Testament, God called out a new people from among the nations to become the Church. This new manifestation of the People of God comes about through the resurrection of Jesus Christ and through the empowering of the Holy Spirit (Acts 2:43-47; 4:32-37). It is as a corporate people of God that the Church has a mandate. And it is as a corporate body of a community of faith that congregations carry out the mission of God. Bruce C. Birch stresses that "it is important in the modern church's congregational life to see faithful community as a response to the grace which comes from God, and not the source of God's grace itself."[3]

The Mission

All congregations have the same mission: to be the body of Christ in the world, participating with God in the redemptive work of restoring all people to unity with God and each other in Christ. While all churches share in the same mission, congregations are not monolithic. Each congregation has a distinct identity, resides in a particular context at a particular time in history, and is a unique embodiment of the body of Christ. Therefore, to the extent that a congregation is faithful to its calling to be the Church in its particular context, however it chooses to work out the mission and mandate of God, that unique identity is an authentic expression of the Christian Church. The numerous elements that combine to make up a congregation—its history, size, location, member demographics, identity, and culture—means that no two congregations are likely ever to be the same, though many may share similarities. The challenge for congregational leaders, then, is to give constant attention to the congregation's interpretation of, and faithfulness to, its calling to be the body of Christ in its particular context.

Congregations are never as boilerplate as some denominational bodies seem to prefer for their member churches. This is because congregations are more shaped by the common expectations in their local institutional environment about what a congregation should be like than by the denominational office. In spite of centralized programs, programmed themes, and common denominational products that congregations consume, local churches are never, as Penny Becker puts it, "some simple or straightforward imprinting of a larger denominational culture or religious tradition."[4] The social context in which a congregation exists has the greatest influence in determining the mission of its members.

In addition, the social networks that structure the lives of the congregational members, whether they live in the immediate neighborhood of the church building or travel in from a distance, will inform how the congregation shapes its mission.

One important and informing cultural orientation for congregations has to do with their stance toward the Church and society. H. Richard Niebuhr's classic typology of images that reflect these particular orientations between "Christ and culture" remains a helpful way to understand how culture shapes a congregation's expression of mission. Niebuhr identified five orientations that congregations take toward their surrounding cultures: rejecting, accepting, leading, living in paradox, or transforming.[5] What congregational leaders must appreciate is that, in the hidden life of congregations, members make commitments to their local congregation's mission based on their images—their latent theological understanding—of the Church and on their contextual stance toward the relationship between Church and culture. Because this stance forms part of the congregation's identity (see chapter 7), attempting to change a church's response to the call of God to mission by addressing the congregation's practices, habits, and traditions (what it does and how it does it) directly will tend to prove fruitless.

The Functions

Every congregation has a mission and needs a vision. I'll talk more about vision in chapter eight, but for now, I'll examine the mission of congregations and its relationship to a church's functions. As noted above, every congregation, regardless of its culture and context, has the same mission. Congregations do many things—so much so that the besetting sin in most congregations is busy-ness. But it is important for congregational leaders to help the church discern which, of all of the things a congregation does, are those that are essential to its nature. In other words, what is the "primary task" that a congregation needs to be about because, as an organization, it is an expression of the Church and not of something else? According to congregational researchers H. Barry Evans and Bruce Reed, a primary task "is that one process that keeps the organization existing, viable, and stable."[6] Too often, congregations and their leaders fall into the temptation of defining themselves by secondary factors—the size of the membership, their worship style, a doctrinal belief, and so forth. This reveals an understanding of themselves as Church and of their mission that is egocentric and inward-focused. When a congregation defines itself in these ways, it nurtures an ideal of a congregation as something apart from the community in which it exists, with little expectation of a relevant relationship between the congregation and those outside of its walls. It does not take long for this uncritical point of view, divorced from the universal mission of the Church, to give rise to structures that inhibit processes aimed at mission and instead foster processes of self-preservation, self-care, and complacency.

Paying attention to the structures of a congregation is important, because structures inform the processes of the congregations. The structures of a congregation are those formal elements of congregational life such as policies, buildings, creeds, curricula, boards, and committees, as well as the hidden, informal relationship structures of cliques, networks, norms, and roles.[7] When a congregation loses sight of its universal mission—the one they share with all congregations everywhere—the tendency will be to put in place uncritically structures that foster processes and functions that are at odds with what a local church is to be about. The tragic end result is that activities and programs which cannot achieve those ends usurp the primary functions of the Church—worship, fellowship, teaching, proclamation, and ministry. Ultimately, then, a confusion of aims and tasks arises. In their busy-ness churches continue to engage in tasks—activities, programs, and so forth—with little critical thought as to whether those tasks are helping to achieve the aims that a church strives for. It is a tragic fact that people can attend a congregation for years and never grow in grace or compassion. Some members attend one educational program, workshop, study, or class after another, and never learn how to become a Christian disciple. Youth can attend church activities for the duration of their adolescence, and never experience significant maturity in their spiritual lives.

Congregational leaders need to ensure that the structure of the local church facilitates the processes that are consistent with the nature of a community of faith context in the light of the primary task of the Church. The mission of the Church must be expressed through the ways the congregation performs its basic functions—worship, fellowship, education, proclamation, and ministry—to achieve its mandate. While most congregations carry out all of these functions to one extent or the other, being unclear about the Church's universal mission may reduce these to activities which may not be appropriate to realize the mandate every congregation is under. While a congregation's programs and activities evolve in context and are guided by local vision and culture and conditioned by local history and circumstances, congregational leaders must strive to ensure their authentic relevance to the mission of the Church.

Becker's Models of Congregations

In her study of congregations in conflict, sociologist Penny Edgell Becker identified four "models" of the congregation as an organized institution. These four basic models help illustrate how congregations pattern the matrix of context, beliefs, mission, and function in ways that give shape to the relationship system. These four basic patterns are worth reviewing as they have a direct corollary to the hidden life forces of congregational lifespan and congregational size and style that we will review in upcoming chapters. Understanding the model that a congregation adopts helps identify how a congregation carries out its functions, and hints at the ways that programs, practices, and processes come about. Models dictate the manner in which a congregation will go about engaging in its critical mission and functions, like worship, religious education, outreach, fellowship, and witness. In effect, a model is the way a congregation institutionalizes its functions and the religious dimensions of belief, values, and practices. The institutionalization of the religious dimensions informs everything from what and how sermons are delivered, how members welcome strangers, how communal relationships work, to the forms that ritual and liturgy take. In other words, congregational models are important to understand because they are one primary factor in how congregations decide on who they are and what they do.

The four models that Becker identified are: the House of Worship Church model, the Family Church model, the Community Church model, and the Leader Church model. Becker describes the *House of Worship Church* model as a "provider of religious goods and services."[8] These goods and services include wedding and funeral ceremonies and other rituals that give attention to and provide recognition, if not meaning, to life's nodal events. But the primary focus of the House of Worship Church is its corporate worship services and its religious education enterprises. The primary goal of church life centers around providing uplifting worship experiences and in educating membership in the church's traditions, denominational heritage, doctrines, and rituals. According to Becker, these congregations tend to make limited demands on their members' time and minimum participation in the life of the church is not perceived as an indicator of a lack of member loyalty. Congregations in this model depend on pastoral leadership, paid staff, and a committee structure for most of the decisions about programming, development, and practices. Becker likens the member's relationship to this congregation as that of a temple, which is a ritual center mostly, disconnected to the secular lives and practices of its members. In more contemporary terms, the House of Worship Church is a consumer's congregation—if you have need for some kind of religious service or product, you know where to go to get it, but otherwise, it's peripheral to your life. I remember listening to one gentleman addressing his congregation one Sunday during a stewardship announcement. With obvious affection, he likened his church to an automatic hand dryer in a public restroom. Referring to his church, he said that you don't always need it, but when you do, all you have to do is put out your hands and you'll get what you need.

In the *Family Church* model, worship and religious education are also important, but just as important—if not more so—is the intimate personal and supportive relationships that are at the heart of communal life and practice. Members take pride at being a "warm, loving church" where relationships matter more than belief—although they may not necessarily phrase it that way. The intensity of the hidden life force of the relationship dynamic means that personal connections within the system, length of tenure and shared history, and especially one's assigned "place" in the community's structure is more important in determining influence and authority than formal offices or committee assignments. Actual leadership in this church model is provided either by patriarchs or matriarchs, or by a small group of members who have long tenure and who enjoy familial ties to one or more core family units. It is not inaccurate to say that this congregation is an extended family network for two or three family groups. This makes it difficult to separate family values from congregational values. Additionally, the role, function, and influence of the pastoral leader is limited and bounded in this congregational model, a situation we'll explore in more detail in chapter five.

Becker's third congregational model is the *Community Church*. In this corporate relationship system the role that values play is one of the more influential hidden life forces. While corporate worship and religious education remain central to the practices of this congregational model, these, along with the policies that inform process and the programs that are offered, must express overtly the values shared by the members. In the Community Church, these values tend to center around social issues important to the members as a community of faith. Therefore, "Figuring out how to interpret and apply shared values is the most important communal enterprise,"[9] writes Becker. Indeed, the members in this congregational model consider that their most important witness lies in their ability to practice and live out their confessed values by institutionalizing them into life together as a church. The emphasis on shared corporate values often translates to a democratic form of governance in which each member's voice is allowed to be heard. This is such a high value in the Community Church model that a common misunderstanding among members in some congregations lies in confusing polity with process. I remember a leadership conference I was conducting at a local Baptist church during which a deacon took exception to some comment I made by saying, "But Baptists are democratic." I had to gently correct him by pointing out that Baptists as a group have a *congregational* polity. I stressed that, while most Baptist churches may indeed choose a democratic process for their decision making, being Baptist, however, was not equivalent to being democratic.

Becker's fourth congregational model is the *Leader Church* model. This model of congregation has three characteristics that make it distinct from the others. While sharing worship and religious education are central to its life and living, the Leader Church congregation depends heavily on the denomination and authorities for clues as to its corporate values. A second distinction is that its ways of practicing proclamation and witness are more "activist," to use Becker's word. This crusader approach takes witness and proclamation outside the walls of the church into the political arena and the public square, often through social action. Finally, the Leader Church tends to value intimacy of relationships and "warm" fellowship less than it does participation and support of the mission it maintains at the center of its identity.

We will continue to examine models of congregations in the following chapters. While there are many models that congregations adopt, it may not be an overstatement to say that all congregations will fall under one of the four models that Becker so creatively identifies. Being able to identify under which of the four basic models a congregation falls can provide a shortcut to understanding its hidden life dynamics, and will provide a starting place to knowing how that congregation will respond to the leadership function, a topic we will look at in detail in part three.

Conclusion

In this chapter we've contended that all congregations have the same mission, regardless of context, vision, or other factors like ethnicity, size, location, and so forth. This mission has to do with God's purpose for the Church, and with its theological nature as the Body of Christ. The mission of the Church, simply put, is to be the Body of Christ in the world participating with God in the redemptive work of restoring all people to unity with God and each other in Christ. This redemptive mission is tied into the biblical mandate for the Church (1 Peter 2:9-10; Matthew 28:18-20; Acts 26:18; Ephesians 4:12-13; 15-16). The mandate and mission of the

Church, in turn, inform the essential functions that every congregation must provide: worship, fellowship, education, proclamation, and ministry. How a church structures itself—its organization and the model it adopts—will determine how well it will facilitate the processes that will enable its functions to realize its God-given mandate. Because congregations are living relationship organisms, they have hidden life dynamics that impact all aspects of its being and practice: its mandate and mission, its functions, and its programs and ministries. We will turn our attention to those dynamics in the next chapters that make up part two of the book.

PART TWO

Understanding the Hidden Lives of Congregations

IF CONGREGATIONAL LEADERS ARE TO HELP THE CHURCH LIVE UP to its mission and mandate, they must come to understand the power of the hidden lives of congregations. Beyond theology, doctrine, and belief, congregations are about relationships. People join a congregation for basic human motivations and needs: primarily, fellowship and community. They want to be a part of a group that provides intimacy, that shares their faith orientation, and is like-minded and like-hearted. Ultimately, people come together in a community of faith to be in relationship with others, to be a part of a relationship system—a family—in which they can share self, find meaning and purpose, find their place, and give of their talents and gifts according to their calling, beliefs, and abilities. But, like all relationship systems, a congregation is subject to fundamental hidden life forces that inform how relationships work in the system. This hidden life of congregations is where so much of how a congregation "really works" lies.

The Five Organic Relational Hidden Life Forces

Some hidden life forces come into play at the institutional and organizational level of what it means to be a congregation. We will examine four of those specifically in the chapters of this section, namely, congregational lifespan, size, spirituality style, and identity. But there are five more fundamental organic relational dynamics (or forces) at work in the lives of congregations. A *dynamic* is an interactive system or process that involves energy, motion, change, activity, and force. Sometimes a dynamic involves interaction between conflicting forces. The interaction of these forces with each other within the context in which the dynamic exists may be patterned and predictable, or chaotic and unstable, and therefore uncertain. The nature of a dynamic involves continuous change, at times in the form of progress, but at other times in the form of regression.

51

A dynamic also has qualities like intensity, which describes the amount or extent of force, energy, influence, or change that exists at any given moment.

These dynamics are *relational* in the sense that they both inform and are influenced by the relationships within and outside of the organism. They are *organic* in the sense that every living organism, from a single-celled organism to a complex relationship system exhibits these dynamics. Because congregations are relationship systems, they are in a real sense organic. That is, they are made up not of static objects, but of living human beings who interact with each other and work at organizing themselves in ways that exhibit all of the characteristics of a living organism. For example, a congregation organizes itself, grows, develops, and evolves or declines. This is not only an important way to approach understanding the hidden life forces of a congregation, but a necessary one. Viewing a congregation primarily as an organization, management system, or institution leads ultimately to toxic approaches to congregational leadership and to tragic ministry practices. The five organic relational dynamics that are at play during the lifespan of a congregation are: Systemic Anxiety, Energy, Organizing, Controlling, and Relational.[1]

The Systemic Anxiety Dynamic. Systemic Anxiety in relationship systems has to do with the emotional and physical reactivity shared by all protoplasm. It is evidenced in responses that are automatic and instinctual rather than mediated by thinking or principles. Systemic Anxiety is neither "good" nor "bad," it just exists as part of all emotional relationship systems. However, systems in which high anxiety is chronic—by becoming patterned and ultimately structured into the system—tend to suffer from its debilitating effects. The fact of the matter is that all relationship systems are or will become anxious. Anxiety is dynamic and "free floating," but it does have a tendency to seek a place to rest in predictable patterns and positions in the relationship system.

Anxiety can be informed by the hidden assumptions of the congregation. The most critical hidden assumptions in a congregational relationship system tend to be those between congregational members and leadership—either the pastor or the lay congregational leaders. People maintain many kinds of expectations and assumptions about the relationship they are in, and likewise, a congregation can hold several expectations or assumptions at the same time. For example, *reciprocity expectations* have to do with the congregation's belief that the church's survival depends upon a person (present or absent), another institution, or an idea of God. When members of a congregation have *survival expectations* they may hold to the belief that their survival is dependent on either destroying or evading a perceived enemy—again, a person, an institution, a group, or a belief. Some congregations may hold *belief expectations* in which there is both an assumption and demand for unity in the fundamental beliefs of a congregation—doctrinal, political, or social. Congregations with a *numerical growth expectation* will tend to measure success in ministry and the effectiveness of their congregational leaders on the rate of numerical growth of the membership one year to the next. Another common assumption in congregations is the *togetherness expectation*. This expectation is common in Family-Size congregations (see chapter 5) where intimacy and togetherness is both a high value and a measure of belongingness.

Failure to realize expectations can trigger anxiety in several ways. Often, this depends on the underlying assumptions of the expectations. When leaders fail to behave the way a congregation assumes a leader "should," for example, anxiety may serve as a way for the system to signal that something is wrong and to cause a change in behavior on the part of the leader. More often than not, a peak in anxiety is a signal that the system wants to get back to the norm (to its homeostasis, to use the language of systems theory), or at least to its assumptions and expectations of what the norm should be.

Systemic Anxiety may feel chaotic, but it follows predictable systemic rules. For example, anxiety tends to seek out and rest in persons who occupy one of three positions in the system: the position of the person most responsible (in congregations, that's usually the pastor), the most vulnerable in the system, and the system's most dependent person or persons (those most immature, or least capable of handling change; see chapter 8). Additionally, anxiety tends to affect those relationship systems that have little capacity for change or for challenge.

The Energy Dynamic. The Energy dynamic is best appreciated by its level of intensity. The dynamic of Energy may ebb and flow during the cycle of the year and throughout a congregation's lifespan. For example, most congregations experience an Energy high during the Advent and Christmas seasons, and will experience a level of low Energy during the summer vacation season. Energy tends to be manifested most during the early stages of the lifespan (see chapter 4) and in epochs of high Systemic Anxiety, like during a crisis or when significant persons enter or leave the congregation. Like Anxiety, Energy is an undifferentiated force—it is neither good nor bad. Therefore, a congregation with high Energy depends on the role of the leader to provide focus and direction. Unlike Anxiety, which can be a debilitating force if it becomes chronic, Energy is always an enabling force and therefore a resource for a congregation when they can tap into it. The hidden life force of Energy in a congregation comes through the commitment of its members. Their loyalty, devotion, and continuing support allow the patterns of life to develop.[2] The Energy dynamic is marked by optimism, excitement, enthusiasm, and a sense of open-ended potential and possibilities. Congregations experiencing high Energy are change-oriented and therefore open to challenge and can tolerate momentary inconveniences and uncertainties without succumbing to chronic Anxiety. Energy is a quality whose importance is often overlooked as a necessary sign of congregational health. This is because some churches can go a long time running on momentum, going through routine practices with little Energy or enthusiasm. Congregational leaders who are satisfied that the job "gets done" in spite of a lack of the Energy dynamic have failed to notice a symptom that will lead to eventual decline—regardless of how much work gets done.

The Organizing Dynamic. The Organizing dynamic is universal in all organic systems. "Life self-organizes. Networks, patterns, and structures emerge without external imposition or direction. Organization wants to happen," writes organizational consultant Margaret Wheatley, in her book *Leadership and the New Science.*[3] In the hidden life of congregations, Organizing dynamics take their cues from the basic Church functions: worship, fellowship, proclamation, education, and ministry. Most congregations organize these functions into programs and services for both members and for those outside of the church family. Congregations with a strong Organizing dynamic have an orientation toward action—creating new programs and ministries, starting new ventures, forming new groups, and so forth. In addition, congregations organize patterns of communication and of relationships. Congregational leaders who want to understand what is going on in the congregation will want to pay attention to the patterns and networks of who talks to whom, who meets with whom, and which persons or groups are included and excluded. Because these organizational patterns and networks are closely tied to relationships, they often are the most difficult to change in a congregation.

The Controlling Dynamic. The fourth force in the hidden lives of congregations is the Controlling dynamic. Control in this context has to do with administering the hidden life forces and the resources of the congregation. If the Energy life force is undifferentiated and closely tied to the emotionality in the system, the Controlling dynamic is the rational posture that helps the congregation acquire focus and direction. When congregations work on things like mission statements, goals, objectives, or engage in planning, they are tapping into the rational power of the Controlling dynamic as a resource. Control allows a congregation to determine how to best use limited resources to their greater effect. One way congregations do this is by deciding what structures and processes will best serve to carry out their functions, thereby realizing the Church's intended mission and mandate. Some processes, for example, will have to do with checks and balances, span of control, coordinating, setting boundaries, and ensuring efficiency. The structures that a congregation puts in place facilitate integration, organization, appropriate designation of responsibilities, and effectiveness. Congregations need to ensure that how they use the dynamic of Control matches their particular values and needs. For example, a discerning congregation that is aware of its transitioning into the next stage in its lifespan (see chapter 4) will anticipate putting the structures and processes in place that will facilitate a smooth transition. It will also work at putting in place now the structures and processes it will need later. Most congregations tend not to be able to anticipate these transitions and wind up changing structures and processes only after experiencing much pain and frustration. Rather than being proactive, they wait until they realize that the controlling dynamics in place are actually impeding what they want to accomplish.

Most organizations use the Controlling dynamic with a focus toward their material and physical resources, including their human resources through the application of management. Congregations, too, use management as a mode of controlling their resources, but there is one more important focus of the Controlling dynamic in congregations, and that is *influence*. Congregations are, by their very nature, symbolic organizations, and therefore use normative relationship influences, or "social power" to address the behaviors and practices of their members.[4] Leaders in the congregation, both clergy and lay, use influence, rather than force, coercion, threat, or money, to change behavior and move members to action. They bank on the personal needs for approval, esteem, position, and status, and the corporate needs of belonging and trust, to tap into the Controlling dynamic. While this may seem manipulative and subject to abuse, we are being descriptive here. In order to understand the hidden dynamics at play in congregations, we must begin by appreciating that congregations are subject to all of the dynamics that—positive and negative, healthy and potentially harmful—are inherent to all relationship systems. Despite the reality of how the controlling dynamic works in all systems, congregations can guard against its abuse. The key to being able to do so lies in much of what we will discuss in part three—leadership.

The Relational Dynamic. The fifth hidden organic congregational life factor is the Relational dynamic, which has to do with the relationships among individuals and groups (including congregational leaders) within the congregation and outside of the church. The way a congregation negotiates its relationship networks is one of the most critical determining factors for its identity and its mission. This dynamic can foster maturity among members or hinder spiritual growth. A congregation depends on the hidden life force of the Relational dynamic when it deals with how people are welcomed and assimilated into its membership. Whether or not the church's programs meet the needs of the person over the needs and goals of the institution is a Relational dynamic issue. How effective a church is at calling out its members for personal and corporate ministry, helping members discover their spiritual gifts, and to practice their spiritual vocations in the workplace, are all Relational dynamic issues. In addition, how the church leadership handles issues of power, authority, and conflict are all related to the Relational dynamic of the church. The Relational dynamic in a congregation also informs such values as how warm, inclusive, and hospitable the church is toward its own and toward visitors. The high value that congregations place on fellowship is a function of the Relational dynamic in the church.

This congregational hidden life dynamic will help leaders understand that change in the church is best accomplished by approaching the congregation as a system of relationships in which personal as well as organizational goals are at play. When the congregation is interpreted through this Relationship systems perspective, it is seen as a place where the importance of addressing the relationship needs of the members is probably *more* important than any program the church may produce or any building it may construct.[5] Additionally, the Relational life dynamic emphasizes the corporate nature of the congregation. Maintaining this corporate focus that is at the heart of the nature of congregational relationships will provide an important corrective in that it helps leaders focus on the group life of the church as opposed to the individual experience of persons within or apart from the congregation.

Chapter 4

The Hidden Life of Congregational Lifespan

THE CONCEPT OF CONGREGATIONAL LIFESPAN PROVIDES ONE important lens for understanding the hidden life dynamics of a congregation as a living organism. In this chapter I will explain the concept and identify the stages of a congregation's lifespan. I will show how the inherent hidden life dynamics of the congregational lifespan affect a church's identity, leadership, and mission. The critical implication of this concept is that congregational leadership, especially pastoral leadership, must provide specific and particular functions for the congregation at each lifespan stage. Clergy and congregational leaders must be aware of, and provide for, these critical functions because these functions reside exclusively with those who occupy the leadership positions in the congregation. Failure to do so enables debilitating forces to hinder the health and vitality of the congregation. These critical leadership functions help congregations move in healthy ways toward the next natural cycle of life. Additionally, congregational leaders need to provide these necessary leadership functions during those critical times of transition from one congregational life stage to the other.

The challenges for the congregational pastor and other leaders will be to: (1) accurately identify the life stage in which the congregation is living; (2) understand the corresponding hidden life dynamics affecting the congregation; (3) identify and provide the necessary leadership function unique to the congregation's particular life stage; and (4) be able to equip themselves to minister successfully in the current life stage while concurrently anticipating the leadership functions needed for the upcoming transition, as well as the stage beyond. This chapter builds on the works of Ichak Adizes, Martin F. Saarinen, and others who have developed the concept of the organizational and congregational life cycle.[1] I will emphasize two specific functions here: (1) the leadership functions relative to the effects of the hidden life dynamics on members' faith; and (2) the critical function of education in the church's life.

Members join a congregation at a particular time in the church's lifespan. The organic and organizational dynamics at play during that time in the congregation's development influence relationships, and those relationships in turn shape faith. For example, as stated in part one, the two main activities that congregations use for faith formation are corporate worship and education. These activities change and develop as a congregation evolves through its lifespan. One's experience of Church (and thereby, of faith) through education and worship during a congregation's Formative years is qualitatively different from one's faith experience during a congregation's Aristocracy period. The formation of faith does not happen in a vacuum. The way members acquire faith, incorporate a set of beliefs, form an understanding of ministry (or of the congregation's relationship with the world), and recognize the way one "ought" to relate to other members are all influenced, in large part, by the hidden life of the congregation in which they participate.

The Dynamics of Congregational Lifespan

As with any schema of dynamic development, certain principles guide movement and progress. Understanding these principles helps us discern the hidden life of the congregation's lifespan and how it impacts leaders and members. These principles are based on the dynamic nature of how organic systems grow and develop. They help explain the "rules" that inform the trajectory of the congregational lifespan. In addition, these principles help us understand the parameters of what is and is not possible within the development frameworks and dynamics. Since these development principles are self-evident, I'll just list them with little explanation. They will, however, provide an important backdrop to the description of the lifespan stages that follow.

1. *Growth and decline progress from stage to stage.* In other words, a congregation cannot "skip" a stage. A congregation will progress from its Formatting stage to its Prime only after going through the Adolescent stage. Likewise, once a congregation is in the decline phase it will continue through the lifespan stages—it cannot go back to an "earlier" stage. However, leaders can help the congregation draw on the hidden life forces that can maintain vitality and health during any stage, even during cycles of decline.

2. *The trajectory of growth and decline is not linear.* There is no straight and steady progress from one stage to the next. A cyclical process of

decline and development, progress and setbacks, marks movement during a stage and into transitions. For instance, during times of renewal, enabling forces like the Energy dynamic predominate in the development phase; Organizing dynamics take over and cause the decline phase. Conversely, during times of regression, dynamics like Systemic Anxiety or an overemphasis on the Controlling dynamics will inhibit progress and growth. The cyclical process from stage to stage presents congregational members with critical tasks that must be addressed. The congregation's ability or willingness to perform these tasks not only determines health and vitality during a particular lifespan stage but also increases the potential for healthy movement from stage to stage.

3. Growth and development may be aborted and decline may take hold at any stage. Sometimes this is due to external forces beyond the control of the congregation, like a changing neighborhood or poor national economic forces. But, more often than not, lack of growth or progress is more likely to happen because of internal factors. If leadership fails, for example, the congregation will lack the necessary visionary resources for positive development. Other internal factors that contribute to arrested development include an inability to deal with the seductive homeostatic forces; a presumption of "having arrived," which causes a congregation to lose its edge or sense of adventure; or a failure of nerve—and a lack of faith—that leads a congregation to despair of a hopeful future.

4. Decline and stagnation may be controlled by tapping into enabling life-giving forces like Energy and responsible Control. The presence of courageous pastoral and congregational leadership can provide renewal by renewing the congregational vision or reframing the mission and ministries in response to changing times and environment.

5. During each lifespan stage, there is a unique interplay between the five organic relational dynamics: Systemic Anxiety, Energy, Controlling, Organizing, and Relational. This unique interplay necessitates certain specific organizational functions, including leadership functions, that are specific to each stage. These leadership functions, by definition, must be provided by the leader in the system—the pastor, primarily. As much as we would desire strong and responsible congregational lay leadership, the fact is that congregations are highly dependent on the pastor's leadership position to provide critical relational and organizational functions. Some of these particular functions (like vision) cannot be provided by anyone else in the congregational system; others can be delegated to other leaders in the congregation—staff or lay leaders. If the pastor defects in place and does not provide these leadership functions, the congregational system will lack key resources it needs for survival and development.

6. If the pastor, as leader in the congregational system, is to manage effectively the life and ministry of the congregation—at whatever lifespan stage—and help the congregation realize development rather than decline, he or she must understand and provide the leadership functions needed for that stage of development. This means that effective pastors will need to re-tool continually their skills according to the congregation's needs (or, at the very least, ensure that they can provide through others—an individual or a group—the functions necessary to foster development and arrest decline). One of the most important leadership functions that a pastor needs to provide for a congregation is to help the system maintain resilience in the face of change and challenges. Pastors can do this only if they themselves are growing in their capacity to be resilient and adaptable.

The Lifespan Stages

William Shakespeare identified seven stages of man in his play "As You Like It." In the play, the character of Jacques playfully traces the natural and predictable lifespan of a man going from an infant, "Mewling and puking in the nurse's arms," to the

> Last scene of all,
> That ends this strange eventful history,
> Is second childishness and mere oblivion,
> Sans teeth, sans eyes, sans taste, sans everything.[2]

There are eight lifespan stages of a congregation, which also move from birth to decline and dissolution. We'll sketch each lifespan stage below with an emphasis on two important components in the life of any congregation: the pastoral leadership functions that the congregation needs, and the educational needs of the congregation. Each of these impacts the spiritual formation of the members in the way they shape practices, programs, and processes. Next to the role of leadership, effective education is the second critical element that can facilitate a congregation's progress, effectiveness, and viability. When the educational enterprises of a congregation do not serve to meet the lifespan and transitional needs of a church, the members are denied the second most important resource to their growth and development.

The Establishing Stage

The Establishing stage of a new congregation is exciting and hopeful. For those who are a part of a church's "birthing," little compares to this experience. Members of this new venture, though small in number, have an extraordinary level of energy and enthusiasm. The hidden Energy dynamic provides members with a "can-do" spirit that pervades everything they do. They are the "new kid on the block"—often literally—and take pride in being different and unique. Perhaps never in its lifespan will the congregation be as dependent on the pastor as it is during this stage of its history. Not only do the members rely heavily on the pastor's vision for the church, but the dependency may extend to the pastor's personality. During some lifespan stages the leadership function is primary and the pastor's personality is almost inconsequential. But at this Establishing stage, the pastor's personality may be one of the central components that holds this church together. Founding pastors are often charismatic leaders who can inspire and motivate not just through their competency, but through the force of their charisma.

A constant source of frustration for the church at this stage of life is that the membership base is rarely large enough to support basic ministry and growing organizational needs—much less to facilitate all of the grand schemes and plans that tend to pop up here and there, sometimes fed by the pastor's vision and enthusiasm. Until this congregation reaches a critical mass, it will struggle to rein in the members' desires to have it all *now*. Parents of teenagers will want a full-service youth group and parents of babies and preschoolers will want a fully equipped nursery and play yard. If leadership cannot help the members committed to this new venture take the long view, the church will suffer from spurious enthusiasm and sporadic periods of unresponsiveness—two things it cannot afford since, literally, every member counts. The most urgent need of this congregation is to expand its numbers to ensure its viability. This is tenuous, but not difficult to achieve, since this congregation draws new people through personal contacts, its raw enthusiasm, its sense of "newness" and hope, and through the influence of the charismatic leader. However, this congregation will tend to see a lot of traffic as potential members come and go rapidly.

The most critical leadership functions that the pastor must provide during this lifespan stage are those of *vision* and *connectedness*. A congregation at this stage tends to be very dependent on its pastor for articulating and keeping alive a future-oriented vision in the face of real challenges. Additionally, in this congregation the pastor serves as a hub person. Through his or her relationship with the members, the pastor helps keep the group cohesiveness intact and commitment to the group alive.

The educational needs of a congregation during its establishment stage center around two concerns: (1) communicating a shared corpus of beliefs and (2) training members for ever-expanding and specialized ministry and organizational functions. New church ventures tend to attract a significant number of formerly unchurched members. These people need to be discipled into basic understandings of Christian doctrine, Church history, polity, Bible knowledge, and in how to be a loyal and supportive church member. For some of these new churchgoers this discipleship will happen concurrently with their need to be trained in how to do ministry both in church organizational groups and in any mission activities in which the church engages.

The Formation and Formatting Stage

The time span between the Establishing stage and the second stage of the lifespan, Formation and Formatting, may be brief—as little as eight months to a year. This is because organisms and relationship systems— a congregation being a form of both—seek to find their equilibrium as soon as possible. A system that cannot quickly establish a sense of homeostasis will tend to move toward quick dissolution because it cannot find the center around which to build and focus. The key leadership function at this stage is that of *process management*. The pastor needs to tap into the hidden Controlling dynamics in order to facilitate positive and helpful emotional and relational processes. This includes developing the quality of the congregational relationships. For example, one critical function for the pastor is to help ensure that the level and quality of the Energy dynamic becomes increasingly differentiated by channeling it into tasks that actually benefit the congregation and facilitate good processes and practices. Those relational qualities also include how persons communicate and how open that communication will be. Relationship processes include how well the congregation facilitates inclusion into the life of the church the second and third wave of "new members." The critical function that the pastor provides in forming and formatting these processes and their qualities will have long-term consequences. It is during this period of the lifespan that relational processes, like how the congregational members handle conflict and deal with issues, get "formatted." These processes become, to use a popular (though somewhat inaccurate) metaphor, "the DNA of the congregation," meaning that once in place, these emotional processes will be determinative for the rest of the church's lifespan.

One of the congregation's strengths at this stage is that, with just a little attention, it can retain the open and unrestricted inclusiveness from its Establishing stage, as well as its contagious enthusiasm. This helps maintain the momentum of adding new members and facilitating their entry and full participation in the life of the church. However, due to the limited opportunities beyond basic programs and activities—most of which may be underdeveloped—two things may happen. First, the church may maintain a high level of new-member growth but find that it has few places for them to connect through programs, ministries, and small groups—potentially setting new members into a "holding pattern" from which most will not emerge. From there the church may begin to back off from welcoming new members as it experiences the frustration of not having "room" for them. Because this is the Formation and Formatting stage of development, when either of those two processes takes hold, they will become the formatted posture of a church—either remaining open to new members and learning to live with the frustration of not providing adequate places of connection (in which case it may become a congregation with a back door as large as its front door through which as many members leave as come), or becoming a church that resists welcoming new members for fear of being overwhelmed. The pastor's function then includes establishing processes that can efficiently and quickly create structures to accommodate change and growth. If the congregation can incorporate that posture into its patterned response it will be able to see changes as challenges and not threats, and will be able to respond with resilience and creativity rather than disillusionment.

During this critical formative stage in the congregation's lifespan, articulating an informing theology and establishing attendant practices and habits becomes critical. This will require that the congregational leaders live up to their function as resident theologians (see chapter 8). For example, if a congregation fails to develop for its members a theology of call to participate in ministry and mission (Ephesians 4:4, 7, 11-13), and also does not equip those members for ministry, only with great difficulty will this become a reality in a future stage. This also risks an all-out crisis, as the congregation will need to acquire new values, reinterpret its mission, and restructure its organization and relationships. This focus on equipping the laity for ministry will be a challenge during a time in the lifespan when the pastor and leader need also to work at institutional survival issues. The temptation for leadership will be to give up on the hard work of staying true to theological integrity for the sake of attempting to keep new members happy and comfortable. For congregations that want to remain true to the mission and mandate of the Church, this may prove to be its first challenge to authenticity.

Two additional critical pastoral functions are called for during the Formation and Formatting stage. First, the pastor needs to work at *creating a sense of community identity among the congregation*. The small group of core members, which included the founding parents, has grown rapidly with the inclusion of new members. This is the critical stage in which the pastor needs to help the church acquire and negotiate the sense of "who we are" that includes both the founding pioneering group and the now-greater number of new members. The congregation's sense of "who we are" is closely tied to the perception—if not the reality—of "what we do." Therefore, the second critical function of the pastor is to *help create and develop specific ministries related to the vision of both who this church is and who they will be*. These early ministries are more critical to both identity and mission than most pastors may realize. The first significant ministries that a congregation chooses form part of its sense of mission, which relates to the member's identity in the sense of being "who we are" because of "what we do." In some congregations, the choice may come down to creating ministries that will shore up the church institutional organization or creating an equipping ministry structure with the theological focus of sending members into the world on mission.

The specific ministries that the pastor helps the congregation put in place contributes to the formatting of systemic myths in the congregation. These myths take hold between the Establishing and the Formation and Formatting stages and will remain part of the congregation's self-identity throughout its lifespan. These myths relate to, and will eventually give shape to, a congregation's stance (see chapter 7). One church that I know of created a medical ministry to indigent workers during its Formation and Formatting years. This free clinic was created by a group of church members still in the grips of the "can-do" attitude remaining from the Establishing stage. Challenged by the pastor's vision to be a servant church to the needs of the community, this group rallied members to purchase a building with ease of access to migrant workers and the indigent. Doctors, nurses, social workers, and other volunteers who were members of the church staffed the clinic, along with non-church-member volunteers from the community. For several years this truly was a mission of the church—run and maintained by the members of the congregation. It helped create a sense of identity about who they were as a church—compassionate, hands-on, innovative, and pioneering. They saw themselves as a servant church, because that was indeed what they did—they served the community through their corporate ministry and direct involvement.

Several decades later, this church became affluent and moved to the suburbs as they outgrew their original facility. Time and development had moved them into a different stage of the lifespan trajectory. They still thought of themselves as a servant church, and the "story" of the clinic remained a vital part of their sense of "who we are." In fact, that story, that "myth," was a centerpiece in their presentation to prospective members in the new-member orientation classes. Indeed, the name of the church was still associated with the clinic, which decades later was still in place and still ministering to the migrant population. But now, no church members actually volunteered at the clinic anymore. Doctors from local hospitals and agencies tended to the needs of those who came for help at the clinic. Despite the fact that the reality changed— the congregation was not engaged in the practice of hands-on ministry and the new suburban members were far detached from the lives and needs of the people who benefited from the clinic—they maintained the myth that they were a servant church, and really believed that they were doing missions through the clinic as they had decades before. In that church, the early pastoral leader was able to put in place a ministry that shaped the identity and formatted the myth of the servant church. But subsequent pastoral leaders had failed in their leadership function of ensuring that the myth was also a reality.

The educational needs of the congregation during the Formation and Formatting stage become a challenge for the church—especially because they may still lack the resources to meet their expanding educational needs. Few churches can afford a resident full-time educator at this stage, despite the fact that this is the stage during which most churches need one, perhaps more than at any other time. One need is for the congregation to put in place regular and formal educational programs. In most congregations, these will be traditional—Sunday school or Church school, adult Bible studies, children's and youth programs. Ambitious churches with in-house resources may add discipleship and small-group programs and ministries. As specialized groups and ministries begin to form and grow larger and diverse, more formal and effective training needs to be offered. Ministry groups like the diaconate, the ushers, caregiving groups, committees and ministry group chairpersons, program directors, choirs and worship leaders, teachers, and faculty all need training in order to do their job well. And, just as importantly, they need to be trained to do their job in keeping with the vision, identity, and ministry foci of the congregation. Done well, this conscientious training will result in a culture that supports community values. Done poorly, or not at all, will result in a lack of coordination, inconsistency in quality, and a confusion of means and ends. Either result will become formatted in the system and the congregation will benefit or suffer from one or the other for years to come.

The Adolescence Stage

Emerging from the Formation and Formatting stage, congregations enter into the next lifespan stage of Adolescence. This remains a high-energy stage but the programming dynamic becomes more important and prominent. A necessary pastoral leadership function for this stage is that of tapping into the Energy dynamics present in the congregation and focusing them more intentionally into programming and ministries. In addition, a congregation at this lifespan stage begins to require more services for its membership. Energies that once were directed at mission-related programs now begin to be diverted to creating more inward-focused programs and services. This is appropriate and necessary, and both pastor and congregational leaders need to turn their attention to institutional development. Numerical growth continues in most congregations during this stage—either steady or explosive—which brings with it demands for more specialized programs and services. These member needs may cause a subtle but definite shift in member expectations. An influx of a large number of young families and target groups—like single adults, divorced parents, students, and special-needs populations—may mean that there will be a shift of mission emphasis from ministry outside of the walls of the church to ministry to meet the growing needs of those inside the congregation. In most congregations, this stage brings about a major focus on families with children and youth, requiring the hiring of at least one additional part-time staff member—usually a youth or children's program minister.

The proliferation of new programs and ministries makes for a time of great excitement and novelty for the congregation. New leaders emerge during this time who find their niche in the congregation by responding to program and service needs that match their gifts, talents, or their own personal needs. Some of these members may stay in these adopted leadership roles for years, to the point that these ministries and programs become identified with the individual—who may then become an obstacle to future program development or in bringing new people into those ministry areas. If pastoral leadership is not attentive, the fast proliferation of programs and ministries may lead to burnout—on the leader's part, or on the part of the members. Furthermore, conflict may arise if the focus swings too much toward meeting the needs of the members over existing expectations or values related to the church's mission. If the pastor fails to tap into the hidden life forces and controlling dynamics at his or her disposal, things can get unwieldy. Longstanding members may begin to call for a return to the original vision and missions of the church. Newer members may perceive this as a lack of appreciation for their needs or as a dismissive posture toward new ministries in which they've invested a lot of emotional energy and personal resources. This congregation may still be attracted to the "new"—new programs, activities, and ministries—but more and more it will begin merely to pay lip service to actualizing these ministries.

The emerging level of complexity in the congregational organization and structure, as well as in the church's relationship matrix, will bring on the first major pastoral dilemma, which is, simply put, deciding whether to stay or to go. If the current pastor of the church is the founding pastor, the congregation has developed to such a point that he or she needs to deal with several very important issues. First, the pastor needs to deal with the harsh question of whether or not the church that he or she founded is still a good fit. The Adolescence stage requires some critical leadership functions that a founding church-planting pastor may not possess. Specifically, the Adolescent congregation needs a lot of attention to institutional development, including financial and stewardship development. Therefore, the pastor's functioning needs to shift from a primarily personal and personality-centered ministry, to one that is more administrative. It is possible that very soon the church may decide that the pastor is more of a hindrance to growth and development than an asset. If the pastor does not reach the same conclusion and willingly and gracefully leave—the resulting conflict may result in the pastor's dismissal.

Second, the pastor needs to decide whether or not he or she is able and willing to acquire the new repertoire of skills and competencies that will allow him or her to provide the leadership needed for the next lifespan transition and then into the next stage in the congregation's trajectory. If the pastor decides that it is time to move on—whether it is because he or she has brought the congregation as far as is possible within their capacity, or because he or she is not willing to meet the next leadership functions the congregation will need—then "leaving well" must be the pastor's primary focus. How the pastor leaves at this stage may well format the congregation's relationship with pastoral leadership for years to come.

The educational needs of the congregation during its Adolescence stage require a more intentional attention to new avenues of ministry. These may mean implementing different educational approaches and pedagogies that go beyond those sufficient for traditional church education programs. One new function of the educational enterprise is to identify congregational needs and assess existing programs. Many programs that have served the congregation well to this point are likely at the point of obsolescence. These need to be retooled to meet current needs or eliminated. Maintaining old programs just because they've been around "since the beginning," but do not meet actual current service or ministry needs, drain scarce but important leadership resources from the church. Granted, this is difficult for congregations to do. People invest emotionally in "their" programs and projects. Some may identify personally with programs they have started or invested heavily in time, effort, spiritual gifts, and money. The proliferation of new ministries and services will necessitate educational programs designed to develop new leadership and resource people, while at the same time equipping members for ministries. This includes putting in place processes and structures to identify needs, help members discover their spiritual gifts and passions for ministry, and then provide training that will equip them to carry out new and emerging ministries, programs, and services.

Another increasing educational need at this stage is the education of new Christians or formerly unchurched new members. In some areas, over half of new members coming in to the congregation are from non-church backgrounds or from other faith traditions. These new members need help in understanding the local and universal nature of the Church as well as the mission and vision of their local congregation. The congregation needs to educate new members in the local church history, traditions, and practices, as well as those of their denomination. This educational function is critical and its importance cannot be underestimated, for it is part of what new members need to acquire a distinctly Christian worldview that is informed by a foundational theological framework.

By now, you've noticed that our treatment of the congregational lifespan makes no mention about two important factors: congregational size and length in years. We'll deal with congregational size in the next chapter. Suffice it to say for now that while a congregation will tend to increase in membership size as it moves along the trajectory of its lifespan, there is no set rule as to what size a congregation "should" be at any given point in its lifespan. In the next chapter, we'll argue that the lower limit in size for a congregation is ten members, but there seems to be no theoretical upper limit to the size that a congregation can be. More to the point of this chapter, however, is the lack of mention about how long a particular life stage "should" last. That's because how long a particular congregation spends at any stage of the lifespan is dependent on too many variables to be able to give a set number of years between transitioning in and transitioning out of any given stage.

It may be safe to say that the transition from the Establishing stage to the Formation and Formatting stage is relatively quick. This is because two organic hidden life forces are at work during this time: differentiation and homeostasis. Organisms in the early stages of development need to differentiate essential functions for survival as quickly as possible—particularly the leadership function. Attaining a level of homeostasis tends to happen so quickly that the transition between these first two life stages may blur and the pastor and members may find themselves well into the transition from one to the next before they realize it. But since there is no set number of years that a congregation needs to spend in subsequent life stages, congregational leaders can work at prolonging certain stages intentionally. Certainly, when a church is in its Prime stage, leaders will want to work at prolonging the tenure of that stage as long as possible. It is possible for a congregation to spend decades at the Adolescent stage and then (theoretically) spend hundreds of years enjoying the Prime stage in its lifespan trajectory. That longevity will depend on leadership's ability to deal with some fundamental hidden life forces, as we'll see below.

The Prime Stage

However long it takes for a congregation to move through its Adolescent stage, at some point it transitions into its Prime stage in the lifespan. During the Prime stage, all of the five hidden dynamics that inform so much of congregational life are at full force: Energy, Organization, Control, the Relationship dynamic, and in its usual ebb and flow, Systemic Anxiety. A congregation in its Prime era is characterized by a certain confident maturity. It has learned to balance internal membership needs with the importance of challenging members to move outward in missions and ministry. The congregation has developed a comfortable stance in its intentional creation of a unique corporate "culture" that shapes a strong identity, yet has retained an ability to be open and to welcome new members. At this stage, however, the congregation's posture toward prospective members implies, "This is who we are. Would you like to join us?" People are less attracted to this congregation by the pastor's personality and more by the church's clear sense of corporate identity and culture. Joining a church in its Prime stage involves being open to incorporating the church culture and shared values rather than expecting that the church will readily accommodate personal tastes and needs. After the manic proliferation of creating programs for any number of actual or perceived needs and predilections during the Adolescent stage years, the church in its Prime has learned to balance its programmatic offerings with its vision. By now, many of the programs created during the previous stage have fallen by the wayside and a smaller number of proven and effective programs and ministries remain, supported by experienced lay leadership and competent staff.

A church in its Prime is not without challenge, however. Congregational conflicts will continue to be a part of being and doing church, some as a result of the natural ebb and flow of Systemic Anxiety, some as patterned behaviors and practices left over from the Formation and Formatting stage. Other conflicts will be over diminishing resources and having to deal realistically with how that affects the congregation's ministries. One phenomenon that many congregations in their Prime stage run into is that they may encounter for the first time problems for which they have no solutions. For congregations that still remember the grand things accomplished during the days of their "can-do" attitude, this is a source of great frustration. It can leave congregational leadership feeling vulnerable, which could lead to timidity in the way it approaches current and future ministry opportunities.

If the church has grown numerically, it would not be unusual for some conflict to settle around the issue of the role of the pastor, who now needs to be more and more involved in administration than with pastoral care or personal ministry with the members. While these critical functions may have been delegated to groups like the diaconate or to individual pastoral staff members, every now and again the congregation will feel the absence of the former warmer and more intimate relationship it had with the person in the pastoral leadership position. One critical pastoral leadership function, then, is for the pastor to help the church learn how to "fight nice." A mature and personally secure pastor understands that conflict is inevitable and cannot be avoided—nor should it be. Helping the congregation learn how to deal with conflict in a mature and responsible manner, and staying connected with all parties involved, will prove to be one of the most important leadership functions the pastor can provide during this congregational life stage. The pastor and congregational leadership will need to work harder and more efficiently at "staying connected," even in times when crises are not at the fore. For one thing, the church in its Prime often begins to feel a loss of intimacy and closeness, especially if it has grown in membership. Sometimes this results from losing a sense of vision or of purpose—which is paradoxical precisely because the congregation has grown efficient and proficient at carrying out its mission.

The danger is real here, and not merely imagined. A church in its Prime can begin to suffer from the presumption that it doesn't need to work at renewal, vision, assessment, and evaluation, believing that things will always be as good as they are now. But a congregation that falls for that illusion would do well to remember what any first year engineering student knows about the Second Law of Thermodynamics—*Energy spontaneously tends to flow only from being concentrated in one place to becom-*

ing diffused and spread out. Or, to put it another way, "things tend to break down." The critical leadership function for this stage is to fight the forces that lead to atrophy and resistance to change. Pastoral leadership will need to tap into the hidden life forces that are the critical resources for combating this settling homeostasis: vision, energy, renewal, resilience, and challenge. To put it succinctly, the most critical function of pastoral leadership at this stage may be to help the congregational emotional system "inhibit the inhibitors and jump start the resources."[3] The constant challenge for the pastor will be to develop and communicate the vision that will tip the church's direction from homeostasis to evolution, from complacency to resilience.

As ever, the educational enterprises of the congregation are a major resource for the congregation. Specific educational functions for this stage in the congregational lifespan include the cultivation of imagination. Since the congregation at this stage will create only a small number of new programs, educators and programmers will need to be creative in providing variations on a theme while maintaining the sound educational processes that ensure effectiveness in existing programs. This creative process includes maintaining a sense of adventure and novelty in existing programs while retooling them as the congregation's educational needs continue to evolve. This congregation will be tempted to attempt to "do more," when what it really needs to work at is ensuring that what is already does is effective. One way that the educational function can help prolong the congregation's Prime stage is by creating the culture of an equipping church and a learning organization.[4]

The Maturity Stage

However long a congregation can exist in its Prime stage, inevitably the lifespan dynamics push the church into the decline cycle. The first lifespan stage on the arch of the decline phase is the Maturity stage. Martin Saarinen, one of the first writers to apply the concept of the life cycle to American congregations, describes a church in this life stage as having a "status quo culture."[5] This is a congregation with well-worn relationship pathways and a set fellowship structure. The use of sound and tested administrative procedures and processes and strong staff support and leadership means that the congregation enjoys a level of efficiency in its use of the Energy hidden life dynamic. This congregation tends not to get too excited about "new" things, preferring the predictable and familiar to the novel. It values stability over adventure. This congregation may exhibit the adult characteristic of "crystallized intelligence," an almost world-weary stance that gives it the ability to choose what it will and will not learn or venture. This congregation knows that it has nothing to prove, so, while it can maintain a sustained level of energetic activity, it tends to be unenthusiastic, and therein lies one of its greatest threats. Feeling secure and being able to make decisions based more on what appeals to them, members may become unresponsive to new opportunities and challenges. As the conditions in their immediate context change they may fail to focus externally to address the needs of those outside of their own circle of relationships—in other words, they may lose the capacity to create a new vision for themselves. If that happens, it will not be long before they become benign and then, ultimately, irrelevant to the broader community context.

The most critical pastoral leadership function at this stage of the lifespan, then, involves leading the congregation to engage in life review—to tell the story of "who we are and how we came to be so"—but with an honest and critical eye. Through honest life review, the congregation can celebrate its heritage, affirm its gifts and strengths, and own its uniqueness, but also engage in honest assessment of the integrity of its mission. If this church is to prolong its tenure in the Maturity stage of life, it will need to restate and refocus both its vision and its mission. Most pastors will find that, while the church may be open to restating its *vision*, the challenge will come in reframing the church's *mission*—what they do because of who they are, or more accurately, *how* they will do mission differently. Old ministries may once again have to be let go and new ministries and programs aimed at meeting the needs of those outside of the familiar circle of church members are needed. It is at this stage that pastors will need to put into practice one of the most critical pastoral skills: courage. Leadership at this point becomes not so much about expertise, but about vision and persistence.

The educational needs for the congregation at the Maturity stage include the creation of new programs, and ministries and services aimed at newer members and prospects as well as to the community at large. While current established members will be satisfied with existing programs that continue to meet their needs, the needs of newer members and of prospective members tend to be very different. There will be points of intersection where an existing program will be meaningful to both established members and new members—but those will be few. This congregation must intentionally work at regularly and periodically creating new small-group learning experiences, ministry opportunities, and services aimed specifically at new and prospective members. This is because, in a real sense, there may be two or three different generational subgroups coexisting in the same church at the same time.[6]

The Aristocracy Stage

For some congregations, the next stage on the lifespan is the Aristocracy stage. While it would seem that to move from Maturity to Aristocracy is a "move upward," it actually is a movement along the trajectory of decline on the congregational lifespan. Saarinen plots this stage as following naturally out of the Maturity stage, but I don't believe all churches attain this stage. In fact, it may be more accurate to think of this as a stage that is achieved by only a certain type of congregation, one that occupies a unique place in the larger neighborhood network. This congregation's profile includes an appreciation for efficiency, professionalism, traditionalism (even if only its own unique traditionalism), and good taste. So named because of its status-consciousness, the Aristocracy stage congregation may enjoy a level of influence, if not efficacy, in its networks. This congregation retains some of its characteristics from the Maturity stage—like the comfort of routines, a presumption of success, the benefit of attracting competent and experienced staff, and confidence in its chosen purposes and practices—but becomes more guarded against changes in its habits, practices, and values. The close-knit and inward-focused fellowship circles now become calcified toward exclusiveness. This results in a dwindling base of support from members—fewer and fewer who may be willing to trade a perceived privileged mentality for actual mission and ministry. While some restless members look back to the "golden years" of the congregation, a faithful but dwindling group will perceive that they currently are living in the golden years. This small group may be influential enough to block attempts at reform and renewal. The most desirable leadership skill for this congregation is that of a "showcase" pastor—someone with a celebrity personality and strong pulpit presence. While administration and control skills are critically important, these may be delegated to associate staff. But the real leadership challenge at this stage in the lifespan is to restore the sense of vitality in the congregation by again envisioning a new ministry purpose that embraces, respects, and celebrates the history of the church.

The Bureaucracy Stage

Whether or not a particular congregation achieves and goes through the Aristocracy stage, the natural progression on the declining trajectory is from the Maturity stage to the Bureaucracy stage. When a congregation slides out of fully transitioning into this stage, it is well on its way to dissolution; the likelihood of turning around a congregation in the grips of the hidden controlling life force through renewal, revisioning, or pure force of will is slim. This is a congregation held captive by the calcification of irrelevant structures and an incipient survival anxiety that leaves it with an inability to dream dreams for itself. Instead, members may fight turf battles over remaining positions, programs, and ministries. This results in an inability to pass on corporate memories, values, and ministry to the next generation of members.

The hidden life dynamic of Systemic Anxiety now takes on a new quality—it becomes chronic. Chronic anxiety is an "exaggeration of a basic rhythm of life: the instinctual, nonthinking response necessary of wilderness survival. . . ."[7] Chronic anxiety eventually takes its toll and the congregational emotional relationships become rigid, defensive, myopic, sometimes hostile, and suspicious. It is not unusual for a congregation at this stage to run through a series of short pastorates because of the unresponsiveness of the members to challenge. For this congregation, no amount of challenge or cajoling will move them from its devotion to institutional structures, even if they are no longer effective or relevant.

If a committed pastor cannot begin to address the issue of the hidden dynamic of chronic anxiety in the congregational system, eventually the congregation begins to personalize the Systemic Anxiety. Systemic corporate problems become personal as members become unable to distinguish their own anxiety from the congregation's systemic chronic anxiety. Paradoxically, a pastor's attempts to deal with the church's anxiety will tend to be perceived as personal attacks by those members who cannot let go of a personal ministry or committee turfs. Only three leadership functions can help this congregation function at a healthier and more visionary level. First, this congregation needs an experienced pastor who is committed to staying for the long haul. The perpetual string of short-term pastorates typical of this congregation will only serve to reinforce the hidden life dynamics of Control and Systemic Anxiety. Until a pastor comes along who is willing to invest in a long tenure with lowered expectations of what this church can manage in the short term, pastoral leadership will not be a resource for this congregation.

Second, the pastoral function will need to work hard at inhibiting the hidden dynamics of chronic Systemic Anxiety and Control forces. This includes managing those members who have personified these hidden dynamics. In order to accomplish that, the pastor will need to practice a kind of redemptive ruthlessness that is out of reach for most ministers. For example, there may come a time when a pastor has to choose vision over relationships, or the health of the congregation as a whole against the narrow and personal interests of a few. The pastor's firm interventions in setting boundaries, confronting dissidents, or containing saboteurs may result in a parting of the ways of individuals or groups. For ministers who value consensus and strive for unity, or for those whose "pastor's heart" values affirmation and warm personal relationships as confirmation of success, taking these uncompromising stances will prove to be an almost paralyzing challenge.

Third, pastoral leadership will need to work at empowering and enabling the resources inherent in the congregation. The function of leadership in this context requires attention to the well-being of the congregational system as a whole and not that of individuals. It may take a good while before these inherent resources—in processes, structures, and persons—are identified, since the chronic system has worked so well at inhibiting them. Educational enterprises in the Bureaucracy stage tend to be benign and nontransformative. Systems with chronic anxiety have an incapacity to learn, and therefore the few educational programs that this church will tolerate are those that merely reinforce the myopic beliefs of the emotional system. If the educational enterprises are to make any difference in this context, leadership will need to make intentional investment in those members who are most willing to change. Only those will be capable of learning and will ultimately be the enabling forces in the church.

The Dissolution Stage

They say that nothing is certain except death and taxes. And while most congregations enjoy the benefit of a tax-exempt status, none will likely escape dissolution, or organizational death. The final and logical end of the congregational lifespan is the Dissolution stage. This is a concept that is difficult for many to accept. The denial of personal death is an existential defense mechanism for individuals and organizations. And, as Ernest Becker has well argued, ours is a death-denying culture.[8] But once again we must make the distinction between a congregation and Church, and resist the temptation to equate the two. The Church will not only survive, it will thrive. What will inevitably change are the forms and expressions of Church and our experience of it. It may come about that the institutional congregational expression of Church will not survive at some point in the distant future but churches—groups of believers who commit to some form of faith community for worship, fellowship, and discipleship—will continue to exist in some form or another. Whatever its institutional evolution, it's a certainty that the Church will always have a corporate dimension to it, will always struggle with institutionalism, will always be caught in the dilemma of being in the world but not of it, will always experience cycles of renewal, will always vacillate between faithfulness to God and being a success in the world, and will always struggle with defining the nature of the roles of laity and clergy.

The remaining faithful members in the final stage of the lifespan have an enormous capacity to delay the corporate dissolution of their congregation—by engaging in institutional life support. But once a congregation reaches this stage, its end as a local expression of the Body of Christ is at hand. Nancy Ammerman's study found that, while commitment makes a positive impact during early stages in a congregation's lifespan, that characteristic becomes a liability in the later stages. She states that "In fact, their very commitment to each other and to the memories their congregation represents may be among the major obstacles preventing congregational adaptation to new circumstances."[9] Despair, loss of hope, and loss of identity will leave members with an incapacity to address even minimal issues of institutional survival. The buildings, property, and programs become mere cultural artifacts, a sad commentary on lost hopes and current failure. If the remaining members cannot extract themselves from the grips of denial they will be unable to choose responsibly and courageously from the few realistic options they have: leaving individually, turning over the remaining assets to a denominational body, allowing itself to be absorbed by another congregation, or closing shop and attempting to begin again elsewhere. If there is a pastor remaining, or if the church finds that rare pastor who is called and gifted in providing a pastoral-care ministry to a dying church, he or she can resource the church through the dissolution process. Ministry at this church is all about helping the congregation "die well."

Conclusion

Congregations are living relational organisms. And, like any other living organism, they have a lifespan composed of stages and cycles of decline and renewal. They are planted or established, and then they go through a formation phase during which the personality, values, and homeostasis of the congregation is established. The subsequent lifespan stages are periods of growth, evolution, stability, then decline and, eventually, dissolution. The concept of the congregational life cycle has been ably treated and interpreted elsewhere. This chapter has focused on the importance of the leadership function during the life stages, and has attempted to identify how the educational enterprises can be a resource to the churches throughout their lifespan.

Chapter 5

The Hidden Life of How Size Shapes Congregational Relationships

ONE COMMON AND PRACTICAL SCHEMA USED TO UNDERSTAND congregations is the congregational-size approach to classifying churches. Looking at congregations through this lens is used not only by denominational strategists in assessing and planning, but also by sociologists who study the role and development of religion in society. In this chapter we will use the schema of congregation-by-numerical-size to understand how the size of a congregation influences certain dynamics in the hidden lives of congregations. My review of current material on congregational size, however, will not advocate a church-growth approach to understanding this material. That is, the purpose of this chapter is not to use the schema as a way to "grow a church" or to move a church beyond a "plateau." Rather, the concept will highlight how the size of a congregation affects corporate relationships, leadership functions, and congregational forces. What I want to do in this chapter is help you to understand the hidden life forces of numerical size in the lives of congregations.

One typical but misguided interpretation of this model is to emphasize church numerical growth with its accompanying necessity for a particular, and narrow, clergy leadership focus. A survey of current literature and training programs for clergy will reveal certain unfortunate assumptions about congregational size, including the one that seems to say that "bigger is better" and that numerical growth correlates to being a "successful" or an "authentic" church. Clergy and denominational leaders who rely too eagerly on popular business models of organizational leadership will readily assume that growth in such indicators as numbers—or in business-oriented indices like market impact, product, and facilities—signifies effective leadership. But the fact of the matter is that there is no *theological* reason for insisting that a congregation needs to grow in numerical size. If one were to ask the average pastor or congregational lay leader, "Why do you want your church to grow numerically?" the reason given may have to do with marketing, strategy, organizational matters, or even ego, but it will not be theological.

Most presentations that focus on the congregation-by-size model seem to fail to understand three things: First, *the schema is descriptive, not prescriptive*. The fact of the matter is that bigger is *not* better, just different. And a small congregation is a *real* church, complete and fully Church, and is not inadequate to its nature because of its numerical size. Part of our obsession with size may be, as author and international church consultant James Desmond Anderson suggests, that American culture has created an ecclesiastical mentality with an entrepreneurial bias toward organizational efficiency and numerical growth.[1] Theological educator Janet Fishburn is correct in stating, "The point is that there is a difference between ministry that is a success measured in numbers and a ministry where spiritual formation and growth of all the people of God is the criterion for effective pastoral leadership."[2]

Second, *this model is only adequate in describing* one *model of Church*. At its worst, this size-related model fosters a congregation-in-a-kit type of church that is dependent on the pastor's personality and on a narrow perspective of the pastoral leadership function: Pastor as CEO and institutional developer. This tends to leave out many pastors whose pastoral strengths are more personal and relational rather than corporation building.

Third, *this model fails to appreciate that numbers are important less because of numerical size and more because size informs us about the nature of the congregation's systemic relationships*. This in turn helps us appreciate the formative processes and possibilities at work in the faith community. In other words, faith communities shape the faith of their members through the nature and dynamics of the relationships that exist in its context; rightly understanding those relationship dynamics created by numerical size informs us about what leadership functions a particular congregation requires.

I am indebted to the good studies of Arlin J. Rothauge, Alice Mann, Loren Mead, Gary L. McIntosh, Carl Dudley, and Beth Ann Gaede for their treatment of and continuing development of the concept of congregation size.[3] All of them are quite useful, especially in their treatment of the dynamics of transitioning from one size congregation to another. If you are familiar with their work, you'll recognize their influence in this chapter. I'll use a slightly different schematic organization in order to highlight the hidden life forces that are the focus here. I will divide congregations into three major categories: small congregations, large congregations, and size-independent congregations. There are two distinct types of congregations within each of the first two categories, which I will identify in terms of their unique hidden life forces. In the third category, the size-independent congregations, I will highlight particular hidden life forces inherent in those congregational contexts.

Small Congregations

Small congregations are churches with an average worship attendance of between 10 and 150 members. The term *members* in this schema does not refer exclusively to names on the official church register or roll. The hidden life dynamics of congregational size has also to do with how "belonging" is defined—that is, who "belongs" to a congregation and who does not. From an organizational reference point, membership may refer to the names on the roll (including even persons who are inactive, have left the area, have disappeared, or have died). But congregations are more than an organizational entity, and membership must therefore be understood in a way that provides more integrity about what it means to belong. Therefore, meaningful *participation* in congregational life may provide a better gauge for what it means to "belong" than a name on a membership roll. In most congregations, one does not need to be an official member to be able to participate significantly in the life of the congregation.

The Family-Size Congregation

The smallest-size congregation, with its accompanying styles of practices, is the so-called *Family-Size congregation*. Relatively small in number—from 10 to 50 members—the "family" designation is apt. Some church size schemas use the numbers "0 to 50" or "3 to 50" for this category. But I don't believe a number under 10 actually constitutes what we mean when we use the term *congregation*. Certainly, three individuals meeting regularly for worship can be a genuine faith group—but it is not a "congregation" in the institutionalized sense of the word. The individuals that tend to make up these congregations are a family in a very real sense: They all tend to be related through familial bonds. The easiest way to become a bona fide member in this church is to "marry into it." With the presence of resident patriarchs and matriarchs in the congregation, it is not unusual to have two or three influential extended family systems setting the tone for how this church functions. That includes everything from how worship is done (or not done) to how the church makes decisions.

Two hidden life forces are important to appreciate for this size congregation. First, the inclusion dynamics of this congregation make it
essentially a "closed" system. This is a "members-only" congregation with
a strong sense of who "we" are and who "they" are—or perhaps more
precisely, who "is not one of us." Entry and participation in this system is
difficult to achieve—unless you are literally "one of the family," in which
case membership and participation is expected. This congregational
system facilitates the "selective inclusion" hidden life force, as discussed
in chapter 3, through the function of the congregational "gatekeeper."
Often, that gatekeeper is the system's matriarch or patriarch, but sometimes that function is "assigned" to someone else. The resistance to include outsiders into this congregation makes it a tight-knit group
providing a feeling of closeness, of being a part of a "real family."

The second significant hidden life force is the ascribed leadership
function of the pastor. Even when this congregation can afford a full-
time pastor, the system's required leadership pastoral functions are
bounded. That is, this congregation has clear, if unspoken, expectations
of the pastor regarding what it does and does not want the pastor to
provide for them. Mostly, this congregation wants the pastor to function
as a family chaplain who will provide basic pastoral care, officiate at
nodal family events (weddings, funerals, births), and provide crisis counseling. As worship leader, a pastor in this church will do well to foster the
family atmosphere and provide inspiring (but not challenging) sermons
that affirm and reinforce the congregation's beliefs. This congregation
may occasionally feel the pinch of a small congregation's limited resources and begin to talk about growing and reaching more people. The
wise pastor, however, will understand that attempting to take the congregation at its word and moving to facilitate numerical growth will meet
only with resistance. In fact, the string of short pastoral tenures typical
of this congregation is evidence of its resistance to change and its adept-
ness at maintaining its homeostatic structure. What people in a Family-
Size congregation want from their pastor is to be loved and cared for—in
effect, to be shepherded.

The hidden truth about education in this context has less to do with
how religious education is done, than *to what end*. Because of its size and
limited resources, religious education programming tends to be basic,
small-scaled, and run on a shoestring budget. Educational programming
tends to be pastor-initiated and pastor-led. These tend to be family affairs (rarely do outsiders attend educational or training functions offered by this congregation) with basic content that is nontransformative.
That is, the educational intent is not to challenge the faith of the members; rather, it is to reinforce and affirm the family corporate faith—the

beliefs and values that bind the church. This is accomplished primarily through the power of community narrative and storytelling. Additionally, this church will rarely partner with another small church in joint educational ventures. Despite the advantages to such a partnership, this church will resist interacting with other congregations because of the possibility that its own beliefs and values will be challenged.

The hidden life of the Family-Size congregation speaks to how this type of faith community "shapes" the faith of its members. Perhaps in no other model of congregation is the power of corporate spiritual formation more evident than in this intimate system. Faith is more about relationship than about content, such as doctrine, teachings, or theology. In other words, faith is more about *who* you know than about *what* you know. Therefore, ministry is more important than missions in this church—but ministry is defined by what the members do for each other and for the community because of their place in "the family." This translates directly to the single most important hidden life force in this relationship system: identity. If there is one thing that the Family-Size congregation does better than any other type, it is to provide its members with a strong corporate identity of "who we are," accompanied with the formation of a strong personal identity to its members about "who *you* are among us."

The Shepherding-Size Congregation

The second type of congregation under the small-churches category is the *Shepherding-Size congregation*. This church has between approximately 50 to 150 active members. I refer to it as a "shepherding" church because it is highly dependent on its pastor for leadership (in contrast with the Family-Size congregation whose leadership functions center around patriarchal or matriarchal relationships and functions). Additionally, the primary leadership function of the pastor is akin to that of a shepherd caring for the flock. The members in such congregations get their spiritual needs met primarily through their personal relationships with the pastor. In fact, the majority of new members in this congregation will likely join the church as a direct result of the pastor's influence, either his or her ministry style or personality, or the pastor's direct efforts at reaching out to potential members. In this size congregation, it is likely that if the pastor is not reaching out to bring in new members, few in the congregation will do so.

One of the hidden life forces of this congregational type is just how dependent the church is on the pastor, not only for leadership functions but also for ministry tasks and missions activities—so much so that this can be called the "burn-out" church for clergy. Clergy in these congregations are overworked and overburdened. This congregation tends to attract overfunctioning pastors who mistake busyness with effectiveness. This congregation depends on the pastor not only to bring in new members, but also to grease the skids for their entry into a church that does not receive new members easily. This happens often more through the force of the pastor's personality than through any formal structures and processes. While membership in this congregation is more easily granted than in a Family-Size congregation, inclusion into the core life of the church is more difficult. This congregation can maintain a sense of "family." It is small enough to ensure that everyone knows everybody else, and it values the fact that the pastor knows everyone and can provide highly personal pastoral care. In fact, one of the chief obstacles to growth for this congregation is the unwillingness on the part of its members to receive pastoral care from anyone other than the "chief shepherd." Many a new pastoral associate in this size church learns this lesson when, at the conclusion of a hospital visit to a parishioner, he or she is asked, "And when is the pastor coming by?"

In the Shepherding-Size congregation, religious education enterprises also remain highly pastor-initiated and mainly pastor-led. As this congregation reaches the 150 mark in member participation, it may hire part-time, if not full-time, program staff for youth or children's ministry— or a combination configuration depending on perceived needs (youth and music, children and family, education and administration, and so forth). Even so, its educational offerings will likely be basic Bible studies and traditional church programs like Sunday school, Vacation Bible school, home Bible studies, and perhaps a support group or two. But this congregation will occasionally partner with other local churches to pool resources and make an attempt at organized outreach.

Most Shepherding-Size congregations will reach their ceiling at about 150 members and then stop growing numerically. At that point, they become one of the infamously labeled "plateau churches." The fact is that the majority of congregations in the United States have an average membership of less than 100.[4] But when a Shepherding-Size congregation nears the 150 membership point, it seems to become anxious about its inability to grow larger. Several reasons may contribute to this, including our culture's success-oriented mentality that assumes that "bigger is better" and that the goal of any organization is to grow as large as it can. The "celebrity status" given to the so-called megachurches certainly contributes to this, including the often-misguided attempt among denominational leaders to duplicate the megachurch model as the norm. Add to that the feelings of insecurity that clergy suffer when their efforts at "growing the church" continue to fail in spite of their best efforts at following the recommended formulas for success—starting the right programs, adopting the right styles, and putting in place the correct strategies they are told will ensure success in numerical growth.

At 150 members, the Shepherding-Size congregation hits its first real plateau in terms of numerical growth. But I suspect that there is a hidden life force in the congregation that suggests that the reason for this has less to do with a lack of faithfulness on the part of the congregation, or a failure of leadership, or a lack of competence on the part of the pastor, or even the implementation of misguided strategies, and has more to do with the nature of the systemic relationships that are at play in the Shepherding-Size congregation.

Malcolm Gladwell, in *The Tipping Point,* presents the concept of "The Rule of 150" to explain the phenomenon of why groups have difficulty moving beyond the 150-member "tipping point."[5] The Rule of 150, says Gladwell, is the "tipping point" for any organization or group, because, when more than 150 persons are involved, structural matters impede a group's ability to agree on issues and to act with one voice. And if there is one value that churches with a sense of family desire, it's a sense of unity and oneness. Gladwell suggests that the dynamic behind the Rule of 150 is not merely organizational; 150 seems to represent the maximum number of individuals with whom we can biologically have a genuine social relationship, which goes with knowing who the people in our group are and how they relate to us. Gladwell cites the practice of the Hutterites, who, whenever their community reaches 150, split the community into two in order to maintain the intimate communal relationship dynamics.

Anyone who has had some experience in sales is likely to have endured any number of "pep talks" from sales managers and supervisors. One common pitch to starting salespersons is the message, "You can go out that door right now and sell 150 of these! How do I know? Because you know 150 people well enough to sell them this product." I worked my way through seminary as a manager in a funeral home. The home had two viewing parlors with a large sitting area in between. Each of those parlors would seat 300 people. Why 300 and not 150? I suspect because no one likes to go to a funeral by him or herself! The average size of the typical funeral is 300 people.

The hidden life force that drives this Rule of 150 phenomenon is what Gladwell refers to as the role of *transactive memory*. Transactive memory is a type of communal-corporate memory that involves the kind of information we store with other people in our group. This instinctual sharing of knowledge is a big part of what intimacy means: Knowing others well enough to know what they know and to trust them to know things for us. It's why, at any given moment in any number of places around the globe, someone in a household is turning to another person and saying, "Honey, where do we keep the ___?"

My favorite personal example of this is the time I was in my study at home working on a class lecture. In the course of typing the lecture notes it occurred to me that showing a video clip from the movie *Ferris Bueller's Day Off* would provide an effective illustration of the point I wanted to make. Without even thinking or taking my eyes off the computer screen, I called out to my youngest son, "Thomas, would you go down and get me the *Ferris Bueller* videocassette?" My son went downstairs and in less than three minutes was in my study with the tape. The hidden dynamics in that little scenario did not occur to me until later. Like most families in suburbia, we have a cabinet crammed full of videos in no organized system, long having exceeded its maximum capacity. When I wanted the video of *Ferris Bueller's Day Off*, I instinctively knew that if I tried to go down to the den and look for that one videocassette, I'd spend a fruitless half hour trying to find it. And, just as instinctively, I knew who in our family would *know* where that one videocassette was in that chaotic mess: my youngest son. That is the power of transactive memory! Our family never called a family council when the kids were young, sitting around the kitchen table with a notepad, saying, "Now Mom, you're in charge of housewares and landscaping; Dad, you keep track of the tools and auto maintenance. Doug, you're the oldest, so you're in charge of the household pets, and Thomas, you're the video guy." Families and intimate communities don't work that way! Intimacy, and the role of transactive memory, means that while I don't know where certain things are in my home, I know who does, and I trust them to have that knowledge for me.

The hidden life dynamic of why congregations tend to plateau at 150 is that the nature of the systemic, communal relationship will change beyond the tipping point and thus alter emotional processes like transactive memory. Churches intuitively know this. Growing larger will mean risking the loss of the way they know each other and the way they are known. In an intimate small congregation, you don't need an organizational and administrative manual to find out certain things. All you have to do is ask the right person and you'll get the information you need—and the systemic nature of relationships ensures that you'll likely know who that right person is.

The systemic relational dynamics of intimacy and identity are part of the hidden life forces that explain why change in terms of numerical growth is resisted and is such a challenge for the Shepherding-Size congregation. Numerical growth will mean a loss of intimacy, and a loss of the feeling of "church" as people have come to experience it.

In terms of pastoral leadership, there are additional hidden life forces at play that provide reasons why so many churches plateau at around 150 members. First and foremost may be the sense of loss that the pastor feels about his or her ministry. As the congregation grows in numbers and the relationship dynamics get more complex, the pastoral leadership function shifts. The practices and habits of ministry that sustained and made the shepherd pastor so good at providing ministry—"caring for the flock" through intimate personal relationships—become increasingly difficult to maintain. And in fact, in a larger congregation that highly personal pastoral leadership approach becomes ineffective as the need to give more attention to increasingly complex management functions becomes critical.

If the congregation grows numerically the pastor will need to spend more time on ministry development and organizational maintenance. This includes the creation and launching of homegrown ministries along with the necessary lay leadership development. Often, this entails bringing on staff persons, which means that the pastor now must function as a head-of-staff supervisor. In conjunction with this, the pastor now has to help shift the decision-making structure to facilitate a more democratic process. More and more people need to be involved in decision making, which is quite a challenge for a pastor who previously had the convenience and the mandate to be the "decision-maker" for the congregation.

With the increased complexity in the system, the need for new and intentional ways of communicating becomes critical. This in itself is a challenging shift in both the ways people relate to each other and in how they do things. Formerly, when a decision was made in a committee or in a staff meeting in the office, no one had to think much about or work hard at "getting the word out." Everyone knew that, upon leaving the meeting, no memo needed to be written, no announcement needed to be made, and it really didn't need to be reported in the church newsletter. If what was decided in a committee or staff meeting was important, the system of relationships was intimate and efficient enough to ensure that, one way or another, everyone would know sooner or later. Rarely would anyone be left in the dark about important decisions. But as a congregation grows numerically, with an increase in complexity, more specialized committee or board functions, and new relational configurations, the pastor and staff need to work differently and intentionally to ensure that everyone's on the same page. This means setting up information networks where they did not formerly exist. While this is best done proactively and in anticipation of the needs of the organization, most congregations don't deal with this until one or two unfortunate miscommunication crises.

The two additional new pastoral functions that the Shepherding-Size congregation needs to undertake are critical, complex, and time consuming. First, they must forge a more formal networking relationship with the church's denomination at both the local and national level. Second, they must develop the physical plant needs, which for a growing Shepherding-Size congregation will mean building or relocating. The level of pastoral leadership required for giving effective attention to both of these pretty much ensures that the pastor will have little time or energy to maintain a shepherding relationship with the church. Some members will perceive this as a distancing on the part of the pastor—correctly sensing that the pastor is not as available as she or he once was.

Given the hidden life dynamics inherent in the Shepherding-Size congregation, is it any wonder that most congregations plateau at this stage? But understanding these hidden life dynamics may help us appreciate that there may be legitimate reasons for this plateauing. These reasons have less to do with a lack of faith, a lack of commitment to the mission of the gospel, or with a lack of pastoral competence, and more to do with the nature of systemic relationships present in that size congregation. Rather than perceiving a Shepherding-Size congregation that maintains itself at 150 members as a failure, we need to appreciate that it maintains its size to provide the very things people want and need from their church: intimate relationships among the members, a sense of belonging with a clear sense of one's "place" in the church, and a caring, intimate personal relationship with a pastor who is easily accessible. Why would a church want to lose that? Apparently, given the numbers, most churches do not want to lose that communal intimacy and find ways to ensure that they do not.

Large Congregations

The names we'll use for the two types of congregations that fall under the "Large Congregations" category are: the Programmed-Size church and the Corporation-Size church. Large churches have memberships of 150 or more. This makes them fewer in number in terms of the demographics of all congregations, but they tend to be more prominent and influential, if only in terms of how they are perceived. Large congregations exhibit a higher and more complex level of institutionalization, which bring about hidden life dynamics not present in smaller congregations. These emergent dynamics call for different functions and foci in both leadership and in the congregation's educational enterprise.

The Programmed-Size Congregation

Should the Shepherding-Size congregation navigate numerical growth well enough to break the plateau barrier, it may follow the trajectory of morphing into a *Programmed-Size congregation*. The number of active participants in this congregation runs between 150 to 350 members. A Programmed-Size congregation tends to be more democratic in organization and in its decision-making processes because more members actively participate in leading a myriad of programs and activities. While the pastor remains at the center of these programs and activities, his or her involvement is more as a planner, catalyst, and supervisor. Effective leadership functioning sometimes involves getting out of the way once a ministry or program is launched and in the capable hands of lay leaders.

One relational shift that happens once the transition to this size church is made is that the pastor becomes less accessible to the members for personal pastoral care. While the pastor will still visit church members in times of crises or during nodal life events, most of the time he or she will be available "by appointment." I remember reading a blurb in a church newsletter of a congregation that had just moved from a Shepherding-Size congregation to a Programmed-Size congregation. The notice, framed by a thick-lined box for emphasis, announced that, from now on, the pastor would be available by appointment only, and gave the contact number for the church office. I'd never seen this relationship shift so overtly announced, and could only chuckle at thinking about some lifelong church members saying, "I've been a member of this congregation for twenty-five years, and you're telling me that if I want to see my pastor I have to make an appointment?!"

One hidden life dynamic in this congregation is that the pastoral function needs to shift from interpersonal pastoral caregiving to programmatic management. When additional paid staff are hired to help oversee and lead program and ministry emphases, two critical pastoral roles emerge. The first is to provide the binding vision that will lie at the center of multiplying activities and ministries. The second role is that of "resident theologian," in which the pastor interprets the mission and ministry of a church that is getting busier and busier. The role of resident theologian serves to remind the members of the *why* behind the activities and practices in which the church engages. Additionally, to the extent the pastor can provide the function of resident theologian, he or she provides the congregation with the important ability to be discerning—to make appropriate decisions in legitimate ways not only about *what* to do, but also *what not* to do.

The members and potential members of a Programmed-Size congregation relate more to small groups and ministries for their spiritual and personal needs, and become less and less dependent on the pastor's personality and direct intervention for these. It is possible that one hidden life shift for the Programmed-Size congregation is to become what sociologist Penny Edgell Becker calls the "House of Worship Church," in which members find identity and meaning primarily in corporate worship events and church programs rather than intimacy of relationships.[6]

As the Programmed-Size congregation grows larger, its need for additional varied and multi-tiered programs makes it highly dependent on competent paid staff. Excellence in staff performance becomes an issue—whether in musical performance, program design, administration, worship leadership, or running a meeting. Expectations rise for staff professionalism, evidenced in matters like spoken or written communication. This becomes critical because new members in this congregation will be attracted by the quality of the programs it offers. Investment in quality staff—finding them, keeping them, and developing them—is critical for this congregation's continued success. As Programmed-Size congregations become more specialized and localized, they tend to develop a "niche." This means that this congregation will depend on a competent and professional staff that has the ability to craft and create programs and products specific to its context as the church discovers that it cannot depend on religious publishing house products or their denominational office for their specialized programming needs. This becomes more so if the congregation takes seriously its calling to impact its local community context.

In its hidden life dynamics, the Programmed-Size congregation shapes the faith of its members by providing a myriad of opportunities and programs to meet the multitude of needs of a widening diverse membership. The repertoire of educational approaches expands as Christian education programs are created to realize a myriad of learning needs (teacher training, lay leadership development, group leaders, pastoral care, ministry specializations, and so forth). Strong leadership development programs become critical, and laypersons are challenged to spiritual maturity through their participation in leading ministries and in their growing competence as spiritual leaders for their church. Because of the complexity in relationship dynamics that numerical growth brings, the creation of small groups becomes critical to maintaining intimate relationships. Staff in this size congregation need to provide seven small groups for every 100 active members. Maintaining this ratio helps ensure that the programmatic structure is able to absorb and accommodate newcomers, by increasing the likelihood of face-to-face, intimate, small-group relationships among the members, as well as providing the diverse kinds of groups necessary to meet the various needs and interests in the congregation. A small group may consist of anything from a traditional Sunday morning Bible study class or a weekday mother's book reading group to support groups or a men's mission action group. Because of the nature of small-group dynamics that cause any group to become a "closed" group soon after its formation, this type of congregation also needs to ensure that new small groups are continually developed and begun. It is easier for "new" members to join "new" groups than established ones.

Additionally, in order to ensure that new members do not get lost in the system, leadership needs to intentionally put in place structures and processes that track new members to ensure that 80 percent of all newcomers (whether formal members or highly participant regular visitors) are involved in a small group within six months. The hidden life dynamic that leadership needs to pay attention to is that newcomers to a church are in a time of transition when they are beginning to create new life patterns. People who are new to the church are making lifestyle changes and choices, including restructuring their time. The window of opportunity that most people allow for that restructuring of their lifestyle and schedules is small. If the church is not intentional and aggressive about helping them make some choices about what they will commit to, something other than church participation will fill up that time vacuum. Getting 100 percent new-member involvement is ideal, of course, but not attainable. Leaders can, however, realistically set a goal of getting 80 percent of newcomers involved in significant ways through intentional programmatic structures and processes designed to facilitate moving people from the periphery toward the center of congregational life.

The Corporation-Size Church

The second type of congregation that falls under the "large churches" category I call the *Corporation-Size congregation*. This congregation has an active membership of 300 to 500 members or more (although its official membership roll can be in the thousands). This is a more complex and diverse congregational system with a pastor who functions much like a CEO of any other corporation. He (but rarely she) may be unknown personally by most of the members yet serves as an important personified symbol of this congregation's vision and character—sometimes even enjoying a kind of celebrity status if his or her influence extends beyond the boundaries of the congregation's ministries.

Some Corporation-Size congregations develop the characteristics of what Becker calls a "Leader Church." This type of church makes a qualitative shift away from the relational community dynamics exhibited even in the Programmed-Size congregation. As Becker describes it,

> . . . intimacy is less valued here as a public good. Providing members with intimate connections or a feeling of belonging are low priorities . . . although here too some individuals can find close friends by seeking them out. These congregations are participative, but they are more like branches of a social movement organization, with a strong mission, than are democracies, which have a more diffuse mission.[7]

This type of congregation is perceived as "big," and members take pride in that, seeing bigness as a sign of God's blessing—if not also a sign of their own abilities to embody effectively what successful church ministry can be. It is this bigness that tends to attract newcomers initially, and the church provides multiple entry points to facilitate a way for people to find a point of connection in a complex and diverse system. Personal relationships, friendships, and formal educational and discipleship networks are fostered in intentional small-group experiences—sometimes with overtly stated high accountability expectations not found in smaller congregations.

Because of its size and complexity, the Corporation-Size congregation tends to have a large paid professional staff, many of whom specialize in focused ministry enterprises. Some of this paid staff may be "homegrown," having received their theological training and practical ministry experience in the church itself. Staffing is a major challenge for this size congregation, which needs to maintain a ratio of one full-time staff member for every 150 members. Specialized ministries, including those that target particular groups and populations, will increase that ratio. The Corporation-Size congregation can grow quite large—at times to the so-called "megachurch" category. And while there may be localized impediments that may limit growth, it seems that a theoretical limit to how large a congregation can grow has not been determined.

Size-Independent Congregations

In the case of some churches, the congregation-by-size schema breaks down and is insufficient to describe or understand their nature. These congregations are best identified by the preeminence of the hidden life forces driven by their locale, their spirituality style, their theology, or their stance (a congregation's stance has to do with how its members view their corporate mission and ministry. Often a congregation's stance is determined by its immediate context, but sometimes it is determined by a doctrinal or a mission task emphasis). Because the hidden life dynamics of these churches create different ways of relating, organizing, and practicing their faith, they may be large or small, but their numerical size will be independent of their systemic nature in the ways that size influences the hidden life dynamics of most congregations. Some are more truly faith communities than the institutional congregational model can contain. One can think, for instance, of communal religious systems like those of the Amish. Other churches are more like organized groups than congregations, ranging from cultic to intimate, ongoing faith groups in which people attempt to live out a more intentional and overt response to Christian discipleship than most congregations can support. Some of these size-independent congregations may seem similar to the Family-Size congregation, but actually are more defined by familial, cultural, missional, or tribal dynamics than by their formal organizational structure.

How Size Shapes Faith

In using the congregation-by-size schema to examine the hidden lives of congregations, I must again stress that the point is not primarily to glean insight into how to help a church grow numerically. Despite all of the hype, print, and anxiety surrounding "church growth," finding ways to cause a congregation to increase in numerical size is almost beside the point. The reason is that there is no theological or qualitatively missional difference between large and small congregations. A small congregation of 70 is no less authentically Church than is a large congregation of 1,000. In other words, congregational size, while neither an indicator of theological authenticity nor necessarily an impediment to carrying out a local congregation's missional mandate, is important because the size of the congregation shapes the nature of corporate relationships. In turn, the nature of corporate relationships shapes the faith of the members in the congregational system.

Congregational size gives rise to the hidden life dynamics of congregations in at least two areas, the first of which is in the role and function of the spiritual leader, primarily, the pastor. As we've seen, the function of the pastor changes dramatically as a congregation moves from one size church type to the next. The two main dynamics that necessitate this change in function have to do with institutional development and relationship dynamics. As a congregation grows in size, the organizational structures and processes grow more complex. The level of intentional control and attention required to maintain and, more importantly, to develop the organization increases. Pastors who reside in growing congregations must become more competent in new managerial skills as the church's leadership needs move from relational to institutional. In addition, as the nature of the corporate relationships change with the increase in numerical size, the pastor needs to make a shift in how he or she relates to both the individual members and the congregation at large.

In congregations transitioning from one church size to the next, perhaps the most hidden life element is the change of pastoral function to the *institutionalizing dimension*. One reason for this is that congregations and their leaders fiercely resist the idea of the institutionalized church—despite the reality that a congregation's nature is in fact an institutionalized expression of religion. Beginning in the early stages of the Programmed-Size congregation, the pastoral leadership functions need to shift to that of institutional developer. This is a challenge to most clergy, who have a strong orientation toward personal relationships with their parishioners and who value intimate pastoral care as part of who they are and what they do. To make the shift in focusing their *primary* responsibilities and attention to the *institution* of church, and not to the individual members, is often too much of a stretch for some pastors. For example, institutional development often means that a leader needs to choose to make an institutional choice over maintaining a personal relationship. This is a tough stance for any leader, but for a pastor who is trained to focus on the spiritual needs of individuals and who has a heart for people, this can be an overwhelming, if not oppressive, decision to have to make.

The second hidden life dynamic of how size shapes people's faith has to do with *the nature of systemic relationships*. Persons exist as part of systems that provide for certain personal needs—ranging from basic survival and safety needs to more existential spiritual needs, such as the formation of values, of a functional worldview, and the acquiring of a healthy self-understanding. How systemic relationships in the congregation provide for those needs depends to a great extent on the size of a congregation. But, more to the point, the way the systemic relationships can or cannot provide for those needs shapes the faith of the members. Smaller congregations, like the Family-Size congregation, shape people's faith primarily through personal relationships that stress intimacy, trust, a strong sense of corporate identity, a clearly bounded world view ("Us" and "Them"), and a genuine sense of community that unapologetically lets the members know their place in the system, if not in the world. In these smaller relationship systems, the narrative structure of the community's story is intricately intertwined with both its members' individual life narratives and with a highly selective faith narrative, biblical or otherwise. In the small Shepherding-Size congregation, faith often is shaped through the influence of the pastor's personality. How one perceives self and God, and one's perspective of the world may be more influenced by the personal views and teachings of the local pastor—for better or for ill—than by a grounding in denominational traditions and teachings. In the systemic relationship makeup of the Shepherding-Size congregation, faith may be more "caught than taught"—and it is caught, in larger measure, from the pastor's personification and example of religious practices.

The nature of the systemic relationships maintained by larger-sized congregations also shapes the faith of their members, but in qualitatively different ways. The experience of faith, and how faith is formed, is different depending on the congregation's size. This may provide yet another insight as to why transitions—especially from the Shepherding- to Programmed-Size congregation—are so difficult, especially for those who've been a part of the congregation for any significant amount of time. The transition will result not merely in an increase in numbers, programs, or resources, but in a change in how people experience faith and in the way their church will shape their faith. When a congregation changes from one size type to the next, certain identity components will change, including symbols, the community story, and the language and communication patterns. These impact people's faith because they are part of the "stuff" of faith. Transitions are as much about a change of faith as they are about a change in organization. They are difficult to live through because, as theologian James Fowler pointed out, "We are a language-related, symbol-borne and story-sustained creatures. We do not live long or well without meaning."[8] If we accept Fowler's understanding of faith as "an irreducible *relational* phenomenon . . . an active 'mode-of-being-in-relation' to another or others in which we invest commitment, belief, love, risk, and hope,"[9] then we can appreciate that the fundamental issue of a congregation's size has more to do with how it will shape its members' faith than with how many members it has.

One suburban congregation had grown from a Shepherding-Size church to a Programmed-Size congregation. In the process, they built a new sanctuary—moving from a 1950s-style, cinder-block starter building to an 800-seat, elegant auditorium. This transition changed many things the church had not anticipated, including its worship style and its theological language. As one member put it, "We moved from being a 'Jesus' church to a 'God' church." This shift in worship theology, culture, and the accompanying growth in numbers, which shifted relationships and the ways the pastor functioned, meant that not everyone who was an intimate part of the former congregation was able to make a transition "into the new building" which they had supported financially and enthusiastically. For years this church maintained connections with members who remained a part of the congregation in their own way, but who never attended that congregation anymore (some never even set foot in the new building, confessing that it just was no longer their church).

Conclusion

The hidden life dynamic of how size shapes relationships, and in turn how relationships shape faith, is that the nature of systemic relationships gives the members the ability to foster a sense of identity that informs them about "who we are," and therefore, "why we do things this way." The shared and highly localized faith culture of a congregation—its system of knowledge, beliefs, practices, habits and custom, and its curriculum of faith—are built up over time, negotiated, and adapted through personal interaction. This contextual faith culture—each congregation has its own—provides a matrix through which a congregation understands its mission and its identity. It is in the way people in a congregation relate to each other that such things as processes and outcomes are decided, what programs develop (and how), and how conflicts are resolved (or not). This complex relational matrix, bounded by the impact of the congregation's size, is what gives shape to members' faiths. These help define the boundaries of what it means to be "a believer" and what it means to "belong." Each size-type congregation provides for these identity and practices of faith differently. And members, as well as potential members, understand this at some instinctual level. This in part explains why people will join one church over the other, and why members will either resist or welcome transitioning into being another kind of church.

Chapter 6

The Hidden Life of Spirituality Styles
of Congregations

ONE WEEKEND, WHILE OUT OF TOWN DOING WORKSHOPS, I TOOK
the opportunity to visit a friend I'd not seen in a while. He is what I call an
"informed layperson," a lifelong churchgoer and astute lay student of
the Bible and of matters ecclesiological: theology, the Church, denominations, and current affairs related to religion and culture. He is a deacon in his church, teaches Sunday school, and has provided significant
leadership to his congregation during trying times when difficult decisions needed to be made.

During the course of catching up with each other, he shared can-
didly about where he found himself in midlife (he was in his mid-forties).
He had just survived a company downsizing, dropped his first son off at
college four states away, is struggling with his newly diagnosed adult
ADD, but, fortunately, is managing to keep his depression under control.
He is supportive and encouraging to his wife, a recent college graduate
who is entering her professional field in midlife after raising a family. As
a result of work with an ongoing support group, he is making a trip to
reconnect with his younger sister as part of his family-of-origin work. His
sister is lesbian, but that remains the "family secret" that he suspects has
kept him cut off from her and has resulted in several difficult relational
dynamics in his own family.

In the midst of all this, he expressed frustration and dissatisfaction
with his congregation. He was insightful enough to say, "It's not so much
that the church has changed, but that I have changed." The issues and
concerns that take up so much attention and energy in the congregation—of which he was an integral part in the past—hold little interest
for him. The questions that his fellow church members are dealing with
he finds of little importance to him personally, and some he considers
trivial. He recognizes that he is in a different place spiritually, and he
struggles with the real possibility that he may leave the congregation in

which he can no longer find meaning or satisfaction. My friend seems to be growing in awareness that the church he's known all his life can no longer sustain him spiritually. He is in a "different place" than where most other church members find themselves. He is a classic example of someone whose spiritual orientation, his spiritual style, may be outgrowing that of his congregation. It is not that he is "more spiritual" than his fellow church members, nor is it that he has "more faith" than others in his church. And it isn't that he does not believe the same things that his church confesses. As he puts it, "I just believe those things differently than I used to."

The Nature of Faith

As one of my teachers was fond of saying, "There are things we say we believe, and then there are those things we really believe." This is true even in matters of faith. How can we know if we really believe something? In order for someone to really believe something, four components (or domains) must be operative to some degree. When all four of these components are operative, then *effectual faith* exists. Effectual faith is a qualitative designation that suggests that the issue is not "how much" faith we have (Jesus said as much in the Parable of the Mustard Seed), but rather, *what kind of faith* we have. A qualitative understanding of faith accepts that, as many scholars and theologians claim, faith is a normative human dimension—everyone has faith. Effective faith is the kind of faith that makes a difference—has an effect—on the way we live our lives. That is, effectual faith is a particular kind of faith, the kind of faith that has an overt effect on our lives: the way we behave, the way we think, the way we make decisions, the values that we hold, and the responses that we make to life. The four necessary domains of effectual faith are the:

1. AFFECTIVE (feelings, emotions, values);
2. COGNITIVE (knowledge, understanding, comprehension);
3. BEHAVIORAL (actions, conduct, skills); and
4. VOLITIONAL (will, conviction, intentionality).

We can say that a person has an "effectual faith" to the degree that all four components are operative in that person's life. Having an effectual faith means that a person really believes something (whether a value, an idea, a dogma, a doctrine, or an opinion). To the degree that any one of these four key components is not operative in a person's life, then that person does not really believe.[1]

Congregations shape the spirituality of their members in how well they address each of the four components of effectual faith. Through teaching, worship, and relations, churches impact the first three domains—cognitive, affective, and behavioral—relatively easily. For example, in the *cognitive* domain (that part of ourselves that deals with the cerebral, such as information, concepts, ideas, and facts), congregations teach beliefs. Through educational enterprises, they guide members through the stages of recall (memorization), comprehension, application, analysis, and evaluation. Likewise, effective teachers and leaders can lead members through the stages of the *affective* domain (that part of ourselves that deals with feelings, emotions, attitudes, and values) with success, from receiving to responding to valuing to organization to characterization.[2] The affect of the congregational members facilitates things like devotion, decision making, commitment, and loyalty. And while changing the attitude of a person or congregation is harder than inculcating a belief or passing on a doctrinal stance, it is not all that difficult. We've all experienced an "attitude adjustment" at some point in our lives. That can happen gradually and gently, as in coming to appreciate a new hymn or music style, or we can be shocked into a change of attitude through confrontation and challenge.

As for changing people's behavior, any child psychologist (or dog trainer for that matter) will tell you that it's not all that difficult. Whenever congregations need to teach a learner a new skill, a new method, or a different way of doing something—from helping ushers take up the offering differently, or helping deacons learn pastoral-care skills—they are causing change in the behavioral domain. But changing behaviors, while relatively easy, can be deceptive. Just because there has been a change of behavior does not mean there has been a change in belief. As faith communities, congregations are very effective in changing behavior—so much so that they risk teaching pagans to behave as Christians. Again, unless all four components of the affective, cognitive, behavioral, and volitional domains are operative, then there is no real effectual faith—that qualitative faith that has an effect on how we live our lives. In part, this explains why techniques-based diets, seminars to quit smoking, or workshops on the spiritual life are ineffective—they tend to focus almost exclusively on the behavioral domain.

The fourth domain of effectual faith, *volitional* (will), requires some additional comments. More than any other, this is the domain of the Spirit. This is where the deeper relationships are operational. Congregations may or may not overtly address issues related to the volitional domains, whose dynamics include relationship, trust, will, honesty, and openness. Congregations and their leaders will do well to respect the

AFFECTIVE   COGNITIVE
(heart)   (mind)

EFFECTUAL
FAITH

BEHAVIORAL   VOLITIONAL
(hands)   (will)

Dimensions of Effectual Faith

boundaries that define this domain over which they must not cross. No amount of manipulation or techniques can make members want or will to learn or to change. That is the prerogative of the individual church member. Members of a congregation have the personal freedom to learn or to choose not to learn or to embrace a belief. It is worth respecting the truth that while God's greatest desire is for us to love God, God will never coerce us to love God.

Nevertheless, congregations fall short in *not* addressing matters of volition as an aspect of hidden spiritual styles. Maybe this is because it is the one domain that cannot be taught in one lesson, or in the course of one quarter's worth of Sunday school classes, or in a Sunday morning sermon. This is the domain that requires an intentional commitment from congregational members if it is to have any meaningful impact in their lives together. While it is true that any intentional action to directly affect the volitional domain is inappropriate—and in some cases is a form of spiritual abuse—congregations can have an impact in that domain. Relationships mediate movement in the volitional domain, so the way congregations impact it is through the corporate and individual relationships that they facilitate and foster as a community of faith.

The Nature of Corporate Faith

James Fowler's theory of faith development can help us understand certain observable facts about congregations as faith communities. While Fowler's theory is one schema among many for understanding issues of faith and congregations, it is more rigorous in its methodology and conceptualization than other theories seeking to understand the nature of faith and spirituality. Since its introduction in 1981, it has stood the test of critique from scholars, academics, and practitioners in theology, psychology, and education. First, we'll examine Fowler's theory, and then we'll raise questions and implications concerning the hidden spiritual lives of congregations.[3]

According to Fowler, faith is a human universal and therefore is a part of what it means to be human.[4] Fowler identified six "stages" of faith, a misnomer he admits is regrettable. I prefer to think of these six distinct categories of faith as "styles" or "stances." The stages describe ways of relating and making meaning that are grounded in a person's psychological development and faith orientation. Identifying what stage a person is at in his or her faith development will give congregational leaders increased awareness of how the faith stance of the individual members of a congregation affects the corporate spirituality of the church system. This understanding will allow them to draw upon the very resources of the congregation's hidden spiritual life to help it resolve problems commonly encountered in the course of living and worshiping together and dealing with critical issues. Simply having the knowledge of what Fowler's theory involves will be useful to anyone working in the areas of spirituality, faith, and congregations.

Fowler's theory is relevant to all areas of religious concern—theological education, academic exploration of individual development and learning, as well as personal and corporate spirituality. But his work may be particularly important for congregational leaders—clergy, staff, and lay leaders—who are charged with ministering to, teaching, and training congregational leaders. Understanding faith development theory will provide insight into the hidden spiritual lives of congregations by looking specifically at the way people construct their faith. Fowler puts emphasis less upon the content of one's faith (*what* one believes) and more on the way in which one structures his or her faith (*how* one believes). Pastors and congregational educators should understand the implications of Fowler's theory at the very least so that they can teach effectively in congregations full of people who may be at different stages than themselves, and therefore may see things from a different perspective.

Needless to say, clergy who lack this understanding will fail to appreciate some basic realities of the hidden lives of congregations.

Fowler defines faith development as a sequence of stages by which people shape their relatedness to a transcendent center or centers of value. These stages indicate that there is an underlying system of transformation by which the self is constituted as it responds to questions of ultimate meaning. Fowler concludes that the seven stages of faith are hierarchical, that people have to progress from one stage to the other. The first stages are a process of finding self and establishing one's own identity. The later stages describe the situations in which the person learns to give from him or herself and moves from viewing self, life, and relationships in egocentric ways. The theory's observation about the nature of adult faith holds critical implications for understanding the hidden lives of congregations.

Fowler's work is very academic and at times hard to understand, but he is thorough in providing evidence to support his conclusions. Fowler's concept of faith development is much more comprehensive than other theories that address faith development. In addition, the premises on which the hierarchies of faith Fowler developed are quite different from other theories of faith or spiritual development. His reframing of the concept of faith from a focus on belief (content) to a way of knowing (an epistemology) and relating helps us unlock important aspects of the hidden spiritual lives of congregations. While the earlier stages of faith—Stages 1 and 2 and the "pre-stage" of Undifferentiated Faith common to infants—exist in congregations, they belong primarily to the children in the congregation. While important to the hidden spiritual lives of congregations, these stages are more acted upon by the community through education and formation, and therefore the impact of these stages of faith on the hidden lives of congregations is not as directly influential in the same way as in our primary focus on the hidden life of corporate spirituality. Fowler's Stage 5, Conjunctive Faith, is an adult faith that emerges, if at all, in midlife, and is rare in congregations. In fact, congregations have such difficulty addressing the needs of this stage that, to overstate the matter, "there are no congregations for Stage 5 people." Nevertheless, for the purposes of understanding the more typical congregational faith styles, it is helpful to understand the parameters of a Stage 5 faith.

Fowler's Stage 5 is a more "interior" and individual faith than the earlier stages of faith. The believer can now see herself as not only *a part of* the community, but also, at the same time, *apart from* the community that shaped her faith. This way of faith goes beyond surface self-awareness and self-criticism of the perspectives, beliefs, and worldview that have shaped the individual as part of the faith community. Not only can this person be critical about the assumptions, myths, and symbols of the faith, but also she can at the same time embrace these in a deeper, non-critical way that recaptures the essence of each. In the language of Carl Jung, a symbol is no longer merely a sign (if you don't understand that, it's unlikely you're a Stage 5, so don't worry about it). Unlike members at previous stages who seek, and need, certitude and loyalty to mutually agreed-upon interpretations of creeds, doctrines, and beliefs, the Stage 5 person can comfortably maintain paradoxes of faith and belief. They don't need definitive answers to every unresolved question or mystery of faith.

Another paradox of Stage 5 is that while it is an "interior" faith that is comfortable with its own center of authority, at the same time it looks outward toward a wider embrace of a more universal understanding of Church. Therefore, to faithful church members, it may appear that the loyalty of the Stage 5 church member is suspect, since he or she can affirm the beliefs, perspectives, and practices of other faiths and groups that are seemingly at odds with those of the church to which the person claims membership. To oversimplify, the Stage 5 member's internal authority gives its loyalty first and foremost to God, and only secondarily to the local faith community, its members, and their local beliefs, identity, and practices. This can seem like a loss of faith or disloyalty to members of a congregation who value oneness of spirit, consensus of belief, and adherence to local practices and habits.

Obviously, Stage 5 is complex and multidimensional. It is no surprise, then, to read Fowler himself claim, "I have not found or fabricated a simple way to describe Conjunctive faith. This frustrates me. I somehow feel that if I cannot communicate the features of this stage clearly, it means that I don't understand them."[5] We will restrict our focus to the two stages of faith that can best inform our understanding of the hidden spiritual life of a congregation.

Stage 3: Synthetic-Conventional

The Stage 3 church member (beginning when the person reaches adolescence) sees the world through the lens of the peer community. People are socialized into their faith community, "catching" their values and ways of thinking unconsciously from their peer group and subculture. In this stage people are immersed in the thinking and valuing system of their faith community, like a fish that does not perceive the water in which it swims. This, in part, is what we mean by "formation," the process of becoming a particular kind of person as a result of one's exposure and experiences with one's environment and relationship networks: familial, social, and communal.

Stage 3 appears to be the adult faith stage of most people in our congregations and society. It is estimated that two-thirds of adults in the United States function at Piaget's Concrete-Operational level. This means that they have a very limited ability to work with abstract concepts. This directly impacts a person's ability to attain a more mature faith since the "stuff" of faith is all made up of abstract concepts: salvation, redemption, sin, justification, God, faith, hope, and love. A person's inability to understand or "grasp" the deeper meanings of the "stuff" of faith results in an inability to attain a deeper, more complex, and more nuanced faith posture. Once the culturally accepted ways of thinking of the groups to which we belong become part of us, we tend neither to question them, nor the authoritative sources from which they derive. This is especially true of the congregation as faith community, which relies on a shared narrative matrix of beliefs and practices to inform corporate identity—which, in turn, provides for such things as a sense of intimacy, belonging, and clarity about "us" versus everyone else. At Stage 3, one's identity is based on being part of a group with shared history, traditions, and values. Without people in Stage 3, congregations, denominations, or cultures would have little cohesiveness or continuity. It is the faithful Stage 3 church member that supports the congregation and helps it thrive through his or her loyalty, commitment, and financial support. These are desirable qualities that help create the sense of "family" and/or "community" that congregational members want in a church.

Group-based identity, however, is also a cause of conflict. It is hard to deal calmly and rationally with issues that touch on one's identity. This is why it is only the naïve new pastor that messes with the liturgy of worship during the first year of his or her tenure in a congregation. Liturgy, like all other "practices" that a community creates and participates in, is directly linked to the negotiated corporate identity of the group. Congregations do what they do because of who they perceive they are. Clergy commonly joke about the seven last words of the church: "We've never done it that way before." But they fail to appreciate that there is a legitimate reason for that. This is a homeostatic mechanism that protects the continuity of the faith community's identity. Doing something in a new or different way forces a disconnect with accepted and assumed understandings of an acquired corporate identity. Because the hidden spiritual life of congregations includes the idea that "how we do things is an expression of who we are," the natural legitimate question to raise when someone wants to change a practice is, "Why are we doing it this way now?" Unfortunately, a lot of people get hurt in the process of trying to maintain the continuity of practices that are associated—whether consciously or not, legitimately or not—with identity, and many others get trampled by ungentle attempts to challenge or impatiently prompt members toward more mature spiritual growth before they are ready or willing to be challenged. Adult Stage 3 believers, then, tend to be loyal and support the congregation and its beliefs. They embrace and perpetuate the lifestyle practices that create a shared corporate subculture. They may react strongly if they perceive any of these things are under attack, since their identity is tied to them.

Stage 4: Individuative-Reflective Faith

In contrast to the corporately focused Stage 3, usually people at Stage 4, Individuative-Reflective faith, have little interest in the marks of church subcultural identity, because with these people there is a moving away from group-based identity, as well as from dependence on external sources of authority. Thus, Stage 4 believers are extremely irritated by the traditional "Sunday school answers." They do not require the assurance of assent that those familiar and uncritical answers provide for the group, but instead perceive those handy answers as an impediment to dealing with the new questions they desire to ask.

Adult believers in transition to Stage 4 may experience deep disappointment and anger at finding that some of the beliefs they had based their lives on do not stand up to scrutiny. They find little satisfying response to the new questions they are now willing to risk asking in the answers the faith community relies on to interpret life and living. The meaning-making hedge of the corporate milieu with which a congregation surrounds itself, that includes a set repertoire of explanations, interpretations, metaphors, and stories, feels suffocating to a Stage 4 seeker. Some become restless and impatient with the congregation's failure to deal with their questions and ultimately leave. Others may nevertheless remain in the church if they can reinterpret their faith along reasonable lines and find a supportive local church community with Stage 4 church-role models. A congregation with even a moderate tolerance for diversity and ambivalence in its members' faith exploration process can provide a home for the restless Stage 4 members. But congregations with leaders, teachers, and members who insist on having 100 percent of the church agreeing with all doctrines or creeds as a condition of retaining membership—however broadly or narrowly defined—are unwittingly demanding that all Stage 4 believers leave the congregation. In doing so, the congregation will lose the resources not only of a maturing and moderating influence, but also will run the risk of casting out those capable of providing the "prophetic voice" in the congregation.

Because congregations are complex and generally open communities of faith, they will at any given time have any number of stages of faith and faith styles in the congregation. With people at all stages fully participating in the life and practices of the church, finding ways for them to coexist in harmony is a challenge. To those at any given stage, the next stage looks like loss of faith. And the previous stage, the one that has been "outgrown," is unattractive and appears naïve. To people in Stage 3, Stage 4 sounds like disloyalty and a moving away from essential beliefs necessary for maintaining a unity of spirit and mind. To those in Stage 4, Stage 3 looks like unthinking traditionalism and Stage 5 like mystical mush.

Faith Styles and Theological Orientations

Understanding how faith styles, or stages of faith, inform the hidden lives of congregational members can help inform us about how congregations work. For instance, certain stages of faith (or faith styles) relate more specifically with certain theological metaphors for the Church. Churches do have operational-functional theologies that inform members about what kind of church they are (which in turn informs a congregation's identity). The congregation that embraces primarily a "Body of Christ" theology is different in significant ways from a church that embraces primarily a "Community of Faith" theology. Some denominations cluster around a "Kingdom of God" theology while others identify with a "Priesthood of Believers" functional theology. While all are biblical metaphors for the Church, each is only partial, incomplete, and certainly inadequate by itself to encompass the totality of the reality it seeks to describe.

There may be no end to the number of "spirituality styles" we can identify, nuance, and classify. Because the gospel always manifests itself in context and relationships, in a sense it is not inaccurate to say that every context and relationship is an expression of spirituality with its own unique style. But the corporate nature of congregational spirituality seems to provide a smaller repertoire of prescribed spirituality styles. This manifests in the ability to seek out and find congregations that feel "familiar." The experienced churchgoer can get very adept at recognizing a congregation's spiritual style shortly after walking through the front door of the church building.

A few years ago our family moved to our current home, only two hours away from our former home and place of ministry. In our context, two hours distance was enough to experience a qualitative cultural divide. When our family experienced a disconnect in how we were used to things working, one of our boys would inevitably say, "Well, I guess we're not in Kansas anymore." (To which the other one would respond, "How would you know? We've never *lived* in Kansas."). Like many families, one of the first things we did as part of restructuring our lives was to find a "new church home." This was an experience that was both frustrating and fascinating. One of the fascinating parts of this experience was watching our two teenage sons navigate the process of visiting, assessing, and choosing a congregation in which to participate. One of the most important factors for them in feeling their way around a congregation was the spiritual style of a congregation. These styles are so palpable that even my teenagers were able to make an assessment based on "first impressions" of how a congregation's style communicated beliefs and values.

Congregations adopt clearly identifiable hidden spirituality styles—based on anything from theology or doctrine to local culture or, more and more, a niche marketing strategy. Congregational researcher Jackson Carroll argues that the particular theological beliefs in a congregation are "elected" or selected by the members of a particular congregation because they have what he calls an "affinity" with their social worlds.[6] These spirituality styles are part of the hidden life of the congregation in the sense that they are not matters of overt intent; rather, they seem to be acquired somewhere along the way. If we were to ask a member of a congregation what his or her church's "spirituality style" is, that person would most likely be unable to answer. At best, they would tell us about "how we do things here," or "what we believe." Some hidden spirituality styles are chiefly influenced by the founding mothers and fathers, and perhaps especially by the founding pastor. Some congregations adopt the hidden spirituality style of their denomination, and others take on the spirituality style of an ideological or cultural segment of their denomination. For some congregations, the acquisition of a spirituality style is not a covert affair, but rather, an intentional decision about what approach to faith they consider more authentic. Some of these congregations may have had to split from a parent congregation in order to accommodate and practice freely what they perceive as a "better way" to be church. Such splits, all too common across the congregational landscape, rarely are about issues such as administration, aesthetics, or even practice—although they may be understood as such. Passions strong enough to move a group of people to cut off from each other find their impetus in things that are much deeper: ideology, cultural values, and often, a particular corporate spirituality that insists on its way of believing and practice, with little ability to tolerate challenge.

By way of illustrating what a corporate congregational spiritual style is, and how it is part of the hidden lives of congregations, we'll identify six distinct styles. None of these styles exists in a "pure form" in congregations, but they are common and identifiable enough to be able to show that each can be an informing spiritual dynamic that shapes the faith of congregational members. The six spiritual styles are: (1) *cognitive* spirituality, (2) *affective* spirituality, (3) *pilgrim* spirituality, (4) *mystic* spirituality, (5) *servant* spirituality, and (6) *crusader* spirituality. The names are merely descriptive and arbitrary, though some have found popular acceptance as ways of identifying personal and congregational spirituality styles. Professor and spiritual director Corinne Ware, to whom I'm indebted for the basic concept of corporate spirituality styles here presented, rightly points out that while any and all of these spiritually styles may be present in any given congregation in the lives of its members, the corporate congregational identity will tend to take on a dominant and identifiable spirituality.[7]

Cognitive Spirituality

Given our Western context in which rationality and scientism influence so much of life, it may not be an overstatement to say that the spiritual style of most congregations—especially of mainline churches—tends to lean toward cognitive spirituality. This "spirituality of the head,"[8] as Corinne Ware calls it, tends to emphasize, perhaps overly, the cognitive component of effectual faith. Congregations with a cognitive spirituality tend to focus on concepts and doctrine. Right belief rightly interpreted is a high value, whether that belief is traditional orthodoxy or a particular and localized one. Corporate worship tends toward the liturgical and is informed by attention to the text. Leadership in worship may seek to provide an elegant, literary, and challenging experience for the members. The minister's preaching has an overt teaching posture, and a well-educated, if not degreed, pastoral staff is valued by the membership—who themselves tend to be educated. A congregation with a cognitive spirituality values a strong education program, one that not only serves to perpetuate orthodoxy, but that can at the same time provide for opportunities to think seriously about critical issues of faith and of living.

Congregations that embrace a cognitive spirituality style can tolerate and make room for sincere seekers, pious skeptics, and doubters. While the members may demand respect for orthodoxy, they are not threatened by questions whose intent is to understand or even to challenge misunderstandings or misinterpretations of the faith. This is because members not only value knowledge and its pursuit, but they have confidence in their beliefs, which have stood the test of time, and have a sense that those beliefs can stand up to the scrutiny of those who need to question and test them before being able to embrace and affirm them.

At its best, the cognitive spirituality congregation takes seriously the importance of encouraging a critical faith on the part of the members. This is an important characteristic of a more mature faith and can be a rich resource that facilitates responsible discernment when decisions need to be made.[9] This congregation can train its members in a more responsible apologetic stance regarding what it believes and why (1 Peter 3:15), enabling them not only to value their tradition more deeply, but also to appreciate the beliefs of others. At its worst, however, this spiritual style may neglect the more emotional needs of its congregants if it fails to recognize that not all of faith resides in the cognitive domain. Uncompromising insistence on adherence to a narrow orthodoxy can exacerbate the posture of what "we believe" versus what "they believe"— even among the membership. One danger in this stance is in confusing "cognitive" with "rational." Failure to appreciate that effectual faith requires attention to the affective, behavioral, and volitional components of faith as much as the cognitive may result in a skewed understanding of what it means to be a believer and how we need to relate to those within and outside of the congregation.

Affective Spirituality

Historically in the West, and in our culture, movements and groups that have reclaimed for spirituality a seat in the heart have been a breath of fresh air. In doing so they have promoted a more affective, pietistic, and a more devotional dimension to faith and practice. Spiritual affect is primarily about values and attitudes, but also includes feelings and emotions. For affective spirituality, the latter two may become the focus of its style of practice. Experiencing the faith is very important to the members of an affective spirituality congregation. Warm and intimate fellowship is important for members of a church with a predominantly affective spirituality. Close relationships affirm feelings of intimacy and belonging among the members. Feeling affirmed, loved, and cared for is what is most important for this congregation, and the pastoral skills desired of its pastors and spiritual leadership are those that provide such qualities.

Because corporate worship is a formative event that serves to reinforce the congregational spirituality style, the affective spirituality congregation's worship experiences tend to be events of celebration, with high emotional energy, unapologetic enthusiasm, and joy—"praise" is the operative component here. Singing is important to congregations in most faith traditions, and each tradition will reflect its particular spiritual style through its music. The congregational spiritual style of affective spirituality provides a contrast to the cognitive spirituality style. If the "head spirituality" style gives overmuch emphasis to the cognitive component of effectual faith, then this style tends to invest too much of its spirituality on the affective domain. Unlike the cognitive spirituality congregation where hymns are valued for high aesthetics and for intelligent and elegant text that supports orthodoxy of belief, the affective spirituality church may choose hymns and songs more for emotional impact than for the message of the text. One typical reaction on the part of liturgically oriented visitors to the music at so-called "contemporary praise services" has to do with the words that accompany praise choruses. These visitors will turn to each other after singing the text of the chorus (often after the seventh go-round) and in a bemused tone ask, "What does that *mean*?" What they may fail to notice is that regular participants really are not as concerned about whether the text is poetic or literary, or even if it actually makes any sense, as much as they are about whether the music "rocks" them. Music in the worship experience for an affective spirituality congregation serves the primary function of providing a religious experience. In the same way, the kind of corporate prayer preferred by this congregation is impromptu, "sincere," and personal. It is not unusual to hear worship leaders use the first-person singular rather than a corporate "we" when addressing God during prayer in a corporate worship setting.

In an affective spirituality congregation, the emphasis of worship and programming can be on evangelism and the need for conversion, or on affirmation and hope. Evangelism may require evidence of heartfelt repentance. Affirmation stresses the unconditional love of God toward each and the stress on hope may address feelings of anxiety, worry, and uncertainty. Either way, Christian spirituality is marked by an upbeat optimism and a perpetual spiritual buzz from the belief that God is in heaven and all is right (or at least eventually will be) with the world.

At its best, an affective spirituality congregation shapes a hopeful and optimistic membership with an ability to embrace life's challenges because, after all, there's nothing that cannot be accomplished in God's name and with God's blessing. The freedom to embrace and celebrate emotional experiences and expressions allows members to tap into the spiritual joy of the faith, and that is very attractive to many seeking a meaningful religious relationship with God and others. This meets the need that all of us have to tap into our affect, which is an important part of effectual faith. Attention to the affect also provides a corrective to the too-often cerebral approach to spirituality common in many congregations. At its worst, however, this spirituality can be dismissive of education's importance to faith. This may leave members with an inability to discern the difference between one experience and another. As Jonathan Edwards warned, "No object can come at the heart but through the door of the understanding: and there can be no spiritual knowledge of that of which there is not first a rational knowledge."[10] If "experiencing the experience" of one's faith is the ultimate validation of authentic spirituality, then it may be that one experience is as good as the next. Without the corrective that critical discernment provides, members are at risk of not appreciating that some experiences ennoble us, while others diminish us—even though each may "feel" good.

Pilgrim Spirituality

Congregations with a pilgrim spirituality style of faith may be described as a church for searchers. This is a church that values being "on the journey" in the Christian life. As such, the members of this congregation may be hesitant to put down roots in one location or to commit to one worship style, or to join a denominational body—even if that denomination or congregation holds shared values and theologies. Congregations with a pilgrim spirituality exhibit openness to questions. Worship and activities may be highly interactive and experimental. It will not upset the members of this congregation to see teachings from a variety of religions and faith traditions—including non-Christian ones—represented in the worship services; Native American prayers, Buddhist sayings, Zen thoughts, African American spirituals, feminist textual interpretations, pseudo-Celtic rituals—all can contribute to enrich and enlighten members on the journey. This type of spirituality style tends to be found where community is small-group based. Even in a large congregation with this style spirituality, small groups become the primary way members interact and work out their life together. This small-group approach facilitates a focus on the relevance of faith to personal daily living. Belief and action are closely linked and more easily facilitated through the structures and processes this type of congregation puts in place.

At its best, this hidden spirituality style fosters openness and tolerance in its members. Through the intimacy of its small groups, this congregation provides many opportunities for its members to develop deep friendships. But, at its worst, this hidden spirituality style may weaken its members' ability to take stands and be prophetic because of its reluctance to appear provincial or closed minded. Being open to all, they may lose the ability to value their own faith traditions and beliefs. This style congregation will not long retain members who need a more affirmative claim to confession or belief.

Mystic Spirituality

Another spirituality type identified by Corinne Ware is that of mystic spirituality. The mystic spirituality style tends to describe not so much a churchwide style as it does a subset within a congregation. While the majority of members in a given congregation may not share this spiritual style, it is commonly and widely found in many congregations. Often, only a small group in a congregation embraces this orientation—who are at times tolerated by the majority as a group of misfit but benign members. Congregations that value being a place for everybody tend to support and provide openly for this small group of members who have particular needs for spiritual expression. The outlook of this hidden spiritual style tends toward the contemplative. There is an enthusiastic—but sometimes serious—focus on spiritual disciplines. Silence and listening is more important than making noise (preaching or music). A primary focus of this spiritual style is on inward spiritual formation, which requires a level of dedication and discipline that may put off most members from joining this group. The worship preference for this group leans toward the pietistic, a dimension that their congregation may not provide in the principle corporate worship gathering. Therefore, this group often seeks worship experiences in smaller, more intimate gatherings, like retreats. This style is somewhat similar to that of cognitive spirituality in that the text and the written word are important—therefore, activities like journaling, reading, and group *lectio divina* are valued as both expressions and means.

At its best, this hidden spiritual style attracts those who are serious about their commitment to spiritual maturity. Moving toward a more universalizing faith, this style can be a tremendous prophetic resource to the congregation. At its worst, those who coalesce around this spiritual style—few in number in any congregation—run the risk of practicing and living out their spirituality apart from, rather than as a part of, their congregation. Staying connected and finding ways to call out others who may be ready to engage in deeper spiritual discipline is a challenge. Additionally, this group may unintentionally foster an approach to church membership that finds comfort in withdrawing from the world. When prayer is seen as an activity to perform in private and not something that should compel members to move out and minister to the world, members will run the risk of misinterpreting the necessity to balance the journey inward with the journey outward.

Servant Spirituality

"Faith is action" may be the rallying cry of those congregations that embrace a servant spirituality style. Discipleship that results in ministry to the world is at the heart of what this congregation values. Therefore, membership mobilization through the working out of spiritual gifts, the application of talents, and the sharing of resources for service to the world is a critical part of what it means to be a member. In educational enterprises, teaching is for obedience more than for understanding or for ensuring belief. Educational approaches that facilitate training may be more prevalent than those that give attention to knowledge and learning for learning's sake. A ministry of works defines this community of faith, and the congregation's members work hard at winning and maintaining that reputation in the community. This congregation's theology says that the church is in the world; although working at transforming the world is not the primary impetus for the many ministries outside the church walls, members understand that God continues the work of redemption through the church's service to the needs of the world.

The servant spirituality-style congregation tends to have clarity of purpose. Members receive the unambiguous message that authentic faith gets its hands dirty. Clearly, this hidden congregational spiritual style emphasizes the behavior component of effectual faith. At its best, this type of congregation is a powerful witness to the gospel through its presence and ministry in the world. Both members and those outside of the congregation appreciate that "faith matters" and that the church's beliefs and presence are relevant to the lives of people. The intentionality of moving members to personal participation in ministries facilitates a faith stance that is both courageous and humble as it focuses outward rather than inward. At its worst, however, the emphasis on the behavioral domain of effectual faith runs the risk of creating a works-oriented faith. Lacking a strong theological rationale for *why* they engage in missions, members may misinterpret the nature of their faith. It is a small leap from doing ministry to please one's fellow church members and to feel a part of the community to believing that one needs to engage in "works" to please God. Therefore, this congregation needs to work at keeping the theological imperative for engaging in spiritual works in the foreground.

Crusader Spirituality

As with the servant spirituality style, the crusader spirituality style also has an outward focus. But this congregational spiritual style is focused on a mission task—not necessarily on the needs of those in the world. The "mission" can be any number of things, and may be determined by any number of variables, from a doctrinal emphasis, a theological understanding, the personality of the pastor, a denominational thrust, a social cause, a reactive posture, an ideology, or a perceived injustice. Any of these, or a combination of these, will result in a "cause" around which the members gather. The congregation with a crusader spirituality style tends to be narrowly focused; there's only one song to sing here, and all others are variations on a theme. All resources are geared toward that task, and everyone is in agreement on that one task. In this congregation, evidence of faith equals commitment to the cause. Distractions are not easily tolerated. Members and paid staff who are perceived as less than committed to the cause tend to not stay long or to lose their influence.

At its best, this hidden spiritual style can powerfully engage the public square. It makes its presence known in an unapologetic way that demands attention. The level of engagement in the arenas that influence the cause for which this congregation fights often is prophetic and profound. The level of commitment to a cause that congregations with this spirituality style embrace has made the difference in changing laws, stopping injustices, launching social and faith movements, starting organizations and services, righting wrongs, and realizing social changes. At its worst, a congregation with this spirituality style has a skewed understanding of the role that willfulness plays in effectual faith. The will component of effectual faith is a volitional stance that cannot be addressed through coercion or through demands. This church's in-your-face engagement in some causes tends to make it difficult for others to hear the prophetic voice it may legitimately bring. Often the crusader spirituality stance is not above winning a battle at any price, but in the end it risks losing the cause by alienating both perceived enemies and actual friends.

Conclusion

The hidden life of a congregation's spirituality is a critical force that informs a local church's beliefs and practices. This hidden life force influences how a congregation approaches its worship of God, how it understands the purpose of gathering for corporate worship, and the expectations it places on its pastoral leadership. What kinds of people are welcomed into the congregation—and what kinds of people a church will attract—are also determined in great part by the spirituality style of a congregation. Early into the welcome process of a potential member, congregations are trying to discern, "Does this person believe as we do?" And visitors who are prospective members are trying to figure out what kind of church they are experiencing. One of the first things a stranger tends to focus on to get a handle on the congregation is to determine what spiritual style the congregation has. This is done more intuitively than analytically—visitors tend to zone in on the "feel" of a congregation when trying to discern "What kind of church is this?" and "Is this the church for me?" They do this by listening for the language of worship, identifying the music and liturgical style used in worship, and observing how members relate to each other. They also take their cues by looking at what the church has to offer programmatically and by assessing the pastor's relationship with the church. Listing the academic degrees by the names of the pastoral staff on the Sunday worship bulletin or church newsletter sends a message, and a visiting prospective church member whose personal faith orientation is toward an affective spirituality is likely to interpret that in a different way than a person looking for a "thinking church."

Understanding the hidden spiritual style of a congregation will help its leaders and members appreciate that no one congregation is for everybody. When I was on the pastoral staff of a congregation, I witnessed a very unusual episode one Sunday morning. One of our deacons was serving as a greeter in the church foyer. A visiting family of four walked in through the front doors and the deacon moved toward them to greet them and direct them to available Sunday school classes. But, as he approached the family, he noticed that each of them, including the children, was carrying a Bible, the father carrying the largest Bible of the bunch. The deacon smiled as he approached and said, in a friendly though sympathetic way, "This probably isn't the kind of church you're looking for." I could only laugh at the outrageousness of that scene. Unlike at other churches where wary visitors are received as potential candidates for membership and handily ushered to Sunday school classes in an effort to help them make contacts with members who may help lead them to joining, this deacon was so attuned to the hidden spiritual style of his congregation that he could guess that a certain kind of Bible-toting, church-hunting prospect would not likely find a good home in that congregation. The clearer a congregation is about its own hidden spiritual style, the better it can serve its members and the more effectively it can move toward providing a more balanced approach to worship, education, practices, and relationships that address all of the components necessary to foster effectual faith in its members.

Chapter 7

The Hidden Life of Congregational Identity

I BELIEVE THAT ONE OF THE MOST CRITICAL DYNAMICS OF THE hidden lives of congregations is the formation of a corporate identity. And I believe that the element missing in the lives of most congregations is a clear sense of their identity, leaving them with the inability to answer the question, "Who are you as a congregation?" Two instances stand out in my mind that illustrate that state of affairs.

The first was a casual conversation with a colleague. He is a fellow faculty member who provides a lot of pastoral interims in local churches (and he seems to have no end of opportunities to do that). He had just started an interim at a large suburban church and was telling me about his meetings with various leadership groups. He shared his surprise and frustration when two leadership groups in the congregation hinted that part of what they wanted him to do during his short time with them was to help them find their identity. One member of the pastoral search committee stated that it would be a good idea if they had a sense of identity for when they started interviewing potential pastors. My colleague friend expressed his frustration at the expectation that he would be able to provide that for them. "I can't give them a sense of identity! How can they expect me to do that in the short time I'm going to be with them?" Then he added, "I wouldn't even know how!"

The second incident that comes to mind is a phone conversation I had with a pastor of a midwestern church. He had called to ask me to lead a retreat for his church leadership group. This congregation with a 100-year history had just completed a long-range planning process where they identified values, wrote a mission statement, identified goals and objectives, and assigned responsibility for carrying out plans and programs to various church groups. But a few months after that process, they were stuck and frustrated. I asked the pastor, who'd been there for over twenty years, what he thought the problem was. After stumbling around for an answer, he finally concluded, "I guess the problem is that we don't have a sense of identity. We don't know who we are."

I have argued previously that the prevailing fundamental deficit in congregations is a lack of a clear and viable theology of Church. The second fundamental deficit of unhealthy congregations is a lack of a sense of identity. The issue is not that a local congregation does not have an identity—all relationship systems have an identity. The problem is that members and leaders get to a place where their lack of self-knowledge leaves them with an inability to know what that identity is. Lacking a sense of who they are leaves congregations at the mercy of, as the apostle Paul said, "the waves, and blown about by every shifting wind of the teaching of deceitful people" (Ephesians 4:4 TEV). Congregations that lack a sense of identity are not self-determinate.

Identity has to do with a congregation's understanding of itself as Church and as a unique corporate body of relationships. Besides those distinctive cultural and local contextual components that make any congregation unique, identity includes the members' collective beliefs, values, and patterns of relating as well as the congregation's symbols, stories, spirituality, style, and stance.[1] Congregations develop their identities soon into the Formation and Formatting stage of their lifespan (see chapter 4). Failure to do so will tend to lead to dissolution because identity facilitates group cohesion and the ability of the members to think and act corporately. This rapid attainment of a corporate identity is what allows the members to define themselves to others, an act which in turn reinforces and clarifies the very identity they seek to define. The members' sense of identity develops over time, through shared experiences and in the ways they negotiate the avenues of meaning-making, like stories, practices, and mutually shared experiences. For congregations at any stage of the lifespan, identity is also shaped by the members' capacity to hope—to formulate an image of the future possibilities open to them.[2] Not only is identity critical to the social and relational dynamics of the members of the congregation, but, according to Carl Dudley and Earle Hilgert, "There is a clear correlation between congregational identity and institutional strength."[3]

Three Components of Congregational Identity

It is worth examining more closely some of the components that make up a congregation's identity. Aside from the myriad number of variables related to history and location, there are three key components of a congregation's identity: its *spirituality*, its *stance*, and its *style*. After examining these selected components of identity, I'll examine briefly the sources of a congregation's identity.

Spirituality

The first component of a congregation's corporate identity is its *spirituality*. Chapter 6 examined the hidden life of congregational spirituality, so I'll not deal with it in depth here. Suffice it to say here that the hidden life of a congregation's spirituality is a critical force that informs much of the life and practice of a local church. A congregation's spirituality influences how a congregation approaches its worship of God, how it understands the purpose of gathering for corporate worship, how and why it participates in ministry and mission, and how it formulates the expectations it places on its members and leaders. The dynamic of the corporate spirituality of a congregation is a key component in the identity formation of a congregation—and, therefore, in the identity formation of its members. A congregation's spirituality style can influence its stance, the second component of corporate congregational identity we will examine.

Stance

A church's *stance* has to do with how it views its mission and ministry and how it relates to the world around it. Often, a congregation's stance is determined by its immediate context—including its geographic location, for example. A congregation's stance informs how it engages the public square on broader social and community issues as well as determining to what extent, if at all, the members of the congregation provide overt and visible ministry to its immediate environment.[4] The identity and practices of a congregation are influenced directly by its locale, the geographical and social environment in which it exists—the residents of the community, the economics, social values, and local history of its setting. As Carl Dudley asserts, "In significant ways, different images of the church are related to the social location of the congregation."[5] The issues, obstacles, and opportunities that a congregation in an urban setting faces are distinct from those that a sister congregation will face in a rural environment. A suburban congregation that enjoys a relatively stable membership base deals with a different set of internal and external issues than does a congregation made up of immigrant members who are striving at being upwardly mobile and whose culture is not as permeable as an "inclusive," upper-middle-class community.

One important point to make about a congregation's stance is that the locale in which a church finds itself often influences its viability more than its members—and sometimes its leaders—appreciate. Nancy Ammerman claims that "The ability to sustain a congregation that is not identified with its immediate neighborhood depends on both the particular identity chosen and the resources available to sustain it. The chosen identity must be specialized enough to distinguish it from others, but not so specialized as to have no possible constituents."[6]

Sometimes, a church's stance is determined by a doctrinal or a mission task emphasis. While a church's stance may change over time or circumstance, it often is a byproduct of the initial "imprinting" of the founding members of the church. Because the early systemic formatting of the forefathers and foremothers is difficult to overcome, a congregation may have difficulty changing its stance when circumstances or its immediate context change and call for a different stance. For many congregations, it's easier to pull up stakes and move to a different geographical location when the neighborhood changes than it is to change their stance. Below are nine common congregational stances that inform the hidden lives of congregations.[7]

1. *The Urban Ministry-Stance Congregation*. This congregation's stance is informed and shaped by its geographical locating in the urban setting. Commitment to "the city" is a high value for the urban ministry-stance church. This is a congregation that at some point in its history made the decision *not* to move to the suburbs as the neighborhood changed around it. The members of this congregation seek to impact the lives of those in their neighborhood, which sometimes is made up of a broad spectrum of ethnic and socioeconomic groups. The members themselves may reflect the varied population that makes up an urban setting: upwardly mobile professionals and homeless persons, professional and blue-collar, educated and unschooled, third- or fourth-generation members of founding church members alongside recent immigrants. In addition, it is not uncommon to find urban ministry-stance congregations with large buildings housing several separate ethnic churches in their facilities. I grew up in an urban ministry congregation. By the time I graduated from high school, our church had six different ethnic groups meeting for worship and fellowship in the building: Swedish, Hispanic, Arab, Haitian, Portuguese, and Chinese.

Congregations with a stance toward urban ministry are committed to the life and welfare of the city. In fact, their stance may appear to be one of actively engaging to redeem the city from itself. These congregations are very active in community ministries, including educational programs like after-school day care, English as a Second Language courses (ESL), literacy tutoring, and even vocational training. Many of these congregations experience little resistance on the part of their members in hosting non-member groups like AA, divorce-recovery groups, sex-addiction groups, and single-parenting groups. In addition, they may even provide office and meeting space for strictly secular support agencies like clinics, career counseling centers, or domestic violence services.

2. *The University-Stance Congregation.* Another stance that is directly influenced by its geographic context is the university-stance congregation. This congregation tends to be in close proximity to a center of higher learning. A significant part of its membership is made up of persons who are part of the university community—professors and teachers, staff, and students. As such, this congregation tends to value education and learning and has a more critical approach to matters of faith than may be found in other kinds of churches. Sermons, for example, tend to lean toward the scholarly and are directed at the well-read and currently informed. It's not unfair to say that its preferred approach to Christian education activities is through book studies and lecture series. Obviously, this stance tends to foster and appeal to a cognitive spirituality style.

This type of congregation enjoys tremendous resources in terms of the caliber of education that its members have. With a savvy staff on the lookout, this congregation will never lack for teachers! One challenge for this congregation, however, tends to be that its financial potential cannot keep up with its taste for excellence in culture and the arts. Let's face it: Neither professors, professional educators, nor students tend to have "deep pockets." Unless this congregation enjoys a generous endowment, financing beyond the essentials can be a challenge. And with a significant portion of its membership—the students—being transient, it may be difficult to develop membership loyalty or to maintain continuity in programs and ministries.

3. *The Country Club-Stance Congregation.* This third category of a congregational stance may be the only one that clergy openly decry, but everyone secretly wishes they had. The terms *country club* and *church* seem to grate when put side by side. And indeed, to say that a church is a country club usually is to intend something derogatory. The country club-stance congregation tends to cater to affluent members, whether "new money" or "old money." Ultimately, what money buys is access, exclusiveness, and distance (the more expensive the house, the longer the driveway). So, to the outsider, a country club-stance congregation seems aloof, exclusive, and disconnected from the world.

In a sense, this congregation may be exclusive in that it is intentional about whom it allows and whom it excludes, but we must confess that all congregations do that. To some extent, after all, religion is about membership. And to admit that this congregation is exclusive in its in-clusion of members does not mean that, as a church, it does not engage in ministry and missions. The members of this congregation may resist or be unable to participate directly in ministry ventures, but they are very generous in financial support to missions, causes, denominations, and ministries. And because money buys access and influence, the coun-try club congregation can impact culture for the gospel in ways other congregations cannot. In challenging its elite members to practice ethi-cal Christian living in the circles of influence in which they live and work, this congregation makes a unique impact on culture and society.

4. *The Community-Stance Congregation*. The community-stance congrega-tion casts a wide net as it seeks to be a place that "welcomes everybody." This congregation strives to live out a "community of faith" theology that values belongingness and diversity. Some community-stance con-gregations are affiliated with a denomination, but you may have to look closely to discern which one. These congregations tend to downplay denominational loyalty and affiliation in order for those not to be ob-stacles to reaching people. Overtly, they foster a sense that theirs is a grassroots, neighborhood church.

Community-stance congregations are unapologetically "in the world" while trying—somewhat—to be "not of it." This congregation celebrates the best of the culture of which its members are a part, and not only recognizes the influence of the culture, but accommodates the parts of the culture that it sees as consistent with its faith values. In this congre-gation, the pastor would not hesitate to use sermon illustrations based on a *Seinfeld* or *Friends* television episode—and it's likely that everyone in the audience would "get it." No parent in this congregation is likely to question that the youth staffperson cancels a regularly scheduled youth meeting because it would conflict with a school sports event or a home-coming (in fact, parents would likely be more upset if the church event were *not* canceled!). This congregation's "creative" educational offerings may include Bible studies along movie or TV-show themes: a "Spiritual-ity of *The Matrix*" study for young adults, a "*Married with Children*" Bible study for young families, a "*Survivor*"-themed youth retreat.

Because the community-stance congregation tries to be a place for everybody, it strives to provide a cafeteria plan of ministry opportuni-ties, programs, and activities options—everything from day care for tod-dlers to art classes for seniors. This provides people with multiple entry points into the congregation. Outreach for this congregation echoes the line from the movie *Field of Dreams*, "if you build it, they will come." But this approach requires the congregation to make a big investment in competent program staff. One major trap for this congregation and its staff is falling into the mentality of trying to provide church for a constituency of consumers. Allowing a "market analysis" approach to outreach and programming, or to creating a certain constituency "type" (parents with children, or young thirty-somethings, or a certain socio-economic group, for example), runs the risk of creating a pseudo-community. Ultimately, the "community" catchword that this congregation strives for becomes defined down because its constituent members center around likemindedness and not around building an inclusive, multigenerational faith community. The trap is in not appreciating that a consumer constituency primarily focuses on what it wants and perceives it needs, and not on what it can give or contribute to the community.

5. *The Mission-Stance Congregation.* Like the outreach-stance congregation (described below), the mission-stance congregation is overtly outwardly focused. The missional value that this type of congregation embraces is to serve the world. To be the church of God is to work to transform the world through active engagement. Unlike what at times happens in the urban ministry-stance congregation, where the mere provision of building space is sufficient to "count" as mission and ministry, the mission-stance congregation takes seriously the belief that every member is called to personal ministry engagement. As such, this congregation is effective in organizing, structuring, and providing processes that facilitate its members' quick and effective engagement in personal or corporate ministries outside of the church walls. In addition, this congregation is very effective in cultivating in its members a theology of call and the value of service through ministry to others.

Because the mission-stance congregation sees active participation as the end goal of Christian discipleship, it tends to have difficulty maintaining a multigenerational membership. This is an "adult" church that does well in challenging adult members to serious discipleship through personal ministry in the world. But because it is so outwardly focused, this type of church may have difficulty in maintaining programs to provide for the needs of more dependent members of its congregation—children and youth. Some mission-stance congregations may get to the point of not trying to address the needs of children and youth—accepting the idea that the primary responsibility for the faith formation of these young ones lies with the parents, and not with the staff or congregational programs.

6. *The Pillar-Stance Congregation.* You can spot a pillar-stance congregation easily. Drive down the main street of any small or midsized town and

look for the solid-looking large church building with the big columns at the front and you'll find it. Pillar-stance congregations enjoy prestige, if not always influence. Sometimes, this congregation indeed may have *influence*, but may no longer enjoy *affluence*. This church is the "grand old man" on the block. With nothing to prove, this congregation knows what it wants by way of being church. Enjoying a rich history and an influential reputation, the pillar-stance congregation often is the epitome of a church in its bureaucracy stage (see chapter 4). Leaders and congregational members of a church with this stance are strong supporters of denominations and of orthodoxy (if not orthopraxy). Members of this stance congregation highly prize professionalism and competence in the pastor and staff.

7. *The Shepherd-Stance Congregation.* A friend of mine once described the shepherd-stance church as "a congregation of social workers." And indeed, this type of congregation seems to attract a large number of caregivers. Because the members of this congregation value mutual affirmation and caregiving, they tend to favor a "family of faith" operating theology. The pulpit ministry in this congregation tends to focus often on the issues of reconciliation, healing, and peace and justice. In fact, the language and metaphors of therapy resonate well from the pulpit in this congregation. The members of this congregation welcome willingly the hurt and broken of the world, offering comfort, healing, and restoration through loving relationships and support. One danger of the shepherd-stance congregation, however, is the potential addiction to pain. Often, there seems to be no room for healthy and mature members who need challenge rather than rescuing.

8. *The Outreach-Stance Congregation.* "Outreach" on the part of a congregation can mean a lot of things. And all congregations, because that is their nature, do outreach in one form or another. After all, proclaiming the good news through word and deed is at the heart of the Church's mission. The outreach-stance congregation, however, defines outreach in the narrower sense of evangelism. This congregation holds reaching the lost for Christ as the ultimate value and highest good. In some outreach-stance congregations, the conversion experience—and some outward manifestation of it—is the ultimate goal of the Christian faith. Consequently, every practice of this congregation is geared toward realizing that goal or reinforcing that value. Every gathering or event is an opportunity to preach a message of repentance with an invitation to respond overtly to the call of God for salvation through Jesus Christ. Even in those times when all who gather for a worship service or an

activity are current members, the chance to preach an evangelistic message with an accompanying invitation is not lost. Events where strangers (and therefore potential converts) are present are opportunities to stress the message of the damning influence of sin, the lost state of humankind, the atoning sacrifice of Jesus Christ, a call to repentance, and an invitation to respond—even if the event is a baby-dedication service, a wedding, a church social event, or a funeral.

While the outreach-stance congregation holds that the highest good is winning the souls of people for God, some also emphasize social concerns. These congregations understand that caring for the body and working to meet the needs of persons also is important and is part of what is means to be a witness for Christ. These practices are part of "bearing fruit," and are understood as part of the outward manifestation of the inward reality of "being converted" to a new life.

9. *The Crusader-Stance Church.* It has been said that the Church does not have a mission; it is God who has a mission and the Church is to carry out that mission. While that may be true, the crusader-stance church does have its own mission—or at least a particular spin on what "the mission" should be. The crusader-stance congregation has what can be called a "Kingdom of God" theology. This congregation embraces a cause and marches under that cause's banner. Additionally, through the impetus of its spirituality, this congregation carries the cause into the public square, engaging in debate, providing a prophetic stance, and ensuring that in a predominantly secular culture, the voice of God is heard. It is important to note that crusader-stance churches exist on either extreme of the theological spectrum.

Style

The third component of a congregation's identity is its *style*. Style has to do with the outward corporate expression of the emotional tone that a congregation embraces. It is no secret that, just like individuals, groups develop their own "personality." Groups take on a repertoire of easily identifiable characteristics that inform how they relate to their members and to those outside the group. I'm always fascinated to see this happen in an academic setting with classes. When I teach the same workshop or course over again, each time is different in substantive ways—sometimes to the extent of feeling like a totally different course. The material is the same, and the teacher is the same, but because when groups come together they quickly form a "personality," the dynamics of the learning experience can change dramatically. In fact, the style of the group can facilitate the learning experience or it can inhibit it to such an extent that the course becomes a source of frustration for all parties involved.

There may be no end to the number of styles we can identify, and more than one of these style elements can exist in a congregation. These styles are an important part of a church's identity and exert influence on how the congregation goes about its work and relates to those within and outside of its walls. Because style has to do with inherent values and habits, a congregation may not be overtly aware of its style. But members will sense when something said or done goes against the adopted style that it is used to and will respond—if not react—strongly.

Styles can be plotted on a continuum. Though congregations will not likely fall at the extreme end of the spectrum described, they do tend to plot closely enough to one end or the other to be readily identified as to which way they lean. As will be evident in the descriptions, thinking about styles this way suggests that falling at one particular end of the continuum over the other is a healthier place to be. Here are examples of some styles that commonly exist in congregations:

Between Open and Closed. Congregations with an open style enjoy a high capacity for honesty and open sharing. The flow of communication and news flows easily in this congregational system. Furthermore, unlike congregations with a closed style, the structures and processes in place in open-style churches facilitate rather than hinder communication at many levels—from casual conversation to crisis-related news. As in all congregational styles, leadership sets the tone for this. One little observation experiment I always conduct when visiting a congregation is to check for its level of openness by observing the staff office doors. Inevitably, in an open-style congregation, staff members tend to keep their office doors open. Conversely, in a closed-style congregation, I'll observe that staff members stay in their offices behind closed doors.

In closed-style congregations, communication is difficult. Some people are always in the know and others seem to be perpetually clueless about what's going on—and the system is set up that way. Messages tend to be indirect and people ask by insinuation rather than overtly. In this system leadership may use information as currency, or as a way to keep people off balance. Suspicion, rather than trust, is the default attitude for relationships in closed systems.

Between Inward-Focused and Outward-Focused. This style relates directly to the congregation's attitude toward its mission. This style demonstrates the truism that "actions speak louder than words." A congregation may say that its mission is to reach out to the neighborhood and to the world, but its actions may reveal that it believes something else altogether. Simply put, an inward-focused congregation is more concerned about maintaining internal relationships than identifying and meeting the needs of those outside its walls. It may be more focused on institutional maintenance than missional action.

Between Inviting and Excluding. This style relates to the "inclusion forces" covered in chapter 4. Inviting congregations accept and seek out new members and welcome strangers easily into the full life of the church community. Excluding churches maintain an "us" versus "them" mentality. This excluding force is so powerful that it is possible for someone to be a church member for years and yet remain a "them."

One parish minister friend shared with me a painful meeting with the leadership of his small church. The purpose of the meeting was an airing of grievances about his performance. The usual complaints were expressed, including the one that says the pastor "isn't visiting enough." My friend corrected that misconception by relating how he'd visited every single person that was in that meeting of the disgruntled. When he shared that just the other day he'd driven two hours to visit with a hospitalized woman who'd become a new member just two weeks before, one woman in the group responded, "But she's not one of *us*." What she meant was that while that woman in the hospital was a member of the church, the pastor's visit "didn't count" because, from the church's perspective, the woman was still one of "them" and not one of "us." Needless to say, the exclusion forces in this congregation were off the scale!

Between Culturally Conservative and Culturally Liberal. Cultural style, whether conservative or liberal, has little to do with a congregation's theology. These styles have to do with mores and corporate lifestyle choices. A theologically conservative congregation may be liberal in its cultural style. Conversely, a more theologically liberal congregation may prefer a culturally conservative style. Sometimes this seemingly paradoxical phenomenon is in response to the broader cultural norms in which the congregation exists. I know of two different churches of the same denomination that are similar in their doctrinal and theological orientation—one on the West Coast and the other on the East Coast. Their pastors are products of the same seminary and their educational and ministry programming is almost identical. However, the congregation on the West Coast is very culturally conservative in its style—largely in response to the very liberal, if not libertarian, geographical surroundings of the congregation. The congregation on the East Coast, however, is very culturally liberal in spite of (or because of) the fact that its surroundings are staunchly traditional and conservative in lifestyle.

Between Professional and Laissez-Faire. The styles on this spectrum can inform elements in the congregation as diverse as management and worship leadership. Congregations with a professional style value order, process, structure, and protocol. These congregations don't like surprises—and they like paperwork in triplicate! Decorum in the church office and in worship leadership is prized and expected. The business side of congregational management is almost indistinguishable from how any other professional business conducts its affairs. In fact, larger churches with this style may have a full-time business manager on staff. Congregations with a *laissez-faire* style can tolerate a lot of "looseness" in organization and practices. No one will care too much if a few spelling errors creep into the church newsletter or worship bulletin (a mistake that, if committed too often in a highly professional congregation, may result in a dismissal of a grammatically challenged staffperson). And if the pastor is gripped by the Spirit and happens to stray from the printed order of worship, so much the better.

Between Conventional and Pioneering. Two other styles that bookend a spectrum on which congregations can plot themselves are the conventional and the pioneering. Congregations with a conventional style exert minimal effort on creativity, originality, or innovation. They have a set idea of what a congregation is and what it is supposed to do and are satisfied at meeting those expectations. The ministries and programs of this style congregation are predictable and perhaps traditional. They may follow their denominational program suggestions closely and, in fact, may be highly dependent on their denomination for planning what and how they go about being and doing church. As I was about to graduate from seminary and in the process of interviewing with congregations for potential ministry positions, I met with the pastor and personnel committee chair of a large church. As they described what they were looking for in their next staffperson, they stressed over and over again that they wanted someone to lead their "traditional" programs currently in place and which were apparently working well for them. They went out of their way to stress that they were not looking for an innovator or an "idea person." They sincerely wanted someone who would fit in with their conventional way of doing church.

In contrast, congregations with a pioneering style are trendsetters and innovators. They pride themselves at being on the "cutting edge" of ministry. Some pioneering congregations do this responsibly through a well thought-out process informed by a studied theology of Church and clarity of their unique mission. Others fall into the trap of being pioneering by virtue of loving change for change's sake. Creativity, novelty, and innovation are ultimate values that they pursue regardless of the effectiveness (or theological soundness) of what they end up doing.

Styles are formatted early in a congregation's development, between the birth and formative infancy stages of the lifespan (see chapter 4). Therefore, these are strong identity factors and difficult to change. Regardless of how large a congregation gets in terms of membership and organization, these styles will inform and influence how the congregation conducts its ministry and management. The wise leader understands that trying to change a congregation's style will be perceived as an attempt to change the congregation's identity. When change in self-identity is required for growth, a congregation's style can be an obstacle to change. For example, if a new pastor attempts to shift the congregation's decision-making process from a *laissez-faire* to a more professional approach in order to facilitate communication, order, and intentionality, he or she may experience a level of resistance unwarranted by the simple motivation to make things more efficient. The wise pastor will understand that this is not a resistance to the commonsense value of trying to make things more efficient. Rather, the reactivity arises because the church's style of making decisions is part of its identity. While the pastor is saying, "Let's find a way to work more efficiently," the gut-level, unspoken feeling from the congregational members is, "You're trying to change who we are." Unless the pastor is careful, he or she may miss the point that what is at play here are the hidden life forces of the congregation.

The Sources of Congregational Identity

Let's return to that important question concerning how a congregation acquires a sense of identity. I've said that congregations already have an identity—what they may be missing is an *overt sense* of that identity. This lack of self-understanding leaves congregations in the unfortunate and potentially dangerous place of feeling that "we don't know who we are." As far as I can determine, there are three sources of a congregation's identity.

Corporate Memory

The first source of identity for congregations is their *corporate memory*. As Roman Catholic educator Thomas Groome described, this memory is comprised of a clearly defined ability to know, articulate, and share in

"Our Story."[8] This source of a congregation's identity speaks to the importance of the roles of the resident historian and of the resident storyteller. This role is sometimes embodied in one person—often an elder but sometimes just someone who has been around long enough to be able to carry the memory of the congregation's experience in his or her mind. The important function that the resident storyteller/historian provides goes beyond merely keeping a clerical record of events. The storyteller function helps foster the oral tradition that interprets the congregation's shared experience. Hearing "Our Story" is how new members adopt and share in the congregation's group-identity. This is likely to happen only if the congregation finds ways to facilitate the frequent telling of that story. The corporate telling and hearing of the congregation's story is what helps move a person from the novice's point of saying "you" to being able to say "we" as it becomes part of that individual's own story and memory.

The power of story—which is the ability to create narrative—is that it facilitates the interpretation of experience. We all need to answer for ourselves the question, "What does this experience mean?" As we move through life, stories mediate experience and meaning for us. The same applies for corporate entities like a congregation. Experiences in and of themselves are meaningless and, as meaning-making beings, we cannot tolerate that for long. We all make meaning of our experiences by making up a story—a narrative—that gives an experience a structure and a "place" in our larger frames of reference, such as our beliefs, values, mores, and understandings. We've all heard the axiom that "experience is the best teacher." Certainly that is true, but there's a second part to that which we aren't taught. Experience is the best teacher—*but then you have to throw away the experience and keep the lesson learned.* The reason that people go to therapy is because they get stuck in the experience. They relive the pain or fear or anxiety of the experience without being able to make meaning of it. Rather than attaining insight, they are stuck in time and unable to move ahead in their lives. The same can happen to a congregation that is stuck on an experience without the benefit of resident storytellers to help them interpret the event—whether it's a crisis, a conflict, a tragedy, or a celebration. Creating "Our Story" is one way that congregations practice the critical discipline of theological reflection—which is necessary to make theological meaning of the corporate experiences that shape us. The most important function of corporate memory in the congregation, says Bruce Birch, is the formation of identity and character. "We are shaped as a community by what we call to memory from our biblical and historical tradition. The importance of congregational activities of remembering is often underestimated."[9]

Corporate Values

Second, as a primary source of a congregation's identity, are the *values* that the congregation holds. These values are elected and negotiated; they are not disconnected from the matrix of the components and dynamics within the hidden lives of congregations, and there is an interplay between their mutual influence. A congregation's values, for example, are influenced to a great degree by the social and cultural context in which its members live and work. For example, as the sociologist Max Weber wrote in his classic work *The Sociology of Religion*, "Other things being equal, classes with high social and economic privilege will scarcely be prone to evolve the idea of salvation. Rather, they assign to religion the primary function of legitimizing their own life pattern and situation in the world."[10]

While culture and class influence the values that congregational members possess, faith communities have great ability to shape its members' corporate (if not always individual) values. Most congregations do this through the formative practices of faith they provide for their members, including the rites and rituals of worship (hymns, prayers, observances), creedal confessions, and social gatherings. But other, more formal venues are available to the congregation for shaping corporate values, like educational enterprises and programs specifically designed for this purpose—from orientation programs for new members to mentor relationships and religious apprenticeships.

Congregations make decisions about policy, procedures, and processes based on their values. Whether the majority of the congregation's programs are directed at serving the members of the congregation or the nonmembers who reside in the community is a value judgment. How staff relate to one another and how potential members are accommodated also have to do with corporate values. A congregation's core values will ultimately determine what the congregation does, as opposed to what it says it will do. For example, a congregation's values—even latent operational beliefs that inform those values—will translate directly to membership norms. Every congregation tends to be very clear about whom they welcome as members—and whom they do not.

Corporate Relationships

The third source of corporate identity is the *nature of the relationships* that exist in the congregation. We've already looked at how the size of a congregation influences the kinds of relationships that the congregation, as a relationship system, can sustain. The size of a congregation matters because it shapes the nature of the relationships the members have with each other. In turn, the nature of the corporate relationships in a congregation shapes the faith of its participants. The larger the church, the more complex and distant the relationship structure and the harder it is to maintain a sense of intimacy and oneness.

One force in the hidden lives of congregations that is related to how corporate relationships influence the members is the concept of *propinquity*. In certain presentations, I tell my audience that I know at least one thing that they may not know about themselves, and that is that the real reason they married the person they did is because of propinquity. I tease them that their soul mate—that one-in-a-million person whose soul resonates with their own in a perfect harmony of passion and being—may be living today on the other side of the world. But they will never marry that person because of a lack of propinquity.

Propinquity has to do with access and opportunity. The reason you married the person you did was because you had access and opportunity to do so. (Unfortunately, propinquity is also the reason people have affairs—they have access and opportunity to do so with another person.) This powerful concept informs many of our decisions, albeit unconsciously. The reason people with financial and social means choose to live where they live has to do with propinquity. They recognize that moving into a certain neighborhood, near a particular school, will give their children access and opportunities to be in relationships that will help facilitate goals, dreams, or values.

Part of the reason people choose to join a certain congregation also has to do with propinquity. People choose a congregation intuitively because they want to have the opportunity and access that the relationships in that faith community will provide. Propinquity forces an increase in the amount of contacts we have with other people. The more time we spend with a person or a group, the more we get to know each other mutually and the more alike we become. The more time spent together, and the more experiences shared, the greater the level of access and opportunity the players afford one another.

Conclusion

One of the most critical dimensions that a congregation needs in order to be viable and healthy is a strong sense of its identity. Congregational leaders who want to help a congregation discover and articulate its identity will give attention to the three sources of a church's identity: its corporate memory, corporate values, and corporate relationships. Over the course of its lifespan, a congregation constructs a corporate identity out of these sources of meaning. It develops an image of itself through which it interprets its experiences and through which it makes decisions about its common life. Jackson Carroll is correct in asserting that "if a congregation's leadership wishes to avoid uncritical conditioning by the social context, and instead desires to be intentional about its ministry and mission, then it is necessary for them to develop clarity about the congregation's identity."[11] Having a clear identity allows a congregation to act with integrity. With a strong sense of identity, members will have the capacity to make decisions consistent with who they are and based on their shared values. They will be able to make difficult decisions based on principles and beliefs rather than expediency or anxiety.

PART THREE

Understanding Leadership in the Congregation

IN THIS FINAL SECTION WE WILL EXPLORE THE IMPLICATIONS AND practices for congregational leadership that our understanding of church dynamics provides. At the outset we must stress that most of what we discuss about leadership will be for all of the leaders in the congregation—deacons, elders, officers, teachers, and staff, including leaders of influence like matriarchs and patriarchs, sages, and those who provide leadership not through elected positions, but through influence—as well as the clergy pastor. Some leadership functions, however, apply primarily to the person in the position of pastor. There's nothing autocratic about this—it merely goes to the necessary function of congregational leadership and to what a congregation needs of its pastoral leader.

Understanding the dynamics of how congregations work enables members to know how to share leadership with their pastors, as well as how to demand effective leadership from their leaders. In the case of congregations with young and inexperienced pastors, for example, this understanding helps members to give permission and to empower an unsure and hesitant novice in providing courageous leadership. In the case of an anxious or insecure pastor, understanding how the members share appropriately in the leadership of their own church can provide a corrective when claims to power and authority are confused with what leadership is all about.

In the congregational context, leadership is a shared enterprise between clergy and the laity who are all called to be ministers. Therefore, the following chapters are written with both clergy and laity in mind, and may provide the best benefit when both groups read this together. While each chapter is directed at all leaders of the congregation, lay readers should not be distracted or dismayed if on occasion the focus is on the pastor specifically. This is only natural, because pastors provide a unique dimension of leadership to the congregation. Being informed about how and why this is so will empower lay leaders to work together with the pastor, and to provide wise counsel when needed about sharing our mutual calling as ministers in the church—both clergy and lay.

Chapter 8

The Functions of Congregational Leadership

WHAT DOES IT TAKE TO BE AN EFFECTIVE LEADER? THAT'S A SIMPLE but perennial question that has spawned countless books, lectures, seminars, courses, and workshops (and countless moments of personal self-doubt on the part of anyone in the lonely position of leader). There seems to be no end to the number of people asking this question—or to the number willing to provide "the" answer. Too often, leadership is treated from a reductionist view understood as a personal and individual matter that needs to be addressed through personal skills and attitude development. Or, more commonly, leadership is approached as an administrative function or as a motivational skill.

I recall two instances during my seminary days that highlight these approaches to leadership. The first instance was when a nationally known motivational speaker visited the seminary campus for a series of lectures. The lecture hall was packed—mostly with businesspersons from the community (you could easily make them out, in contrast to financially strapped seminary students: nicely coiffured, sparkling with power jewelry, and sharply, if not expensively, dressed). While the speaker was terrific—and yes, motivational—I noticed that most seminary students were sitting or standing at the fringes of the room. As I listened to the speaker go on about being a positive, confident "winner," and a people-motivating leader, I could not help wonder if the reason that the theologically oriented crowd seemed marginalized had something to do with an instinctual hunch that there was a disconnect between the speaker's concept of leadership and the theological understanding of pastoral "servant leadership" most of the students were being exposed to at that time.

The second instance was the disconnect between the theological and biblical advocacy for a "servant leadership" approach to pastoral leadership, and the practical ministry leadership courses that were being taught concurrently. It would not be unusual for a seminarian to attend one class that taught the "servant leadership" model and then go to another course the same day that taught corporate methods of institutional management, staff relationships, marketing, and business administration for the church context. These secular business-model approaches to leadership tend to feed the anxious drive toward organizational and institutional growth, typically defined by increased numbers in membership and in bricks-and-mortar additions rather than in terms of ministry effectiveness.

The insight that a congregation is an organic relationship system with hidden life forces dictates that what effective congregational leaders provide for the church are the specific functions for the systemic relational processes in the congregation. More specifically, leadership in the congregational context is primarily a corporate function, not an individual one. It has more to do with the leader's function in the system than it does with the leader's personality or even with the ability to motivate others. Perhaps the most challenging idea about congregational leadership is that it is not that good pastoral leaders have healthy congregations; rather, healthy congregations possess and enable good pastoral leadership. As rabbi and psychiatrist Edwin Friedman put it, "Institutions are emotional fields that generally affect the functioning of their members more than the members affect the field."[1] In other words, effective congregational leadership is less about the individual personality of the pastor and more about the ability of the congregation to accommodate and foster the leadership functions it needs. To quote the German pastor and theologian, Dietrich Bonhoeffer, "The group is the womb of the leader."[2]

If there is one component in the matrix of congregational dynamics and elements that makes the most difference in helping a congregation become effective, exemplary, and healthy, it is the presence of an effective leader. Jackson Carroll cites the study by researchers Douglas and Brunner, who identified "exceptional leadership" as the most important factor that helped churches thrive in their environments where most others failed.[3]

When I speak of congregational leadership I am not talking about what is commonly referred to as "styles" of leadership. The danger in focusing on styles, as the next chapter will show, is that it places undue importance on the personality or pseudo-self of the individual leader. Different patterns of congregational leadership have appeared over the centuries as the Church, as congregation, has developed and changed. Historian Jay P. Dolan is correct in saying that "It is clear that no one type or model of leadership prevailed in American congregations."[4] Seeking to find the "best" or "right" style that will ensure success in leadership is misguided.

In any organization, leaders have two primary functions:[5] First, they help organizations perform better the practices that are in place; this is a necessary and pragmatic administrative function. Second, they guide organizations toward doing what they should be doing, but are not. This is the singular prophetic function that is critical to effective congregational leadership. Clergy and congregational lay leaders can be key agents in the creation of successful church practices. Their power to do so lies within the differentiated functions of the clergy leadership that affect practices. Congregational leadership accrues from the patterns of practices performed in accordance with the overarching theology and beliefs of what the Church is and of what ministry entails in the congregation's local context.

The three broadest corporate functions particular to pastoral leadership in the congregation are: (1) providing theological interpretations of meaning, (2) the formation of a local community of faith, and (3) institutional development. These three interrelated functions serve to unify the hidden lives of congregations by centering all of the congregation's activities and ministries around the informing theology of what it means to be a Christian church. When a pastor, with the lay leaders, provides theological interpretation of meaning, he or she helps the congregation stay true to its identity and uniqueness as a Christian entity. When congregational leaders focus on the formation of a local community of faith, they help create a local expression of the Body of Christ congruent with its mission. Finally, when pastors and leaders work at institutional development, they help ensure that a congregation's practices, ministries, and organization are congruent with its nature. Let's examine six specific roles associated with these three broader leadership functions: (1) providing vision, (2) the leader and crisis, (3) staying connected, (4) the role of the resident theologian, (5) management, and (6) influence.

The Pastoral Leader as Visionary

There is nothing more critical to a congregation's integrity than its pastor's ability to provide vision. While we generally refer to leadership as a corporate function that rests on the position of the pastor and lay leaders, vision is a systemic function that is the pastor's prerogative. This has nothing to do with notions of "authority" or "power"; it merely is the reality inherent in organic relationship systems. All organic relationship systems require the position of the leader to provide certain corporate functions that do not reside in any other part of the system. In a congregation, the function of vision resides with the person who holds the position of pastor. This is in part because, as professor and political researcher David Leege puts it, "It is the pastor who calls and cajoles the laity to responsibility, who affirms or dismisses their huge or humble efforts."[6] In her study *Congregation & Community*, Nancy Ammerman seems to agree, saying, "Having a strong pastor who is willing and able to lead the congregation in imagining its future seems to be a key additional ingredient. Likewise, the educational resources of the congregation itself can be called on to aid in that imagination and to bridge cultural gaps of various sorts."[7] It is important to underscore Ammerman's point that, next to corporate worship, Christian education is the single most important enterprise that a leader uses to shape the congregation's vision.

"Where there is no vision, the people perish," wrote the ancient sage (Proverbs 29:18 KJV). In his study of six leadership styles, psychologist Daniel Goleman concluded that, overall, a visionary approach to leadership is most effective. "By continually reminding people of the larger purpose of their work, the visionary leader lends a grand meaning to otherwise workaday, mundane tasks."[8] Simply speaking, vision is a blueprint of a desired future state. It is an image of that state of being and living that the congregation will work to achieve in the future. But vision is not to be confused with wishful thinking. Responsible congregational vision is based on an intimate and realistic knowledge of the congregation's identity and potential on the one hand, and of the bold calling of God to be the Body of Christ in one's time and place on the other. Vision keeps a lookout on the far horizon while casting a watchful eye on the realities of the hidden life forces that may inhibit a congregation from getting to that horizon.

Vision is a function of leadership, and it is the leader who must provide it. Vision is directly related to the values of the leader and to his or her willingness to commit every resource available to realizing that vision. Vision, therefore, requires courage. "You cannot be a true leader unless you are capable of charting a desired destination for your followers," says religious researcher George Barna.[9] Some local church pastors seem unable, or unwilling, to be assertive in casting a vision for their congregation. They seem to fear appearing autocratic or willful by being clear and overt in saying, "This is what I think God is leading our church to do and be." But whatever insecurity may drive that timidity, what they fail to realize is that casting a vision is their necessary leadership function and is something the congregation desperately needs of its leader. A congregation will look to its pastoral leader for vision—especially in times of crises, uncertainty, or transition. As I often say to young pastors who seem insecure in casting a vision for their congregations, "This isn't about *you* as much as it is about what your church needs from you."

What is required of a vision is a clear image in the mind of the leader of what the preferable future of the congregation will look like. This includes an understanding of the way things in the church *should* be like based on the ideal of what it means to be an authentic community of faith that reflects biblical foundations, the call of God for the people of God, and the locale in which the church exists—including its geographical location and its culture. A vague idea or a fuzzy image is insufficient as a vision. Unless the pastoral leader can provide the members with a clear idea of where they are headed, the likelihood of the success of any endeavors to reach the horizon will be limited. This, of course, requires that the leader first be clear in his or her mind about the future that is envisioned for the congregation.

One common leadership error is to confuse vision with mission, but vision is not the same thing as mission. Mission speaks to the religious practices and purpose of a congregation because it is by nature Church. As such, the mission of congregations will not vary much from one to another, regardless of culture, context, size, or of lifespan stage. As we say, the churches don't have a mission—it is God who has a mission—churches merely carry out God's mission. A vision, however, is specific to the context of a church, and therefore distinctive to each particular congregation. Furthermore, congregations need a sustaining vision at all times, not just for when they are struggling with crises or systemic anxiety. Even when the congregation is in a good position and enjoying stability and affluence, vision is needed—perhaps especially more so due to the presumptive hidden life forces that will pull a congregation on the downward slope of its life cycle.[10]

Vision is not acquired by consensus—it is an exclusive function of leadership. The vision will enable the congregational system's ability to reach consensus, however. Vision will always be resisted initially. Let's face it, no one likes to be changed—regardless of messages to the contrary. How many pastors have naïvely taken a congregation at its word when they've said "we want you to help us grow," only to discover that it takes only a dozen new members joining the church to cause the congregation to balk and complain that "it just doesn't feel like our old church anymore"?

Vision brings risk, and it will challenge the pastor and the congregational leaders to grow into areas unfamiliar to them. It will cause the pastor to develop skills he or she never had or had need for until now. A genuine vision helps create a *new* future reality for the congregation. But if what a congregation calls a vision is merely something that has been done before, perhaps elsewhere, it's not a genuine vision. This is one instance when congregations confuse mission with vision. Too often, a congregation will identify a deficit condition—a lack of pro-grams, a lack of growth, a perceived lack of prestige—and then will seek out a leader who can address that deficit, one who can "fix the problem." Often this comes about when a congregation compares itself with an-other congregation down the block who seems to be attracting mem-bers. The congregation will find another church that is doing what it feels it needs to be doing, then hires the pastor from that church to "do here what you did there." A fundamental mistake on the part of that new pastor will be to assume that doing what he or she has already accom-plished at a previous congregation, and then doing it all over in a new congregation, is a vision. It is not. A vision creates a particular future reality unique for each congregation.

Vision leads to action. It gets people unstuck and enables them to say "yes" to new things and "no" to those other things that will be an obstacle to achieving the vision. A congregation's vision also serves as the chief evaluative tool for assessing the ministry actions it performs. For example, taking attendance at an educational program is not an accurate measure of effectiveness. It really means very little how many people show up at an event—at the very least, all it indicates is how many people a facility can hold. At most, it may indicate how popular an event is—but popularity is not an indicator of effectiveness. Lacking a vision of the purpose for offering that educational program, how can one know if it is making any difference in the lives of its participants? If a church adopts a vision of discipleship that results in changed lives and in the evidence of spiritual fruit, then the touchstone for assessing effec-tiveness will be how overtly people's lives are being changed, not in numerical attendance at programs and church-sponsored events.

Vision will help get a congregation through the tough times every church inevitably experiences. Being focused on vision provides strength, direction, motivation, and perspective. A clear vision empowers a con-gregation in not settling for matters out of convenience or because it's "more affordable." There's an interesting phenomenon I've witnessed in several churches and businesses that happens when they are experienc-ing financial shortfalls. Faced with the reality of limited means and gripped by anxiety, leadership loses its vision and takes its eyes away from the horizon to focus on micromanaging the immediacy of the crisis. One symptom I look for, which seems to be a universal reaction, is a focus on cutting back on expenses. This often begins with mandates to cut back on the number of copies made on the copying machine. Some-one is charged with "keeping count" of how many copies are being made, and maybe even to keep a list of who made the copies. A secretary may be assigned to call in a sales rep from the copier company to see about renegotiating the service contract. This kind of reactivity is the result of failing to focus on the vision. Paradoxically, this kind of response does more harm than good, because in times of crises the importance of keeping communication open and flowing is critical. The reactive stance, of course, is to shut down communication, get secretive, and hunker down—the very thing that will hinder the congregation's ability to navigate the crisis well. This is where the critical function of courageous, ethical, prophetic, and visionary leadership becomes important. Leaders help to fight off the self-destructive forces and practices that make congregations focus on itself to the extent of losing its redemptive stance in the world. When self-preservation is the paramount value, the congregation ceases to be relevant.

Another way to determine whether one has an authentic vision is to consider that a genuine vision will outlive the visionary. Vision is not about organizational development, effective management, or measurable results. A true vision is generative, it is about investing in the present to create a future. Or, as one friend of mine puts it, it's about "planting trees under which I will never swing, but under which my children and my children's children will." An authentic vision is about changing people's lives—their way of thinking, what they value and how they relate to each other and to the world. Vision is not about methods; that is, it's not primarily about *what* and *how* the congregation will do things. How a congregation's vision gets played out will change and will continue to evolve long after the leader is off the scene—but the vision that informs and drives *what* the church does and *how* it does it will live on.

Vision and Identity

By now, it should be clear how important it is to know realistically the context in which the leader shapes the corporate vision. A genuine vision is unique to each congregation—even while all congregations everywhere share the same mission. This is why the leader's understanding of the hidden life of the congregation is critical. This is also why pastors cannot even begin to formulate a vision until well into their fifth year of ministry at the church. I continue to be amused at the impatience on the part of pastors to "give the church a vision" during their first or second year at a congregation. And it is frustrating to encounter their lack of understanding as to why they cannot do so. Until a pastor has been at a congregation for at least five years, he or she does not know the congregation well enough to shape a vision.[11] It takes that long to get to know the hidden life of the congregation and to get clear about one's necessary leadership function in that particular context. I was amused to overhear one observant young women say to her recently appointed pastor, "Do all of you clergy really need to do that vision thing as soon as you show up?"

The necessity of understanding the congregation's context and grasping how the hidden life of a congregation affects its life and work has a lot to do with the important role that pastoral leadership plays in addressing the congregation's identity. The context in which the congregation exists, and the way the hidden life forces impact relationships, in great part creates the culture of the congregation. Culture is a powerful hidden life force in and of itself and it impacts the church's identity significantly. Cultural forces can work against the intention of a congregation in terms of vision and mission. In order to avoid that, congregational leadership needs to develop clarity about the congregation's identity. This can only be accomplished when the pastor works with the congregational leaders and members toward that end.

Identity is what gives a congregation the ability to practice autonomy and self-determination. Just like individuals, only systems with a strong sense of their own identity can be autonomous, meaning that they can act for themselves and decide on the basis of who they are, what they will do, and what they will be. Therefore, the better the leader helps a congregation know its identity, through providing vision, the greater the congregation's potential for self-direction.[12] What exactly is identity? Dudley and his colleagues define identity as "the persistent set of beliefs, values, patterns, symbols, stories, and style that makes a congregation distinctive."[13] In other words, a congregation with a clear identity knows what it believes, is informed by clear values, exhibits integrity in its practices, knows what it stands for, remembers and celebrates its past, and is unique unto itself.

The ability of the leaders to foster and maintain the congregation's awareness of its identity will help make the church's decision-making process become smoother and healthier. When congregational leaders are clear about their congregation's identity and can affirm it unapologetically, they will have the capacity to make wise decisions about their future. When congregations make decisions about their mission, the *what to do* and the *how to do it*, based on their clear sense of identity, they will do so with integrity about the decisions they make and the goals they pursue. Especially when those decisions are difficult and the attainment of goals is uncertain, a congregation can move ahead with confidence about the integrity of their decision.

When I first started doing consultations with congregations, I was dismayed at how difficult it seemed for a church to shape a vision. Congregational leaders and their pastors would get stuck and frustrated about what a vision was and what they wanted their vision to be. Often, conflicting visions would arise, resulting in two factions competing for attention. Rather than negotiating a vision through consensus, the leaders would push for a "vote" after arguing, cajoling, and politicking. When I realized that this tended to happen only with congregations that lacked a sense of their identity, I changed the process for working with churches that were stuck on articulating a vision. I invested the major part of the time helping the congregational leaders clarify their identity. Only the last portion of the consultation, and a small one at that, was reserved for articulating the vision. But what I discovered was that once the leaders were clear about who they were, that is, about the corporate identity of their church, the vision came easily. In fact, there have been times when the church leaders took only about ten minutes to articulate and reach consensus on a vision for their church. Once they were clear about *who* they were, the issue of what they were to be about became self-evident.

Discovering the Vision

Providing vision is the leader's prerogative; in a congregation, that leadership function falls to the pastoral leader. The pastor will of necessity work with other congregational leaders to help shape the vision, but ultimately, the congregation will look to its primary pastoral shepherd to help it discover its vision. Discovering what that corporate vision should be will take a while to discern. I've cautioned that it will take a pastoral leader at least five years to be able to begin to do that work. But once a congregational leader knows the congregation and has identified how the hidden life forces impact its relationship system, how does the leader go bout discovering the vision? While there is no one way to do this, the essential task can be broken down to a four-step process.

First, *highlight and keep alive the church's history to help the congregation remember and celebrate its past.* A congregation that forgets its history loses its identity. Reviewing the church's history includes identifying and celebration of the church's founders, heroes, sages, and prophets. Every congregation has a pantheon of these important persons. Their anointment and celebration provides tangible human examples of shared values and beliefs. The courageous pastoral leader will remember that, in many congregations, this may mean the reclamation of former pastors who have "not left well," primarily because the congregation needs to remember and own up to how it handled the parting of the ways. In many churches, that pastor may be the founding pastor who was not able to make the transition with the congregation into a later stage of the lifespan cycle. Reclaiming that pastor's role and contributions—rather than discounting or denying his or her influence—can help the congregation remember and embrace those foundational values that influence its relationships as a hidden life force. Creating a juxtaposition of past and present corporate life can create a shared sense of new direction and vision for the congregation.

Second, *articulate the shared values that are particular to the congregation.* What a church "stands for" needs to be a matter of shared concern. The leader will need to tap into the symbols, rituals, and artifacts that represent the intangible values inherent in the congregation. In one congregation, the new pastor's wife spied what appeared to be a rather ugly candleholder on a Lenten display in the church foyer. And indeed, it was apparently an amateurish, handmade piece, chipped and cracked, that had seen better days. The new pastor's wife, who had an eye for the aesthetic, removed the candleholder from the centerpiece display and replaced it with a more elegant one. This innocent action caused no end of misery to the pastor, as he faced a backlash from members. What both newcomers were unaware of, and failed to appreciated, was that the ugly candlestick was a church artifact, not a poor piece of art. A long-time church member had created it during a memorable time in the life of the church. This church member had died of cancer just two years before the coming of the new pastor, and so the artifact served as a symbol for the members of both an important Lenten season in the past and as a memento to a much-loved and now-departed church member.

Pastors and leaders must tread lightly as they seek to understand the values particular to a congregation. Effective pastoral leadership is related to the use of those church values embedded in artifacts and images, and in the language and behavior that the membership understands and supports. Carl Dudley argues that "the relationship of the leaders and members is symbiotic: each makes demands upon the other, and each responds to expectations of the other. Therefore, trusted church leaders promote, articulate, and embody the values which the church claims for itself."[14]

The third step in the process is to *reinvigorate rituals and ceremonies.* The rituals and ceremonies of the congregation provide regular and special occasions for learning, celebrating, and binding individuals to traditions and values. For a congregation to make the ancient and universal rituals and ceremonies of the Church their own necessitates reinterpreting them in the local context. It is not sufficient for the members to appreciate what a ritual means in the universal Church. They must also appreciate and embrace what it means that they are the ones performing this ritual.

The leader can facilitate this by practicing the fourth step in the process: *telling good stories*. People earnestly desire to talk about their faith journeys—individual and corporate. Sadly, we don't give them enough opportunities to do so. Furthermore, people *need* to talk about their faith. The good leader appreciates the importance of narrative for making meaning out of shared corporate experiences and for shaping identity.

Good leaders know how critical it is to create the environment and facilitate the processes that enable formative relationships to take place. That includes creating opportunities and structures that make intergenerational relationships possible. Telling stories, and hearing stories from those who were here before us, is important because who we were is a big part of who we are. We are meaning-making creatures, and our faith is a significant part of that. Most people think more about faith, God, and the meaning of life than we assume, but don't use our polished theological language when they express those thoughts. If we don't listen for it, we sometimes fail to recognize it. Congregational leaders need to provide the opportunity for people to tell their stories, to put it on the calendar and make it part of the church's practice and of its living curriculum. If they don't, it's unlikely to happen. A church minister shared his insight about this after talking to a church member. He was surprised to learn that this church leader was seeing a therapist. When he commented that he was not aware that she was going through difficulties, she replied that she was not in any distress. She explained that she went to see her therapist mainly to talk about her faith. The minister confessed his bewilderment at why she would go talk to a therapist for that, to which the woman replied, "I go to my therapist to talk about my faith because I don't get to do that at my church."

Working with the resident congregational priests, gossips, and storytellers is an effective way to tap into the corporate narrative of shared meaning. Every congregation has a group of people who hold these unofficial functions. Often, it is the secretaries, volunteers, or custodians who occupy those roles. During times of crises, or when challenging changes are proposed, these often overlooked people must be intimately involved in telling stories. In many churches—given the high rate of clergy turnover—these people carry the corporate memory through insider stories of shared experiences. The wise pastoral leader knows how to tap into this fount of corporate memory to cull the interpretive narrative of the congregation.

Actualizing the Vision

After discovering the vision for the church, the congregational leaders must actualize the vision. The first step in actualizing a vision is to *personally value the vision to the point that one can "visualize" the vision.* Unless the leaders can visualize the future, they will be unable to communicate it to the congregation in sufficiently concrete ways. Second, *the leader must give opportunity to the congregation to reflect on the vision.* This period of reflection, which is a corporate spiritual discipline, leads to owning the vision. Goleman stresses the importance of "intuition" in visioning and decision making, calling it an essential leadership ability. Intuition—a part of the discipline of reflection—helps make meaning out of the information and data-overload that can overwhelm a congregation. Intuition includes giving attention to our emotions; as Goleman states, "Emotions, science now tells us, are part of rationality, not opposed to it."[15] As leaders are called to build the church by creating the future rather than investing in the past, "vision matters more than ever. Vision requires what looks to others like a leap of faith: the ability to go beyond the data and to make a smart guess."[16]

The next step in actualizing the vision is to *articulate the vision in ways that move it from a conceptual dream to concrete actions.* This is accomplished by planning for the vision and developing strategies and goals. Finally, the leader helps to actualize the vision by *mobilizing people to make the vision a reality.* The process of actualizing a vision is not as sequential or hierarchical as this suggests, however. And the length of time it takes to actualize a vision may leave the eager and impatient congregational pastor frustrated. It's important to remember, however, that in order to realize fundamental change in complex relationship systems, attention to process will determine the outcome.

The Leader and Crisis

No one likes a congregational crisis. Despite all our attempts to put a positive spin on crises by assuring ourselves that crisis is an inevitable part of life, the fact of the matter is that none of us wants to be in the middle of it—especially if we're the leader sitting on the hot seat. Part of the reason for that is that crises tend to force the leadership function into action. When crisis hits, the leader must act. According to Bowen systems theory, Systemic Anxiety tends to seek out and settle in three predictable places: the most dependent in the system, the most vulnerable in the system, and the most responsible in the system, the leader. The "reason" an anxious system in crisis focuses on the least-differentiated or most dependent in the system is to cause the leadership position to respond to the acting out (the symptomology) so that the system can get back to a more comfortable homeostasis. That is, when the persons in the leadership positions defect in place or underfunction—and thereby do not provide the system with the leadership functions it needs—the hidden life force of Systemic Anxiety will come to rest on predictable systemic positions (on the most vulnerable or the ones with the least capacity to tolerate anxiety or change) in order to create sufficient symptomology to cause the person(s) in the leadership position to get back on the ball and do what he or she is supposed to do for the system: to help regulate it.

The hidden life force of homeostasis requires the leader to help the system regulate Systemic Anxiety. If the person in the leadership position refuses to step back into his or her functional role when the system exhibits symptomology, then something interesting happens: The leadership functions may arise from elsewhere in the system other than in the officially designated leader. In congregations, the leadership function may rise from among lay leadership—a legitimate leadership group (the diaconate, a church council, or a presbytery) or from someone who is willing to take the position of leader in the midst of a crisis. But given the nature of a congregational system, where the leadership position is legitimately and necessarily embodied in clergy pastoral leadership, how healthy can that be?

In one sense, it is a sign of health that a lay leadership group would take responsibility for the leadership functions of the congregation when a pastor defects in place. In such cases, the amount of authority granted the group will be in proportion to the degree of threat perceived by the congregation.[17] But this is a scenario fraught with danger if it becomes patterned. Any group that needs to step up during a crisis to provide the leadership functions that the pastor rightfully needs to provide may set up a dangerous precedent no future pastor would want to live with—and certainly this is a pattern that is not healthy or helpful to the system in the long run. Both clergy and laypersons need to remember that leadership is a shared, corporate function, with each playing a part. Congregational leaders, during times of crises, may need to help the pastor to get focused and to function well, but they run a risk in allowing individuals or groups to usurp the pastoral leader position in the congregation.

The congregational pastor does not enter a vacuum when he or she joins a church as leader. In a real sense, the pastoral leader comes in at the middle of the story. And despite the accompanying optimism and high hopes that flavor the advent of a new pastor, the pastoral leader gradually settles down and loses interest in bringing about necessary changes in the congregation. Especially in churches in the Prime, Aristocratic, and Bureaucratic stages of the lifespan (see chapter 4), an unspoken agreement regarding change exists between pastor and members in these "settled" congregations. According to pastor and professor C. John Miller, what happens is that the congregation agrees to give the pastor special status and authority in certain things as long as the pastor agrees to leave the congregation alone when it comes to the church culture, members' personal lifestyle issues, or expectations about authentic Christian living involving values (like money), vocation, or participation in missions and ministries. When this happens, says Miller, "We have surrendered our hearts to the familiar forms of our religious life and found comfort of soul, not in knowing God, but in knowing that our worship practices are firmly settled and nothing unpredictable will happen Sunday morning."[18]

To overcome this ecclesiastical ennui, the pastor needs to tap into the Energy hidden life force and adopt the function of visionary leadership. When a pastor lives out the function of visionary leadership that leads to an actualization of the vision, change will happen. But change tends to be resisted, if only because of the hidden life force of cultural and relationship homeostasis. Change that lacks the focus of vision can create existential havoc because it introduces disequilibrium, uncertainty, and makes day-to-day life chaotic and unpredictable. People understandably feel threatened and out of control when the processes and structures that they've depended on are dismantled or are taken away.

Visionary leadership is especially needed when a congregation is adrift, during times of transition, or in those periods during the lifespan when there is a dire need of a fresh vision. But the leader also knows that change involves existential loss. People become emotionally attached to symbols and rituals, patterns of relationships, and positions of assumed power or prestige. Congregational members develop attachments to values, heroes, rituals, ceremonies, stories, gossips, storytellers, and other cultural players. When change alters or breaks these attachments, the congregation's usual avenues of making meaning are removed or modified. The wise congregational leader will be sensitive to this, and will respect the potential systemic anxiety it can produce.

Unresolved change and grief either mire people in the past or trap them in a meaningless present. The unhealed wounds following a change—as a result of either a transition or a crisis—can weaken the corporate culture in the congregation. Visionary congregational leaders will work to heal the wounds and repair ruptured meaning through transition rituals that will help the members to bury and mourn what has been lost, and then to celebrate the new forms that begin to emerge. Change in congregations is difficult because it alters cultural forms that give meaning to congregations and to the various groups that make up the faith community. For good changes to take hold, the congregation needs transition rituals to transform meaning, to graft new starts into old roots.

Despite the difficulties and potential crises that visionary change will cause a congregation, pastoral and lay leaders must weather those storms of uncertainty and doubt. No congregation will survive if it clings blindly to old structures and systems while the society around it changes. But institutional survival is not the primary issue, ultimately; rather, it is relevance. When a congregation fails to respond to visionary leadership and to the challenge to minister faithfully in its environment, then it runs the risk of becoming irrelevant. And that is the unpardonable sin for a congregation that is called to be the Body of Christ in its small corner of the world.

As leaders bring about visionary change in the congregation's culture, effective leaders must develop sufficient resilience to make changes also in their leadership style and function as circumstances warrant. Sometimes this will be due to the situational context, but sometimes this is due to the shifts in congregational developments, like a transition from one lifespan stage to another or a jump from one church size category to another, or a shift in mission and ministry emphases due to actualizing the vision. The insight that the leader must change his or her leadership function as he or she works at bringing about visionary change in the congregation is a critical one. Matching the leadership function to the very particular needs of the church culture, context, lifespan stage, and style can spell the difference between effectiveness or failure. As congregational researchers R. Paul Stevens and Phil Collins stated, in terms of a leader's failure, "The most common reason is not doctrinal differences or moral scandals, but mismatched leadership styles."[19] If the pastor is to continue to be effective as the congregation changes in response to visionary leadership, he or she must change along with it.

Staying Connected

One of the most important leadership functions that congregational leaders must provide during times of change is that of staying connected. This is especially true when change challenges the homeostasis of the congregation and brings the hidden life force of Systemic Anxiety to the forefront. The tendency of most leaders seems to be to hunker down and fly under the radar—hoping to become a less-visible target for the more vocal and resistant members in the congregation. This is unfortunate, because what is most needed at those times is for the leader to stay connected to those very persons.

Visionary leaders understand that their effectiveness depends more on relationships than on official status or in the office they hold. Effective church leaders stay in touch with people in the congregation, even if those people are critics of the very things the leader is trying to accomplish. Staying in touch does not mean finding opportunities to make a case for the vision or changes. Staying in touch is an emotional process that seeks to connect with people where they are in order to listen, affirm, and challenge in genuine ways. It means showing authentic care and concern for their point of view while challenging them to responsible behavior. Staying in touch means listening to the members—especially the critics—in order to understand the congregational culture and in order to discern how the hidden life of the congregation is being played out in the relationships in the congregation. The effective leader knows to respect the church's culture while at the same time challenging it according to the shared corporate vision it is working toward. Failing to understand the church culture will almost ensure that the leader will not be able to stay in touch with the congregational members at meaningful relationship levels.

One way that pastoral leaders can stay in touch during times of change and crises is to live fully into the functional role of priest. The priest in the community of faith is the one who leads the people in celebrating the sacraments or ordinances of the church, mediates rituals and traditions of meaning, and incorporates individuals into the community of faith through baptism and rites of membership. In this way, he or she brings people together around the central symbols of the congregation, and provides a means for all to "stay connected" through the elements and practices that bind the culture of the congregation.[20]

Christ is the head of the Church, but, in a real sense, the pastoral leader is the head of the congregation. This means that the pastoral leader must stay connected, but remain differentiated from the body as the head; only then can the leader provide those functions that only the head can provide. The pastoral leader who can stay connected with the members and neither seeks to dominate the members nor allows the members to dominate him or her, helps provide the relationship that facilitates right functioning in the entire congregational system. When the system senses that the leader is in place, is connected, and is emotionally engaged in the lives of the members, the Systemic Anxiety forces tend to be better regulated. The congregational system is then better able to listen to the challenge of visionary leadership and is better able to navigate the uncertainty of change.

The Leader as Resident Theologian

Perhaps few leadership functions are as critical to the congregation as that of the resident theologian. Without this leadership function, the congregation will tend to try to resolve its most pressing concerns— usually having to do with the morale of its present membership or with survival issues tied to diminishing dollars and shrinking membership— based on what is expedient rather than what is theologically sound. When doing so, the congregation will likely never really address the more fundamental questions of its mission in the light of community needs and the gospel imperative.[21] Vision must be informed by theology. Because a vision will reflect the congregation's values and beliefs, it must also reflect the theology that informs the members of what it means to be Church. Therefore, it becomes critical for the visionary leader to fulfill his or her role and function as resident theologian.

It is during periods of crises that the importance of being grounded in an informing theology becomes most critical for a congregation. The pastor that does not provide the function of resident theologian fails to give the congregation the most important resource it needs to be discerning in the choices it makes. Lacking a theology that informs its understanding of self and its practices, one decision is just as good as another as far as an anxious congregation is concerned.

I know of three congregations where anxious reactivity trumped theological integrity in the same way. In each of these congregations conflicts between the pastor and certain congregational groups led to both parties being entrenched and determined to win—or at least, to not lose—at the cost to congregational peace and tranquility. Then, in each of these congregations, something amazing happened: a group formed that decided to end the conflict and tension by going to the pastor and offering him a "severance package," paid by the group, if he agreed to leave quietly. In each case, the pastor agreed. So, problem solved, but at the expense of theological integrity. All parties were at fault here: the group for intervening in a willful way in a conflict between the pastor and the congregation, the pastor for taking a payoff as a way not to deal responsibly with conflict, and the congregational leadership for not taking a stand on the inappropriateness of the misguided action by a few. Because none of the parties was able to ground themselves in theology (a failure that must first be accounted to the pastor's failure of theological leadership), they ignored fundamental theological and ethical issues like calling, reconciliation, accountability, and integrity. Instead of solving the problem, they created a bigger one. How can these congregations approach the issue of calling their next pastor with theological integrity? How can these pastors enter into a call process with another church, having lacked the capacity to leave their last congregations with integrity?

For the past three years I've been engaged in what I call "my obnoxious experiment." Whenever a pastor tells me that his or her congregation has started a new ministry or program, or has begun a contemporary worship service, I ask, "And what theology informed that decision?" Inevitably, I get one of two responses. The first is a blank look that suggests the pastor lacks any notion of why theology needs to inform church practices and the decisions the congregation makes. The second reaction is a blank look that morphs into a look of enlightened surprise. This reaction comes from those pastors who experience an epiphany and realize that the congregation made the decision to begin a new ministry based not on an informed theology, but on a different basis—usually a marketing posture or in response to some Systemic Anxiety force current in the congregation. If a conversation follows, I try to help the pastor discern whether or not he or she was aware of the necessity of being the resident theologian in the congregation. In the three years I've been engaged in this little experiment, not once has a minister of a congregation been able to articulate a theological reason for what the congregation decided to do.

Pastoral theologian Don Browning suggests that part of the problem is that most ministers are not trained how to do practical theological thinking. At best, seminaries offer seminarians some aspects of systematic or biblical theology, who are then expected to be able to apply that knowledge in their future congregational contexts.[22] This is an example of what I call "pretend learning," which includes the assumption that what is taught in a classroom will transition to its intended context. Theological thinking is philosophical and critical and can only happen in the context in which it is required. In the congregational context, the pastoral leader engages in the life and living of the congregational culture where he or she leads the congregation in faith seeking understanding. Like so much of ministry and of the Christian life, practical theology is learned in the living and practice of it—not in the studying of it. Pastors cannot afford to relegate the practice of theology to the academics or scholars.

The function of resident theologian includes the important task of interpretation. A lot of what a pastor does in the course of performing his or her pastoral duties—preaching, designing and leading worship, teaching, counseling, and organizational leadership—is aimed at assisting the members of the congregation to reflect on and interpret their personal and corporate experiences in the light of God's purpose in Jesus

Christ. Jackson Carroll says that the "pastoral task is that of standing with individuals or the congregation as a corporate body in these experiences, helping them to face them and give meaning to them in the light of the gospel."[23] Creating opportunities for church members to experience community life together is important—from celebrations and victories to crises and mourning. But experiences in and of themselves have no meaning; they are just experiences. The critical function of the pastoral leader as resident theologian is to help members reflect on these experiences, framing or reframing them in terms of the gospel and exploring responses to them in ways that express their corporate congregational identity. Only through theological reflection based on a uniquely Christian interpretation of their shared experience can congregational members arrive at an understanding of what it means that they've shared an experience corporately. Only then can they incorporate that meaning into their identity. We are what we've experienced, but only to the extent that we've interpreted a meaning to the experience.

As authentic faith communities, congregations rely on their memory and vision to inform their identity and mission. But a congregation must do this theologically, and it relies on the pastoral leader to lead in this task. "Both memory and vision are necessary to an adequate theology of church for every congregation," explains Bruce Birch.[24] And it is in that sense that a critical part of the resident theologian's function is that of storyteller. The retelling of stories and local legends, the extolling of past and present heroes through stories, reinforces highly valued norms of the faith community.

The Christian faith is a story-oriented faith. The identity formation of the Church, and of congregations, lies in the structure of the narrative traditions of Scripture—from Genesis to Revelation—and in the subsequent story of the history of the Church. Stories are narrative accounts of the development and growth of persons and people. Stories are told in narrative form because narrative is the primary way in which people make meaning of events. The Bible is basically a faith story, a narrative account of a people called of God, the response they've made to that call, and of the journey they've made as a part of that response. In the telling of the local congregation's story, the storyteller seeks to intersect and extend the biblical story.[25]

Narrative contains the metaphors by which a community interprets its common life. Every member of a congregation, from preschooler to senior adult, relies upon story to interpret life and experiences—both individual and corporate. The narrative that the resident theologian as storyteller relies on consists of the news that the members share about their common life—the stories that members tell of themselves (their "testimony," to recall a seemingly forgotten practice), and the stories they tell of each other. Some of these stories are remembrances, others are more akin to gossip, and some stories told may now be legends having grown larger than life by having been wrapped and rewrapped by layers of interpretations and embellishment. Professor and theologian James F. Hopewell argues that for many members in the church, the telling of stories in the church sets the stage upon which they witness the story of the world being played out: "Narrative recovers the metaphors that connect local to larger events; it represents the recurrent drama of humanity; it evokes the microcosm. It shows that structure of human imagination. For a surprising number of people, involvement in a local church embodies their week's most sustained imaginative activity."[26]

The five basic elements that make up narrative are easily recognizable and can be efficiently gleaned from the content of the life of a congregation: (1) The *speech* commonly shared in the congregational culture, or the "idiom" of the community; (2) *themes*, which are the ideas, concepts, doctrines, and dreams shared by the culture of the congregational members; (3) *conflict*, consisting of the tensions, fears, and challenges that confront the community (this includes episodes of a lack of faith, times of threats from within and from outside, and times when a lack of resources may have deferred a dream or impeded a plan); (4) the *invitation and initiation rites and rituals into the life of the community*, which have to do with the congregation's theological understanding of who does and does not belongs and who is "us" and who is "not us"; and (5) *issues and stories of belongingness,* which deal with what it means to be a part of the community, what roles are assigned, and which are negotiated. This also includes the members' shared identities with their self-understanding of "who I am because I am a part of this group."

When telling the stories that interpret meaning and shape identity, the pastoral leader must use the idiom of the congregation—that is, he or she must speak in the vernacular. Using academic theological language will diminish the power of the narrative. This is because storytelling enables a prophetic leadership function. Like the Old Testament prophets, the voice of criticism must come always from within a community already shaped by Torah. The voice of conscience always speaks as a community member, with all the accents, verbs, and metaphors that such a membership implies. It cannot be an alien voice, or it will not likely be heard. Though the prophet speaks his or her conscience—often speaking against the destructive or unregenerative practices of the community—he or she must still speak as one from among the community. Pastoral leaders, who, because of a lack of confidence, hide behind the jargon of academics or stand behind the façade of "professional" language, will speak in technical accents too foreign from the interior life of the community to be heard. The root of the trouble is that the leader speaks as an outsider, and not as a part of the congregation. The soul of a community listens for its own language, and will find it in its shepherd's voice.

Storytelling in the religious community is the primary source of memory for the life of faith. And it is primarily in its local congregational form, says Birch, that the church is the bearer of biblical and historical tradition.[27] This tradition is part of the theological corrective that a congregation needs to remember when developing a vision or making decisions about how to live out its mission. If the pastoral leader fails to develop this corporate long-term memory in the life of the congregation, the church risks being unable to connect the urgency of the moment with the history of its experience. Plainly speaking, it leaves a congregation with an inability to learn from its life experience. The work of the resident theologian then is to invest in the lay leaders and in the congregation the narrative of interpretation that will nurture the corporate memory of the community of faith. Congregations cannot risk depending solely on pastoral leadership, who often come and go with regularity, for its corporate memory.

Storytelling is an educational function. Visionary congregational leaders teach the members how to tell their own story. In so doing, the leader releases the power of the people's narrative to weave and mend the net that binds them together. Storytelling, says Don Miller, is the process of repairing and reweaving the net of memory that ensures integrity of identity.[28] The teaching function may not be a prominent part of the leader's role in most contexts, but in the congregation, it is critical. Historian Janet Fishburn rightly voiced concern over the divorce of the teaching function from the clergy's preaching and pastoral responsibilities. She questions whether pastors can give adequate spiritual guidance and leadership to a congregation if they are not teachers as well as preachers.[29] The professional separation and compartmentalization of the biblical office of Pastor-Teacher has been unfortunate and detrimental to the well-being and effectiveness of congregations. Congregational leadership has a pedagogical component to it. If the members of a congregation are to have a common understanding about ministry, they must be familiar with biblical stories, language, and images as a part of their corporate identity. And in the systemic nature of the pastoral leadership position in congregations, it is the primary pastor who must provide this teaching function through storytelling and narrative as well as through direct involvement and participation in the educational enterprises of the congregation.

The Leader as Manager

Most books on leadership tend to fall into one of two camps, the ones that focus on the relational aspect of the leader as one who leads people, and the ones that focus on the effective management of organizations through process, procedures, organization, and the control of resources. One of the unique challenges of congregational leadership is the reality that pastors and lay leaders must be effective in both camps if they are to help the congregation fulfill its ministry. As we've noted, a congregation is both a corporate relationship organism and a social/cultural organization. The argument that the congregational leader must give primary attention to the corporate body—the system—implies that while management remains an important congregational leadership function, it must be understood in a peculiar way in the church context. Stevens and Collins rightly argue that a more appropriate understanding of the pastoral leader is that of the shepherd of the system. Pastoral care, they wrote, is the "care of the church as a living system, not just the care of all the individual saints."[30] This implies also that the focus on management in the congregation needs to be on regulating the system, the hidden life of the congregation, and changing the culture when necessary.

Certain hidden life forces of the congregation need to inform the management function. The hidden life forces at play in the lifespan stages, for example, call for different levels and styles of management. Obviously, the congregational leader's ability to practice management becomes critical during transition times, but also becomes prominent during the Prime and Bureaucracy stages. As the hidden life of congregational size suggests, the complexity of relationships in a large congregation means that a more rational style is essential for effective organizational leadership. Congregational leaders who serve in a large corporation church during its Prime stage of the lifespan need to practice a professional management style marked by efficiency. They need to be punctual about keeping appointments, both with members and outsiders. They need to be efficient and task-oriented in running meetings, sticking to the agenda and minimizing the personal. Programs need to be planned thoroughly, and everything from public performances to worship is rehearsed to ensure professional execution. The management needs obviously differ in a younger, smaller, family-oriented congregational system. But in those large churches where management is a high value, leaders can take justifiable pride in their professionalism and performance, even if they are lay volunteers. Without them, the church organization would be disorganized and ineffective, to the detriment of the relationship systems, and inhibit the congregation's ability to carry out its mission.[31]

Success in congregational management hinges on a leader's capacity to orient his or her functioning to an overarching understanding of the congregation's purposes (its mission) and of the church as a relationship system. Managing a congregation includes coordination of all activities and groups that make up the congregation's life while also giving attention to the corporate business of the church's property, resources, assets, and finances. The importance of giving attention to the effective management function of leadership is so that members of the congregation can have the resources to live out their calling as the people of God in ministry in their locale. As such, wise and responsible management by pastoral leadership is not something that can be delegated, nor is it something a pastor can choose to defect from if he or she is to fulfill his or her role in the congregational system.

Management includes finding ways to organize the congregation. Being grounded in vision and in an informing theology will allow congregational leaders to manage and structure the local church in ways that are authentic to the nature of the community context in light of the congregation's purpose and primary ministries. Theology will help ensure that the congregation—however organized—reflects the nature of the organic, relational nature of Church. Vision will help ensure the wise use of resources toward appropriate ends. And both vision and theology will help shape the structures appropriate to the church's culture and locale. A congregation in a rapidly transient, highly diverse community, for instance, requires a different structure from one that is in a suburban, stable, homogeneous community.[32] A congregation whose identity of what it means to be church is that of a small, intimate community must be managed more along lines of relationship networks than through management techniques. Adopting a management approach that respects the hidden life of that congregation, along with a vision of Church as family, and a Body of Christ theology will help ensure that this congregation can be as effective and authentic to the mission of the Church as is any larger congregation. In those smaller congregations, management is more relational than administrative. It looks more along the lines of what Goleman described as "relationship management."[33] Relationship management involves being attuned to people's emotions, and practicing influence with a purpose in order to move people in the right direction. This in turn requires that the leader stay connected emotionally with the people.

The Function of Influence

If there is a prime function of leadership—one that is more critical to develop than all other skills or abilities—it is influence. One of the best definitions of congregational leadership was provided by Stevens and Collins: *"Christian leadership is the God-given ability to influence others so that believers will trust and respond to the Head of the church for themselves, in order to accomplish the Lord's purposes for God's people in the world."*[34] When it comes right down to it, effective congregational leaders induce followers to support and work toward the goals that represent the Church's values and purpose through the influence they exert on the relationship system of which they are a part.

The congregation's all-important hidden life force of Energy comes through the commitment of its members, which includes their loyalty, devotion, and continuing support that allows the culture and patterns of life and practices to develop.[35] The leadership function of influence, therefore, includes the need to move people with a compelling vision of their purpose for being. Influential leaders get people excited about the congregation's common mission. They help the members catch the fire in their eyes, whose source is a passion for responding to God's call to minister to and through the Church, because they understand that what people value most deeply is what moves them to carry out their ministries in the world most faithfully.

When we speak of influence, we are not talking about manipulation, nor are we talking about a characteristic of a "charismatic" leader. Manipulating people into participating in ministry through coercion or guilt is a form of spiritual abuse. This willfulness does not appreciate the necessity of the volitional response to God's call to ministry on the part of the members of the congregation. Willfulness is an expression of a lack of faith in God's ability to move people to fulfill their appropriate function in the Body of Christ. Influence is not the result of a personal characteristic along the lines of the myth of "personal power." Influence is a leadership function that is the result of two systemic factors. First, *influence is the result of the position the congregational leader has in the system*. The differentiated position of leader in the system means that the person occupying that position has influence, not by virtue of authority, power, or personality, but by the very fact that he or she occupies a position in the system that the members look to for certain functions. Second, *influence is the result of the leader's ability to stay connected in significant relationships with the members*. It is not enough to occupy the position of leader in a system. One must also work at developing the emotional, volitional relationships that facilitate the hidden life of the organic relationship system.

Conclusion

In this chapter we've explored the function of congregational leadership by highlighting six specific roles. While these six roles are not the be-all and end-all of what a congregation needs of its leaders, they do represent what we consider to be the most critical. Those six leadership functions are: providing vision, managing crises, staying connected, practicing the role of the resident theologian, management, and influence. These six functions are subsumed under three broader leadership functions of (1) theological interpretation of meaning, (2) the formation of a local community of faith, and (3) the function of institutional development.

A visionary orientation to congregational leadership stresses that both rational and emotional-relational functions are necessary in the congregational setting. These mutually interdependent dynamics of leadership connect with the hidden lives of congregations and facilitate the ways that the local congregation maintains its vision and mission while providing prophetic challenges to the culture when appropriate. In order to understand congregational leadership, it is more helpful to focus on the *function* of the leader in the system than it is to concentrate on the development of personal styles, skills, or management strategies. If we are to honor the reality that the congregation is first and foremost an organic living system of relationships, then congregational leadership must provide the functions that cultivate the corporate nature of the Church as congregation. This will happen only when we cease to understand leadership as a function of the individual leader and, rather, appreciate it as a corporate function of the congregational relationship system.

Chapter 9

Leading from the Self

AUTHENTIC LEADERSHIP BEGINS WITH SELF. IN THIS CHAPTER I WILL attempt to reframe leadership for congregations by exploring certain popular myths about the nature of leadership that depend on external illusions of authority, power, or competence rather than leading from the self. A biblical and congregational reframing of spiritual leadership for the church rests on an understanding of the dynamics at play in the hidden lives of congregations, chiefly, that pastoral leadership takes place in an organic relationship system that is only secondarily an institutional organization. That means that congregational leadership is primarily about the leader's corporate relationships. And when it comes to being in relationships, understanding self is paramount.

To say that authentic congregational leadership requires leading from the self is not to suggest the notion of "looking out for number one." Giving attention to self is not the same thing as being selfish or self-centered. Leading from the self is a matter of integrity and authenticity; it is a matter of providing genuine spiritual leadership. Leading from the self is tied into a biblical theology and understanding of the Church. If the leader has an institutional view of the Church, then his or her leadership approach will likely manifest itself around control, top-down management, and misplaced concerns about institutional development. But if the leader views the Church as a living relationship organism, then he or she will understand that the best a leader can do is to be in the kind of relationship that influences people toward maturity and responsible responses to the visionary challenge offered to the congregation. Leading from the self in a relationship system means that the leader understands the corporate nature of the leadership function. In this type of leadership, pastors and other congregational leaders are set free from the tendency toward willful influence and coercive methods because they understand that leadership in the church is not about personal goals. Leadership is a corporate function and therefore must be accomplished within the nature of the corporate relationships in the congregation.

Myths about Leadership

Because there are so many misunderstandings about what leadership is all about, some myths about congregational leadership are worth examining. Pastors and lay leaders alike are subject to an enormous amount of mixed messages about what leadership is and what it entails. Some lay leaders tend to import their ideas about leadership from the secular workplace. No doubt, many are effective leaders in their corporate settings, and their motives are sincere. But lacking a theological understanding of the nature of the Church and the context it creates, they may wreak havoc on the congregation by trying to lead in the same way as they do at a company. Laypersons and pastors who apply these myths about leadership in the congregational setting often do get some things done, but ultimately they may accomplish the task by doing more harm than good.

Myth #1: Leadership Is about Motivating People

One of the most prevalent myths about leadership is that it is about motivating people to do things. This view of leadership is based on two fundamental misunderstandings about people. First, it assumes that people are not self-determinate and are incapable of making choices about what they value and will work toward. Second, this view of leadership can lead to a willful and manipulative approach to dealing with persons. A major shortcoming of this approach to leadership is that while external motivations can move some people to action, their effects are short-lived. People who are easily moved by external motivators have a short attention span and will soon need another novel motivator to sustain movement, or they will seek the next motivating force that captures their attention. Another major shortcoming is that, conversely, some people will never be motivated to action. An almost guaranteed short path to burnout is to assume that finding the right words, or the right techniques, or dangling the right carrot will get a certain kind of person to respond. But the reality is that it is almost impossible to motivate the unmotivated, and leaders who believe that it is their job to get those kinds of people to change will be fighting a losing battle.

The most interesting aspect of the motivation myth of leadership is that external motivators do not even work on the best people in the system. Those who are already participating in the life of the congregation and who have found their passion for ministry do not need leaders to motivate them—which makes the leader obsolete if motivation is what leadership is all about. As Daniel Goleman said, "Wherever people gravitate within their work role indicates where their real pleasure lies—and that pleasure is itself motivating . . . no external motivation can get people to perform at their absolute best."[1] The most detrimental aspect of this view of leadership, however, may be that it assumes that the leader alone knows what's best for others and therefore must work at motivating people to do those things the leader has in mind despite what the person may want for him or herself. Leadership is more about *influence* than *motivation*. Influence happens when the leader knows his or her own values and owns his or her own vision and is in an authentic enough relationship with another to allow that person to choose to participate in the vision.

Myth #2: Leadership Is about Personality

The personality myth of leadership is from the school of thought that says, "Leaders are born, not made." The fact of the matter is that leadership is about function, which, in great part, is a learned skill. Daniel Goleman, in his book *Primal Leadership*, identified eighteen competencies of outstanding leaders from an emotional intelligence viewpoint. But he argued that even those competencies are not innate talents. Rather, they are abilities that can be learned to enable a leader to be more effective.[2] Personality merely is who you are, or as Cervantes quipped in *Don Quixote*, "Everyone is as God made him, and often a great deal worse." Because leadership is about function and not personality, any congregational leader who does not take into account the context and culture in which the leadership function needs to be applied will fail. A focus on the individual or on personality as key to effective leadership demonstrates a failure to understand the nature of congregational relationships and of the corporate nature of the Church.

Myth #3: Leadership Is about Style and Technique

The emphasis on leadership as style or technique remains popular today. This understanding of leadership often is characterized by an emphasis on highly structured management systems. But current ways of understanding the nature of relationship systems make clear that an emphasis on style—a veneer one wears like a nice suit—or on techniques fails to address the hidden life forces in organizations like congregations. We are beginning to appreciate the necessity of leading out of the self, which includes giving more attention to what leaders stand for and believe in, and their ability to communicate these values and ideals in a way that provides both meaning and significance to others. This relational stance to leadership, which focuses on the leader's function and influence in the relationship system, is more important than how the leader behaves (his style) or on how the leader goes about doing certain things (her technique).

That technical and managerial aspects of leadership have their place is undeniable, but they cannot substitute for leadership itself. In human relationship systems, technical and managerial behaviors should always be subordinate to human needs and organizational goals and should always be practiced in service of the congregation first, and of the needs of the persons who make up the congregation, ultimately. Leading from the self keeps the congregational leader in touch with the most basic realities of the human spirit by emphasizing the importance of meaning and significance that members derive from their congregations and the relationships that sustain them. It avoids the trap of believing that adopting a particular style or applying one management technique over another can address the leadership needs of the congregation and issues of vision and purpose.

I remember visiting a local pastor who was notorious for his long string of short-term pastorates and know-it-all attitude. It did not surprise me, therefore, upon looking over the books in the library of his church study (apparently, he was a packrat, too; he seems to have never thrown out a book, no matter how dated) that you could trace the history of management fads about leadership—congregational and business—by scanning the books on his shelf. On his desk were the latest three volumes on leadership techniques (two of which, I noticed, were philosophically incompatible). This pastor prided himself on his expertise on the subject of being a leader and running an organization. But, tragically, that did not translate into making him an effective leader—evidenced by the number of congregations and staff he left in his wake.

Myth #4: Leadership Is about Authority and Power

One common myth about congregational leadership that leads to ugly consequences is the belief that leadership is about authority and power and therefore about being above and over others. While it is true that the pastor's position in the church system is unique, and therefore different from that of the members, it is not a position that places him or her over them. If anything, a more biblical understanding of the pastor dictates that he or she needs to adopt the position of servant, especially when it comes to leadership. In one of the few references on the matter of authority and power, Jesus was quite clear about this: "You know that foreign rulers like to order their people around. And their great leaders have full power over everyone they rule. But don't act like them. If you want to be great, you must be the servant of all the others. And if you want to be first, you must be the slave of the rest" (Matthew 20:25-27 CEV). Of all the myths about congregational leadership, this one concerning authority and power is most evidently disconnected from the idea of leading from the self. This stance arises from a personal deficit that equates power with authority. In fact, it may be argued that this is an idolatrous leadership practice in that it usurps Jesus' claim to ultimate authority in the Church (Mark 1:11; 2:10).

The fundamental theological misunderstanding of this myth of leadership is the denial that congregational leadership is a corporate reality in which authority is delegated by God to the Church, and then by the Church to its leaders. Congregational researcher Donald Miller contends that authority in a congregation may be given to an ordained minister, a group of elders, the church board, or to the people of the congregation, depending on the dictates of polity and different modes of congregational authority. But the reality is that the hidden lives of congregations dictate that authority is not something that operates out of ecclesiastical fiat. Pastors and elected congregational leaders may have designated responsibilities, but how authority is perceived and accepted may be very different than what the organizational chart may suggest.[3] The authority that congregations grant to their leaders may be formal or informal. But the actual influence of the authority will have more to do with how the members perceive the relationship between themselves and those who make claims to authority.

I remember one hapless seminarian sharing with me the occasion of when he learned this insight. While serving a small Family-Size rural church, he sought to break the "power grip" of a small group of deacons who continually blocked his efforts for reform. At one meeting he suggested to the deacons that the church should adopt a procedure for rotating deacons on the diaconate—to which one long-standing member of the diaconate replied, "Pastor, we don't rotate deacons here, we rotate pastors." Needless to say, the young seminarian's tenure at that congregation was short-lived.

Myth #5: Leadership Is about Being Innovative and Creative

Few things seem to be as prone to faddishness than the topic of leadership. Peruse the business and leadership section of any local bookstore and you'll find everything from the leadership secrets of Attila the Hun and Machiavellian approaches of management, to the supposed CEO secrets of Jesus. This craving for novelty in leadership styles leads to the myth that an effective leader needs to be constantly innovative and creative and his or her main task is to usher in the "new" while doing away with the old. Creativity and innovation do have their place in the leadership function, but novelty tends to be overrated in some contexts, and innovation certainly is not an absolute requisite for leadership effectiveness. Attempts to be innovative and creative should best be used sparingly and applied only to those congregational contexts that can respond to its challenges.

Being called an "innovative leader" sounds flattering, but in most congregations it's a quick way to burn out the members and staff. Congregational leaders who see themselves as innovative or entrepreneurial tend to be good "idea" persons, but not very good in the details and follow-through necessary to make those ideas feasible. This leaves staff and church members perpetually second-guessing what the leader really wants and with the frustrating and unglamorous work of dealing with the nuts and bolts and the grunt work of implementing ever-changing programs and projects. Too often, these efforts never lead to actualized projects since the leader tends always to be moving on to the next project or "big idea."

I remember, when I worked in a corporate setting, that the company hired a new CEO with a reputation as a creative, cutting-edge innovator. About the only people really excited about this was management—staff and the rank and file were more wary. Their trepidation proved to be warranted. It did not take long for us to be flooded with one new initiative project after the other—none of which ever culminated in tangible products or services. We had to navigate through one "innovative" change of process after another that served only to confuse the employees and lower their productivity (which had never been a problem). It did not take long for staff and employees to lose the ability to get excited about any new initiative from management. They had learned to curtail any investment of energy or commitment to any project because they expected it to be abandoned soon for the next "big idea" coming down from above.

Further, new leaders need to appreciate that congregations which value the rich, formative traditions of faith tend not to value the perpetual pursuit of "the new" for its own sake. Indeed, there is great danger for a congregation that is too willing to uproot itself from the grounding influence of traditions. The long history of the Church and its traditions offers wisdom and correctives to movements and practices that are attractive because of their newness and novelty, regardless of their appropriateness.

Myth #6: Leadership Is about Competence

As Stevens and Collins remind us, it is possible to be competent in ministry and yet quite ineffective.[4] Clergy have one of the most challenging careers anyone can hope to take on. And despite theologies of grace and calling to servanthood, congregations expect performance from clergy. This expectation to perform and to provide "results" can become a point of personal and congregational anxiety. Poorly managed, this anxiety can result, ultimately, in clergy burnout, terminations, and congregational frustration. It does not help that American congregations exist, and often share, in a culture whose values reflect corporate "bottom-line" attitudes and performance expectations of leaders. As a result, very often clergy themselves take on those performance expectations.

I have identified among leaders in both the secular and religious contexts what I've come to call "The Myth of Competence."[5] This myth is fed by the hidden life dynamic of chronic Systemic Anxiety and leads to the belief that personal self-worth, relevance, and meaning reside in the external definitions and assurances of being competent in everything one does. It manifests itself in symptomology of perfectionism and can result in burnout and depression. Pastors and congregations who buy into the myth of corporate professionalism as a touchstone for effectiveness in ministry may be settling for an efficiently run organization at the expense of a relevant one. Professionalism and effectiveness are not equivalent, and neither are success and relevance equivalent.

I know of one pastor whose desire to make an impression in the denominational network led to an emphasis in the congregation of getting as many members involved in the denomination's lay-training certificate program. Indeed, his congregation consistently made the top ten list of his denomination's ranking of churches with the most baptisms, new members, and lay-training certificate achievements. But those success indicators did not reflect the reality of what was really going on. Despite the high percentage of members acquiring training certificates, very few were actually involved in lay ministry or in leadership positions. Despite the impressive record of new members, just as many left the church every year. But for this pastor, tragically, the perception of success in the eyes of his denominational colleagues was more important than the reality of the missional effectiveness of his own church.

Myth #7: There Is One Biblical Model of Leadership

Perhaps the most pervasive myth about leadership in the congregational context is that there is a single biblical model of leadership. This is not to say, however, that the Bible is silent on the issue of leadership. In some of my presentations on leadership, I tell my audience that there are perhaps four classic books on leadership in existence.[6] The first is the Book of Proverbs. Reading this book cold tends to leave one with the impression that it is an eclectic and unorganized collection of wise sayings with no thematic coherence. But if you read the book through the lens that this is the first "how to succeed in business" or "how to be a good leader" manual, then it begins to make sense. This book originated during the height of one culture's civilization, during a time when that nation enjoyed wealth, security, and stability. The culture had developed sufficiently to support a dynasty, artists, and poets, and it was affluent enough to support merchants, trade, and international commerce. This necessitated the development of effective princes and governors for their cities to maintain the peace, to practice justice, and to ensure that commerce continued to thrive. The Book of Proverbs was the training manual for these princes and governors. It taught them how to conduct business honestly, how to deal with conflict, how to avoid the vices of power that lead to downfall and disorder, and even how to find a good wife that will help their career.

A responsible study of scripture, however, reveals that while there are passages that deal with leadership, no one model of congregational leadership is to be found there. The closest that we have in the New Testament to a model of congregational leadership is Jesus' contrast of the use of power in the secular, political world and its use in the Kingdom of God (Matthew 20:25). Jesus, who claimed no status as a model of leadership for himself, referred to himself as a shepherd and demonstrated the stance of one who was sent to serve, not to be served by others. Even in terms of his authority, he defers to the Father who sent him.[7]

Understanding a congregation as a system of relationships reframes the function of leadership. By keeping the hidden lives of congregations in mind, the pastor and congregational leaders can understand that the leadership function will need to change depending on the context of the congregation—its theology, its identity, its vision, its polity, its lifespan state, its style, and its stance. In this framework, a more biblical understanding of the relationship between the leader and the congregation as a relational system is that of *covenant*. A covenant is qualitatively different than a contract. Covenant implies that relationship is more important than performance, that belonging is more important than succeeding, that being is more important than doing.[8] To enter into a covenant one must accept the invitation to do so; in the Church, those who accept to enter into covenant as leaders for the community must enter as servants of those they would lead. In a covenant relationship roles are negotiated and relationship is primary. In a covenant community the leader does not usurp power or authority because he or she understands that, in the system, those are given by the community and are inherent in neither the office nor the person. This implies that leadership is a corporate dynamic that does not reside exclusively in one individual. What the one designated congregational leader, the pastor, needs to focus on in order to live up to the covenant expectations is his or her functioning, not his or her personal style or what "model" of leadership to adopt.

I know of two congregations that have been able to help their entering pastors understand this because they have gotten clear about their theology of calling. Each of these congregations is able to be clear with their new pastors that they believe that the church *calls* their pastoral staff—including the associates—and that it is not a matter that the senior pastor "hires" the pastoral staff. The congregation is clear that they have entered into a covenant relationship with all of their called pastoral staff and that this is not an employer-employee relationship. This requires the new pastor to appreciate that his or her relationship with the staff, and that of the staff with the congregation, is bounded by a theological covenant commitment that is not informed primarily by personalities or working styles. Calling and covenant with the congregation provide the boundaries of the working relationship of staff.

Only the most mature leaders can fully live into the spirit of servant leadership that Jesus calls for. Some take servant leadership to be a model, but it is more accurate to think of it as a value. To make servant leadership a "model" or "style" that one adopts is to be tempted to use it as a veneer one puts on in order to "act" as a spiritual leader in the congregational setting. But when the dynamics of the hidden lives of congregations go into full swing, like Systemic Anxiety, that veneer of pseudo-self quickly melts away and leaders get reactive and willful. And, in doing so, they fail to live up to the leadership functions the congregation depends on them to provide. Effective congregational leadership emerges from being in right relationship with the community of faith and through leading out of one's genuine self.

Leading from the Self

By now, it should be evident that there are several ways to think about organizations, including thinking about the Church in its institutionalized organization as a congregation. And it is also evident that there are a number of ways to view leadership. But understanding the congregation as an organic system of relationships rather than as just a typical organi-zation means that our understanding of the nature of congregational leadership as leading from the self is atypical. Leading from the self is possible to the extent that the leader can know him- or herself, is work-ing at self-regulation, and developing personal spiritual maturity; it ac-knowledges that there is no self apart from community.[9] Therefore, the congregational leader cannot function as someone who is above, apart from, or over the members of the congregation. Congregational leaders can lead effectively only to the extent that they are in relationship with the members and are able to exert influence by virtue of that relation-ship. The health and appropriateness of that influence, in turn, is di-rectly related to the leader's capacity to lead from the self.

I remember with some amusement listening to one young congrega-tional intern expressing her frustration at her new congregation. She was frustrated at her seeming inability to get people in the congregation to do things or to participate in the programs she was creating at their behest. She noticed that when she asked people to do things or to come to events, they often did not respond—but when a pastoral associate who had been there for some time, over ten years, in fact, asked the same people for the same thing, they would readily say yes and commit their time. At first she took this personally, but eventually, she was able to appreciate that what was going on was not about her, personally. De-spite her official staff position, she just did not have the kind of relation-ship with the members that could influence them to respond to her leadership.

Self-Awareness

Leading from the self begins with the leader's self-awareness. Self-awareness includes understanding one's emotions, being clear about one's values and guiding principles, and having a solid sense of personal identity. When congregational leaders are conscious of their own processes of percep-tion and thinking, for example, they are better able to use their strengths. In Jung's terminology of types, for instance, people with a sensing func-tion need to understand their strengths in dealing with reality, in being able to see a situation practically, and in having the ability to make quick decisions. People with the intuitive function need to recognize their ability to focus on the long-range goals of the congregation, to find new ways to solve old problems in the church, to deal with nuances, and to understand the complexities of situations that cannot be addressed by dogmatic doctrinal or theological stances. Self-awareness helps lead-ers articulate their strengths and use them for effective action. Self-awareness includes understanding our basic motivating force; the one that drives us toward or away from people and things, and which therefore informs and shapes our personal goals.

Leaders can work at self-management by understanding self, and understanding the basic motivators that drive them. Goleman writes that self-management, which he likens to an ongoing inner conversation, is a part of being an emotionally intelligent leader.[10] Emotional intelligence helps leaders work on self-management by freeing them from being ruled by their feelings and unexamined motivations. The leader who is self-aware of his or her emotions and primal motivations can think clearer and make decisions based on the necessary leadership function that a situation demands, rather than react based on how he or she happens to be feeling at the moment. Leaders need to understand that regardless of how they feel at the time of a crisis or confrontation, it's how they choose to function that is the key to effectiveness.

Self-awareness of one's motivations and thinking can also help leaders understand why they make certain decisions and why they tend to place certain values on specific tasks as the leader, while at the same time ignoring other tasks critical to the well-being of the congregation. Recognizing that the hundreds of small and large decisions that they make every day are often natural reflections of their own perspectives can help leaders to understand why they take the directions that they do and why other people don't always agree with them. If leaders can understand the importance of the effect of emotions and personal motivations on behavior, then they'll appreciate that it is often futile to argue for the one right way to do something or to bicker with somebody over whether the leader's way is best. While best judgments can be made in certain situations, more often than not the best decision merely depends on the perspective of the decision maker, or worse, on the hidden and reactive motivating forces of fear, the desire to be right, or the need to be accepted.

Emotions are contagious, and because relationship systems tend to take their emotional cues from the person in the leadership position, the leader's first task often is to manage his or her own emotional state. This is where Goleman's concept of emotional intelligence and Murray Bowen's concept of self-regulation play such important roles. As Goleman wrote, "Quite simply, leaders cannot effectively manage emotions in anyone else without first handling their own."[11] And, as Bowen systems theory contends, the better the leader in the system is able to define self while staying connected to the emotional system of which he or she is a part, the more likely it is for both the members of the system and the leader to function from a less reactive posture.

Simply put, self-awareness means having a deep knowledge of one's self, including one's emotions and driving motivation; a sense of one's identity as an individual and as part of the relationship systems in which one exists; and an honest assessment of one's gifts and talents as well as weaknesses and deficits. Only people who are self-aware have the capacity to be honest with themselves and as a result are able to be honest in relationships as leaders and followers. Those who lack this self-awareness will not have the capacity to be differentiated persons—to know who they are as individuals within their relationship systems—and will have little capacity for making decisions for themselves based on their own values and principles. Leaders who lack self-awareness cannot provide the functions that their congregations require of them. They will either tend to be engulfed by the hidden lives of their congregations and become enmeshed in the relationship dynamics of the church, or they will be perpetually reactive by cutting off and remaining emotionally disconnected from their congregations. Either way, they will lose their ability to be effective as leaders.

The leader who works at self-awareness will eventually be able to give up the myth of objectivity. The truth is that the way that persons perceive reality is a product of both personal and corporate dynamics. Reality is a construct, and it is constructed by one's own background and orientation as well as by the relationship system of which one is a part. Furthermore, how a person interprets reality is dependent on what position one has in the relationship system to which he or she belongs. The idea of a socially and culturally constructed reality seems disconcerting at first, but upon reflection it becomes a self-evident truth. We are constantly involved in making sense of our experiences. Making sense and making meaning requires that we interpret experiences in light of our various frames of reference. Different frames lead to different interpretations and constructions of reality. This process of sense-making is influenced by our interaction with others—our relationships—as well as our position in the emotional system and by our identity as individuals who have been formed by our past relationships.

For most people, the context in which they were formed and which shaped identity and frames of reference—emotional, cognitive, and beliefs—is one's family of origin. Perhaps there is no greater source for achieving self-awareness than to work at understanding self through our families of origin. It is in our families of origin that our identities were shaped, our values formed, and our fundamental view of the world and of the nature of relationships fashioned. For the congregational leader, there is a direct corollary between the depth of understanding self in the context of one's family of origin and one's ability to lead from the self in the congregational setting. Of all institutions, other than a family-owned business, no other comes closer to being like a biological family than does a congregation. Regardless of their size—from a Family-Size congregation to a Corporation-Size congregation—churches are organic relationship systems that mirror all of the dynamics of a family system. Bowen systems theory interpreter Edwin Friedman has shown how the interplay of family systems dynamics affects the three relationship systems of which a pastoral leader is a part: his or her family of origin, the congregational leader's own family, and the church family (including all of the families that make up a local congregational system).[12] Those congregational leaders, both clergy and lay, who seek to lead from the self will more likely achieve that stance to the extent they understand how their family of origin intersects the relational dynamics at work in the hidden lives of congregations, with their own perspective of reality (their frame of reference as to what they perceive and feel), and with their leadership functions.

For over a decade I have been working with clergy and congregational leaders in an ongoing leadership program informed by Bowen family systems theory, which provides opportunity for participants to focus on those three key relationship systems. It is interesting to see that the veterans in the program, some of whom have been participating themselves for a decade, often will go directly to looking at the issues in their family of origin when trying to come to grips with a crisis in the congregation. They have learned that the most powerful insights into what is happening in their church and what is informing their leadership function (or dysfunction) will be found there first.

Getting Feedback

Because a leader's frame of reference is never objective, and because one's motivations often are part of the hidden life of the leadership function, getting feedback becomes critical for the effective functioning of the congregational leader. Leaders are prone to becoming victims to what Goleman calls the "CEO disease," which is an information vacuum that grows around leaders.[13] This vacuum is created when people withhold important information from the leader—often because the information is unpleasant or because the news is known to be something the leader will not want to hear. Sometimes, organizational systems that fear conflict will fall into the pattern of feeding the leader only good and positive news. Bad news, however critical, gets "spinned" in order to buffer a reactive or angry response from the leader. However the vacuum develops, the danger for the leader is that this insulating practice can become patterned very quickly, in which case the persons that the leader depends on most for vital information will become the ones who most inhibit his or her capacity to make wise decisions. If the leader does not work at keeping in touch with the hidden lives of the congregation while working at challenging the system toward maturity and honesty, it will not be long before the leader's ability to be effective will be curtailed.

Getting feedback from a good coach or a coaching group is indispensable for congregational leaders who are working at becoming more self-aware and striving to be more objective in their leadership function. No pastor, no matter how intelligent or talented, can succeed in the complex challenge of congregational leadership alone. Effective congregational leaders know that they need others to help them succeed in the leadership task to which they are called. A good coach or coaching group provides the congregational leader with another set of perspectives and frames of references that can help offset personal bias and blind spots. Additionally, feedback from a coaching group can help the leader interpret the selective information that leaders tend to get as a result of the "CEO disease." A good coaching group should share the leader's understanding of the congregational organization and its culture, as well as be intimately knowledgeable about the leader's personal strengths and deficits. This is what makes finding and cultivating a good coaching group so difficult. Being part of a good coaching group requires commitment to mutual accountability, openness and honesty in the relationship, and willingness to be challenged. It may be safe to say that few clergy ever get the opportunity to be with such a group for any length of time. But the benefits are worth the effort of finding or cultivating such a group, for it can make the difference between merely surviving in ministry and thriving as a congregational leader.

Ethics and Principles

Leading from the self requires that the leader be grounded in clearly articulated personal ethics and guiding principles. The ethical character of the leadership function does not derive from a body of technical expertise. It derives, rather, from the fact that congregational leadership is a social practice that is already moral because it takes place in the context of a confessional Christian community of faith. Congregational leaders practice their ministry in a culture with a preexisting ethical framework that informs behavior, practices, and values as to ends and means. The ethical practices that are based on Christian tradition and beliefs serve to both guide and bound the leadership function in the congregation. In other words, it means something to be called a Christian minister, whether by title, or by function (as with lay persons in leadership positions). The ethics of the ministry of leadership will be derived from a clear image of its practice.

The self-aware leader is one who holds clear guiding principles, and principles are what enable a leader to lead with integrity. Integrity simply means the consistent outward manifestation of one's internal beliefs. Those leaders who are guided by principles are constant and consistent in their behavior and in their relationships. Followers know they can trust a principled leader because they know that they can count on that person to act with integrity. Integrity is not only a virtue in leadership, but is an important organizational strength. Leaders who are principled tend to be transparent; they are authentic and open to others about their feelings and beliefs and up front about their actions. Leading from the self means that leaders act on their rational principles and affective values. This gives them the capacity to make difficult decisions based on the necessary leadership function without being swayed by the emotions and feelings of the moment. Principles and values help the leader function out of a commitment to the vision of the congregation rather than out of what may be expedient for the moment.

I remember when I was a school principal how often I had to meet with parents about their child. More often than not, parents would make demands for something they wanted that would benefit their child. But those demands typically would be detrimental to the school as a whole. Staying clear that my primary responsibility was to the school and to *all* of the children in it—and not to any *one* child—was what helped me to make wise decisions, which often involved saying no to the parent's demands and requests. I rarely said yes to parental requests where the primary beneficiary was only one child, and I never acquiesced to requests based on what was convenient for a parent that would be detrimental to the welfare of the school, the child, or a teacher. But I also never had a parent leave my office upset or angry, because I was able to communicate the principles and rationale behind my decisions. They may have been disappointed at not getting what they wanted, but they were able to appreciate the reason why. They recognized that it was not a personal decision against them or their child; rather, they knew it was because the person in charge of their child's school was clear about that school's mission and purpose and had all of the children's welfare in mind, which ultimately included the welfare of their own child.

Few leaders regret a difficult decision made on the basis of a principle; countless are those leaders who live with the regret and consequences of decisions made out of a lack of impulse control or in the reactivity of an emotionally charged moment. The corrective posture that the leader provides for the congregation is the capacity to stand firm at the time of moral testing.

Practicing Courage

One of the most important facets of congregational leadership, which seems in short supply lately, is that of practicing courage. Courage is the flip side to the claim to authority for authenticating one's leadership position. And its source is the leader's capacity to lead out of his or her self based on convictions of principles and the clarity of vision. Courage is what enables the congregational leader to know the difference between real toughness and merely looking tough and acting tough. Real toughness doesn't come from flexing one's muscles simply because one believes he or she has more authority or more power than another. Real toughness is always principled. Ethical and principled leaders, for example, understand empowerment as something that is delegated to them by the congregation. They accept that any personal authority they hold exists only within the frame of reference of the culture of the congregation they are called to serve. That culture is informed by the congregation's core values and beliefs and is further bounded by the leadership function that the congregation requires—no more, and no less.

The paradox, of course, is that the more a congregation invests its leaders with authority, the less mature and healthy a congregation tends to be. The effective congregational leader is one who has the courage of conviction to give back to the congregation those leadership functions that do not belong to him or her. These self-aware leaders are cognizant of their limitations and understand the need both to complement personal strengths with skilled colleagues and to compensate for personal limitations by sharing leadership functions that rightly belong to the congregational members called to leadership. Leaders with a strong sensing style, for example, must often deliberately seek another's perspective on the long-range consequences of their actions. Strong intuitive leaders may need to find reliable people to attend to immediate, practical problems. The ability to accept maturely that one cannot do everything and be everything to everybody is a quality of effective leaders who are self-aware and courageous.

In contrast, leaders who lack the courage to recognize limitations tend to be overfunctioners. They lack sufficient self-awareness to know where the boundaries of self lie, and therefore lack the ability to discern what they are rightly responsible for and what is not their responsibility. For some leaders, a lack of courage is a sign of hubris or a misguided understanding of authority. They truly believe that they and they alone know what is best—not only for themselves, but for everyone else. In their insecurity they give in to the myth of competence and expertise and perpetually feel the pressure of having to have the solution to every problem and the answer to every question. Overfunctioning in congregational leaders is basically a faithless posture—it does not believe that God is capable of working without the leader's help and it lacks faith in the congregation's capacity to take responsibility for its own destiny.

Recently I received a call from a local church pastor asking for some advice. He wanted some ideas about programs for children and for families. He shared at length his vague ideas and those of the various groups he had been talking with in his church about the needs of the children and families and what they wanted to do. I was curious as to the questions he was asking because I had been following the happenings in his congregation for some months. I knew that they were about to call in the next week an experienced and competent new staff minister whose primary responsibilities would be working with children and families. Finally, I had to interrupt him and asked, "Am I correct that you are about to hire a new staff member?" After he answered, "Yes," I asked, "And what will that person's responsibilities be?"

He said, "That person will be working with families and with the children in the church."

To which I replied, "Then why are you doing her job for her?" After an extended pause on his end of the line, I said, "It looks to me like your church is about to do the right thing. You are going to call and hire a competent, professional, and experienced person to do the job you need. Don't you think she can hit the ground running and do the work?" It took a while, but eventually the pastor was able to see that he was overfunctioning due to his lack of trust that the next staffperson knew how to do her job. He was too focused on fixing the problem and address the anxiety in the congregation to be able to see that he was not seeing what was right under his nose: that the church had already solved its problem by calling the right person for the job.

Courageous leaders have the capacity to expect adherence to the common values of the congregational culture, while at the same time giving wide discretion in implementation in practice. They are outraged when they see these common core values violated. The values of the common core are the nonnegotiables that compose the cultural strands, the covenant that defines the way of life in the congregation. Courage is what enables the congregational leader to be unapologetically ruthless when destructive forces or willful persons intent on being divisive or harmful violate these common principles and community values. Pastors provide a necessary symbolic and cultural function that resides at the congregation's center. Church cultures are concerned with the values, beliefs, and expectations that the members share. Congregational leaders help to shape this culture and work to design ways and means to transmit this culture to others; but more important, they behave as guardians of the values that define the congregation's culture.

A central purpose of the leadership function is inducing clarity, consensus, and commitment regarding the congregation's basic purposes. When members know, agree, and believe in these defining values, practices, and beliefs that inform purpose and vision, the reality of community is experienced. From these defining characteristics come not only direction but the source of meaning and significance that members of the congregation find important. When the congregational leader acts as guardian of the congregation's values, the values enjoy a special verification in importance and meaning—they become real-life cultural imperatives rather than theological abstractions.

In her study *Congregation & Community*, Nancy Ammerman identified the presence of effective and courageous leadership as the difference between congregations who were able to turn around toward growth and effectiveness and those that remained nonadaptive and declining. She noted that

> Pastors in the status quo congregations, by contrast, tended not to introduce new ideas and programs. Most provided excellent care for the people in their congregations and performed well the duties expected of them. Most fit nicely with their parishioners, working hard to maintain the pattern of church life all of them expected. If they perceived any need for change, they were unwilling or unable to undertake the difficult (and often conflictual) work of dislodging old routines. A few expressed to us their sense that their leadership skills were simply not up to the challenges they knew the congregation faced. Others simply pastored the best they knew how.[14]

Growth and Change

Self-awareness in the leader leads to a commitment to growth and change. By change, I do not mean reinventing oneself or undergoing a radical cosmetic or personality "makeover." Despite popular notions, the suit does not make the man, and the outfit doesn't make the woman. By change, I am referring to two things: (1) change that comes from personal and spiritual growth; and (2) the change that takes place when a leader is able to function differently as the context and situation warrants. In addition, change requires an intentional plan. Too many leaders drift through their lives and professional careers. Leaders who are self-aware have a personal vision. They ask themselves goal-oriented questions: Where do I want to be in ten years? In fifteen years? What do I want my epitaph to read? At the end of my ministry, what will have been worthwhile? For self-aware leaders, merely being in touch with one's personal deficits and shortcomings is not sufficient. They work at overcoming those limitations by developing new skills, investing in lifelong learning, and constantly retraining and retooling, because they know that an effective leader is not born but cultivated and formed through intentional effort. Becoming an effective leader doesn't just happen; one has to make it happen.

A focus on change is part of leading from the self. But that focus on change is an inward one, not an other-directed effort. One of the most challenging insights that congregational leaders must constantly keep before them is that, despite their positions of influence, the only persons they can ultimately change are themselves. Only to the extent that a self-aware, courageous leader is working at personal and spiritual growth and maturity will he or she be able to make a real difference in the congregation as a relationship system and in the lives of its members.

Vision

Today, perhaps more than at any other period in the Church's history, congregational leaders are called on to build the Church locally by creating the future rather than investing in the past, and to do so by relying less on direction, support, and resources from ecclesiastical bodies and more on themselves. In such a context and in such an epoch, vision matters more than ever. Vision born of knowing the unique identity and culture of one's congregation requires what looks to others like a leap of faith. And such a perception would not be wrong, because a vision is a commitment to a reality that does not yet exist and whose realization depends solely on the commitment and capacity of the congregation to make it a reality. The critical role that vision plays in the life of a congregation, and as the pastor's prerogative leadership function, has already been discussed in chapter eight. But I cannot stress enough that the capacity to provide vision can happen only if the congregational leader can lead from the self.

Casting a vision for the congregation requires the courage that leading out of self enables in the leader. This is because casting a vision is easier said than done—if it is a genuine, God-given vision, casting the vision before the people can be overwhelming and frightening. When the congregational leader casts the vision, there is an implied personal commitment behind it, not to mention a heavy investment of self. This can be overwhelming to leaders because many fear that "owning" the vision will "own" them. Self-aware congregational leaders know that family systems intersect, so an appropriate concern that feeds this fear lies in the realization that a pastor's personal dedication to a vision will affect his or her family life. For those young pastors who are planning a family or whose children are young, this decision is an especially difficult one. Those pastors with established families likely will have negotiated an agreement with their spouses about their ministry and careers, so casting a vision may not be perceived as involving a lot of personal risk.

Self-awareness on the part of the leader is important to casting a vision because a vision is composed of a person's mental image, worldview, internal motivations, and set of beliefs that orient that person to challenges and relationships. All of those factors help to sort out the important from the unimportant, and provide a rationale for guiding actions and decisions. A leader's self-awareness helps to construct his or her reality.

Only when a leader can make a personal commitment to a vision can he or she then share the vision with other congregational leaders and with the members of the congregation. This process involves speaking from a position of high visibility and living up to the appropriate leadership function of casting the vision for the people. Only a leader who is self-aware, understands vision as a function of leadership. Only one who has the courage informed by ethics and principles can risk casting a vision before a congregation (what Edwin Friedman called preaching the "I have a dream" sermon).[15] This is because articulating the vision does not make life easy for anyone—visions challenge the status quo and are made to shake people out of their complacency. Vision makes risk possible. For the congregational leader, commitment to one's vision often results in hard work, long hours, and investment of time, energy, and money in perfecting skills he or she needs to accomplish the vision. However, clarity of vision is what helps leaders discern the difference between being busy and overfunctioning. Overfunctioners are always busy, but they are busy going about someone else's business because they lack the ability to set clear boundaries about their own goals and the needs of others. The leader who has cast a vision may be busy as well, especially during early stages of developing and cultivating the vision. But leaders with vision know why they are busy—they are making an investment in a goal that is their own and which they share with others in the congregation. They know that vision requires sacrifices and a commitment to make the vision a reality. The busyness that the visionary leader experiences is qualitatively different from that of the overfunctioning leader—it is a busyness born out of hope and optimism rather than anxiety and oppression.

The visionary leader understands that casting a vision requires courage, because holders of an organizational vision often have to take an unpopular, even courageous, stand in their congregation. Commitment to a vision provides leaders with a purpose, but it also presents them with a struggle. But visionary leaders seize opportunities. Taking those opportunities—and creating more of them—is an important aspect of the leader's functioning, even if those opportunities present themselves in the form of a crisis. They must confront those in the congregation who are committed to things that will impede change and progress—some of which may be perfectly good things—and thus would hold back others. They must challenge those who lack the courage to move forward due to a lack of faith or an inability to share in the vision. They must be able to "speak truth to power" if necessary. And, at times, they must have the courage of conviction to choose the vision over relationships. Rarely will a congregation that embraces a new vision be able to bring everyone along. Congregations that insist on "not losing anyone" as they move forward in realizing the vision will only succeed in failing.

Conclusion

Effective congregational leaders, both clergy and laypersons, lead from their own personhood. They provide effective leadership not so much because they have a winning personality, or have acquired skills in getting people to do certain things or to feel a certain way, nor because they are "born leaders." Effective congregational leaders tend to be those who have a clear sense of their own identity, are clear about their personal values and principles, and are mature, both personally and spiritually. These leaders not only understand themselves, but they understand the relationships of which they are a part, and they work to ensure the success and growth of those relationships. They commit to ensuring the integrity of the congregations of which they are a part—working toward realizing their corporate vision and congruence between their stated mission and their practices, even if it means challenging the status quo, comfortable presumptions, or values that are inconsistent with their vision of life together. They are never insecure at sharing leadership, but rather, always seek to share it, knowing that in empowering others they benefit themselves and their congregations.

Effective leaders focus on their own self, and recognize that their primary resource for leadership lies within them—not in externals like a style or notions of power or of vested authority or titular positions. "To thine own self be true," cited Shakespeare (and others before him). That's good leadership advice. Effective leaders know that investing in their own personal growth and well-being, and committing to their values and principled living, are their greatest strengths, and the greatest gifts they will give the people and congregations they lead.

Chapter 10

The Focus of Congregational Leaders

LEADERSHIP IS A CONGREGATIONAL RESOURCE. IT MUST BE USED WITH responsible stewardship, because to squander or misuse this important resource will result in dire consequences to the congregation and its members. A theological understanding of the Church as the Body of Christ in the form of a relationship system means that leadership takes on a distinct function in congregations. Leadership is not an individual and personal matter embodied solely in the person of the chief pastor. That is, leadership is not about having the right personality or adopting the preferred style, or perfecting the right combination of skills sets. In the congregational setting, leadership is about providing the right functions at the appropriate time in ways that enable the system to function in healthy ways. Given this understanding, leadership is more of a corporate function than an individual ability. In this chapter, I challenge congregational leaders to reexamine where they need to invest their energies. The dynamics of the hidden lives of congregations hints that effective leaders stay focused on their functioning in a corporate relationship context, rather than focusing on individual traits.

Focus on Lay Leadership

The idea that congregational leadership is a corporate function seems to be one of the most challenging concepts for pastors to accept. Likely, this is because most have been trained with concepts about leadership that focus on the office of the clergy. These approaches to leadership stress authority and power and concern themselves with the individual personality who occupies the leader position. As a result, most pastors exercise leadership in ways that ensure it is disconnected in significant ways from the hidden life of the congregation. Furthermore, the emphasis on the individual role of leadership as a management task that primarily administers the church organization and uses people as the resources to do so runs counter to the nature of a congregation as a relationship system. This renders congregational leadership ineffective regardless of how competent a manager the pastor may be.

One symptom of that congregational leadership approach is the exhaustion that pastors experience as a result of overfunctioning. A corrective to this leadership tendency to take over responsibilities that appropriately belong to the congregation is for the pastor to focus on a more corporate approach to the function of congregational leadership. By cultivating the lay leadership in congregations, pastors can shift the leadership function from an individual task to a corporate function. This is a more biblical approach to leadership, one that empowers the church members and yet does not deny the legitimacy of the biblical church offices (Acts 14:23; Ephesians 4:11; Titus 1:5, 1 Peter 5:1-3). Stevens and Collins advocate this perspective to congregational leadership, saying, "Leadership is a gift given by God to the church and not merely to the pastor. We are advocating full partnership in leadership between pastor and lay leadership, not merely a team of professional staff."[1]

This shift toward a more corporate understanding of leadership will require several things if it is to be implemented in a local congregation. First, the pastor must personally be convinced of the theological correctness of the shared corporate function of congregational leadership. This will require not only the conviction that this is a more biblical approach to congregational leadership, but also a shift toward understanding the congregation as primarily a cultural relationship system—a community of faith—rather than as an institutional organization. Second, it is unlikely that this shift in leadership from a focus on the individual role of a pastor to a more corporate function in the congregation will be effected by leaders who lack maturity and a strong sense of self.

Third, this shift will require pastors to reclaim the biblical intent of the office of the pastor-teacher (Ephesians 4:11). In order to foster the corporate understanding of shared leadership, pastors will need to intentionally and consistently apply the educational function of the pastoral role. They must provide focus and consistency for a congregation by using biblical language and images in every avenue the church uses to educate its members—worship and liturgy, preaching, study, fellowship, and mission and ministry groups—to cultivate the theological value of shared leadership. Historian and author Janet F. Fishburn states that the loss of the teaching function historically associated with clergy leadership has led to confusion about the distinctive nature of pastoral ministry. Additionally, she says this has led to a resentment of perceived clergy power by the laity, and a suspicion among pastors who lack a theology of shared leadership that laity want to usurp their role in church.[2] If pastors do not reclaim this primary educational responsibility for teaching their members in theological thinking and a biblical understanding of congregational leadership, it is unlikely that the local church will be able to make the shift from a perpetual overdependence on the pastor for leadership to taking responsibility for their own ministry, vision, and missions in response to God's call to discipleship.

Successful leaders practice leadership by purpose. Leadership by purpose means that the leader has a clear enough understanding of the context in which he or she leads so that the function of leadership has clear ends related to a commitment regarding the congregation's basic purposes. This enables the congregational leader to form a clear and compelling vision for the congregation's future that in turn informs the actions that need to be taken and decisions that need be made in the present in order to realize that future state. Leadership by purpose means that the leader understands and provides the congregation with the necessary functions of the leadership position and does not merely practice a kind of situational leadership in which a shift in "style" is the focus. Certainly, congregational leaders need to respond appropriately to the immediate needs of a situation and develop a range of task-oriented and people-oriented behaviors to be able to address immediate concerns. But leadership by purpose that focuses on the theological nature of the congregation as a relationship system helps congregational leaders better to recognize that the leadership functions that most help the congregation are those that move the members toward realizing the mission of the Church.

As already noted, no one type or model of leadership has prevailed in the history of American congregations.[3] Because congregations vary in polity, setting, culture, personality, life stage, and vision, then theoretically any leadership style may be appropriate given the context and needs that present themselves. In fact, the most common leadership conflict arising from a "mismatch" between pastor and congregation has less to do with "style," competence, or personality and more with an inability to provide the necessary leadership functions that a congregation needs at a particular time, context, or culture.

I've said that leadership is a congregational resource, and that is true. But the key congregational leadership is a resource that is provided personally by the pastor. One of the most valuable benefits of developing a corporate approach to leadership whereby the pastor shares the function with other leaders in the congregation is that it frees the pastor to focus on specific, critical areas of leadership. Most pastors can give away more leadership functions than they realize. As noted in the previous chapters, the essential leadership functions that reside in the position and person of the pastor as leader tend to be few, though critical. The pastor who can successfully share leadership functions with other competent congregational leaders will be free to focus on aspects of his or her personal leadership that will benefit the congregation in powerful ways. It becomes important for the pastor, therefore, to know on what to focus.

Focus on Culture

A leadership approach that takes account of the hidden lives of congregations will focus on the influence that culture has on both the congregation and on the leadership function. By culture, we mean primarily the emotional process of the relationship system, including its values, norms, and artifacts. Culture helps explain why congregations exhibit common and stable patterns across the variable conditions and contexts in which they are found. Culture gives meaning to ministry activities and the practices of a congregation and provides a symbolic bridge between action and results. It fuses individual identity with collective destiny. For prospective members or those in the broader community, the artifacts of the culture provide the symbolic façade that gives a hint as to the identity, personality, and purpose of the congregation. Culture is where the hidden lives of congregations are embedded, including the underlying assumptions and beliefs that are shared by congregational members that often operate unconsciously.[4]

The renowned sociologist and researcher Edgar H. Schein pointed out that culture in organizations tends not to be directly visible because it is something that the members take for granted and which exists as part of the underlying and unconscious assumptions that have evolved over time to deal with the various internal issues that the group has had to face. But a leader can identify the culture of a system as it is reflected in the overt behavior that is visible in how members relate to each other.[5] In congregations with a strong culture, these assumptions and beliefs give rise to group norms around which there is a high level of agreement. For example, culture ensures that there is high agreement among members as to what constitutes proper behavior in the various settings in which the members meet. I've attended one congregation in which behavior at the corporate worship service was restrained, but where a social gathering at which deacons and leadership participate allowed for a more relaxed and informal atmosphere—and I've been in another congregation where the exact opposite was true.

In congregations with a strong culture, there is high agreement among members regarding what is legitimate authority; and this agreement may be rooted in the traditions of the group rather than some rational formulation (as in a Family-Size congregation that will more readily obey a mandate from the patriarch in the system than listen to the wise council of an experienced and trained pastor). The congregational culture is what facilitates ways for the beliefs and values of the church to be communicated and passed on through a system of rituals and ceremonies, rather than codified in law and detailed rules as in other organizations.

Culture also affects a congregation's inclusion practices. It's what makes staffing patterns relatively stable when there is an expectation for long-term ministry employment of the pastor and other ministers. But culture also makes outreach and recruitment very selective. Congregations with strong cultures tend to follow intensive, if not overtly conscious, socialization processes that move people toward the center of community life. These cultural inclusion practices tend to result in high levels of loyalty and commitment to the values and traditions of the congregation.

Cultural forms embody the ways of a faith community. Therefore, congregational leaders need to give attention to developing and articulating the congregational culture in order to work with the influences of the hidden lives of congregations. The congregational culture includes several components that the leadership can readily identify: (1) the *shared values* of the congregation, often communicated in shorthand slogans that summarize deep-seated core values; (2) the *heroes and saints* of the church—the pantheon of individuals who embody or represent the core values of the congregation; (3) the *rituals* of the congregation—the repetitive behavioral repertoire in which values are experienced directly through implicit signals; (4) the *ceremonies and practices* that are observed—episodic occasions in which the values and heroes are put on display, anointed, and celebrated, such as baptisms, farewell and launching rituals, celebrations and recognitions of tenure; (5) the *stories* that are told—concrete examples of values and heroes and saints who triumph by following culturally prescribed ways; and (6) the *cultural network of relationships*—including a collection of informal "priest and priestesses," gossips, spies, and storytellers whose primary role is to reinforce and to protect the existing ways of the community. As these social components develop in a congregation, they create a strong culture that is extremely powerful in controlling the behavior of participants and is the dominant influence in the hidden lives of congregations. This cultural emotional process is what evokes the cooperative effort normally associated with communities.

Pastors and congregational members who would be effective church leaders must be prepared to go beyond the merely routine techniques suggested by the time-honored models of leadership derived from management schools. They must be prepared to engage in cultural leadership and to develop organizational cultures consistent with the corporate relationship nature of a congregation. Such leaders need to give attention to the creation of a different understanding of leadership through responsible theologies of Church-as-congregation and through different organizational structures that extol the proper place that the congregational members have in sharing pastoral leadership in the church. This requires the hard work of developing new social and cultural norms in the congregation.

Through cultural systemic leadership, pastors signal and demonstrate to others in the congregation what is important, what is valued, and what goals should override others. They create and communicate a vision for others in the congregation describing a desired state of affairs, one better than the present. Through cultural leadership, they can create and communicate a new sense of purpose for the members. Leaders can help members to understand that a new cultural adaptation is essential to the success and relevance of the overall mission and that each member has a role to play in it.

Setting forth this vision of cultural change is necessary, but the pastor and congregational leaders must never assume that everyone will see the whole picture. When a new vision is launched, constant communication through every means must be used, including words (oral and written) and other symbols (such as time, images, media, and personal presence). Congregational leaders must continually emphasize those things in the emerging culture that are important. Leaders will need to make clear to congregational members the connections between what they do and what they want to do in order to realize the vision regarding the church's central values and evolving culture.

The good news is that congregations have a precondition for cultural systemic leadership. But congregational leaders must think clearly about what is important. They must develop a vision about a desired state of affairs that is clear to them, one they can articulate easily and efficiently to others. Indeed, cultural leadership is not possible unless the leader has carefully developed a vision of what should be with some level of concreteness. The vision must have some quality that can stir the consciousness of others and induce their commitment to sharing it as their own purpose. The congregational pastoral leader, after all, stands symbolically for both the existing cultural values of the congregation as well as for its future hope.

Building a new congregational culture means building behavioral norms that exemplify the best a church stands for. It means building an institution that people believe in strongly, that they identify with personally as a community of faith, and that they render their loyalty to gladly. All this gives meaning to the work that the congregational leaders do with the pastor, thus motivating the leaders and other members. To build strong congregational cultures, leaders must not only spend time articulating the congregation's purpose and the mission, but must stay connected with those whose responsibility it is to adapt and build the new structures that will accommodate the emerging culture. The function of the congregational leader, then, involves institutional building, the fashioning of an organism that embodies new and enduring values that reflect the Body of Christ. A high degree of socialization that facilitates a merger of members' individual goals with the espoused values of the organization is the outstanding characteristic of the congregation with a strong core identity.

Focus on Influence

Stevens and Collins define Christian leadership as "the God-given ability to influence others so that believers will trust and respond to the Head of the church for themselves, in order to accomplish the Lord's purposes for God's people in the world."[6] The most effective approach to leadership in the congregational context is one that emphasizes leadership as a corporate function that brings about change through the influence of relationships. Effective leaders know the difference between power over people and the power to influence. Power over others means trying to control people and events so that things turn out the way the leader wants. Thus, power over others is concerned with dominance, control, and hierarchy. Leadership conceived as power over others does not fit the image of biblical pastoral leadership. Practically speaking, it is difficult as well as unwise to focus on programming what people *should* do. To practice leadership conceived as power over others, a leader needs to be in a position of dominance, control, and authority and must have access to the necessary carrots and bully sticks to get people to move. But congregational leaders cannot use carrots or bully sticks to motivate people or to get them to do what they want. Effective congregational leaders recognize that mature and healthy people don't respond to this form of power and will resist it.

Instead, effective congregational leaders are more concerned with exercising the power to influence those with whom they are in relationship. They are concerned with how the influence of leadership can help people become more successful in their lives and ministries, to accomplish the things that they think are important, to experience a greater sense of efficacy. Therefore, effective congregational leaders are concerned less with micromanaging what people are doing, or needing to have people agree with their every idea of what should be done and how, and more with whether they are helping the members of the congregation live out the values and mission of the community.

A leadership approach that focuses on influencing a congregation's culture works for several reasons. From the congregational leader's point of view, it is a pragmatic way to achieve coordinated ministry efforts toward goals in a complex and loosely connected system. Where management schemes fail to link together people and events in a way that provides for successful ministry, congregational leadership that focuses on culture and values—rather than beliefs or personalities—is able to bond people together in a common cause. From an ecclesiastical point of view, ministry unfolds best when members are free to make decisions that are important to them and related to their spiritual gifts and personal callings as disciples. Church members are best served when they use the congregation as a resource and poorly served when they are subordinate to its interests of institutional self-preservation or enlargement. From a motivational point of view, members enjoy greater satisfaction in church and ministry and respond with increased motivation when the church helps them find their personal and work lives a meaningful and significant part of their vocational ministry and calling.

A systemic connectedness exists among the various characteristics and dimensions of cultural leadership. For example, the meaning-making function of leadership and the concept of focusing on church culture are complimentary constructs for enhancing meaning and significance in the lives of the congregation's membership. Therefore, the cultural leadership approach is best understood and practiced holistically. Congregational cultural leadership doesn't work if only some aspects are emphasized but not others. Practicing leadership for empowerment of the laity, for example, without also practicing leadership by purposing and visionary courage results in *laissez-faire* rather than cultural leadership. Further, leaders who hold "worker" views of members and bureaucratic views of ministry as programs and numbers cannot convincingly and meaningfully practice empowerment of members. In both cases the leader's rhetoric and behavior will negate the formation of a culture of shared leadership and of empowering members for ministry.

It is vital that congregational leaders respect the group's cultural values and the organization's integrity as they work at changing the culture. Visions change, but as visions evolve, congregational leaders need to be sure that they protect the "sacred center"—those values that inform the church's identity and hold the members together as a community. The first challenge of the leader, says Goleman, is to know what the sacred center actually is—from the perspective of the members themselves, and not merely the leader's interpretation of what it might be.[7] Only then can congregational leaders discern the vision as to what must change in the culture, even when that is something which is held dear. If core beliefs or culture really need to change in order to achieve the vision, then the members will need to drive that change themselves. Congregational leaders must share the leadership function in enabling these changes through influence, because this kind of systemic change cannot be forced. When the members enter into a change process that involves changing their culture, they need to be personally and powerfully motivated by the vision of how things need to be, and not driven by fear or coercion. "A visionary leader can impact this process positively by honoring the feelings and beliefs of the people around him, while steadfastly demonstrating the benefit of moving toward this dream,"[8] says Goleman.

Focus on Empowerment

In healthy, vibrant, and growing congregations, strong pastoral leadership also means strong lay leadership and a high level of lay participation. Even in the secular setting, according to Goleman, the most successful CEOs spend more time coaching their senior executives, developing them as collaborators, and cultivating personal relationships with them.[9] Effective leaders, in whatever context, practice the principle of investing leadership in others. They distribute the leadership functions among others in an effort to get more influence in return. But their view of influence is sophisticated and relationship oriented; they know it is not influence over people and events that counts but, rather, influence over the achievement of organizational purposes and mission. To increase congregational influence, effective pastoral leaders know that they need to delegate or surrender influence and control over accomplishments. This is extremely difficult to do for leaders who bank self-worth and legitimacy of office in "results" that they can attribute to their own efforts, talents, or skills. The inability to share leadership functions with members and to let go of control over results is a sign of a lack of faith in the member's calling and in the Spirit's capacity to enable the Body of Christ for ministry.

This enabling empowerment needs to come from the systemic leadership position of the congregation's pastor. Nancy Ammerman determined that a key ingredient in adaptation in a congregation's culture is a strong pastoral leader in creative partnership with lay leaders and members who see that leadership as legitimate. Notably, says Ammerman, that pastoral leadership finds its legitimacy through being earned in the particular local relationships of the congregation, and rarely is it conferred by an outside denominational authority.[10]

If there is one primary purpose inherent to the office of pastor—one that is above all others—it is that of equipping the congregational members for their ministries (Ephesians 4:12). Of course, this is unlikely to happen until the pastor him- or herself acquires the conviction that ministry is the work of all the people—not exclusively of the clergy. This requires a refocusing of both the theology and the function of pastoral leadership. Fishburn stated the implication succinctly: "If indeed it is true that the basic responsibility for ministry rests upon every baptized Christian, then the clear responsibility of leadership in the church is to help members identify their gifts, develop those gifts, and make use of them in ministry."[11] While this theological and cultural vision needs to come from the pastor, even here he or she must work with other congregational leaders to make this a reality. Ammerman states that even strong pastoral leadership alone is not sufficient to create certain organizational changes. Pastors need the help of laypersons who are willing to participate in the necessary processes of change in the culture and values of the congregation for the sake of a vision that promises a better way of being church.[12] These leaders will need to respect the power of the hidden lives of congregations that resists this kind of visionary and fundamental change in values, some of which were established during the Formation and Formatting stage of the congregation's life and have become a defining part of the church's identity.

Empowering leaders and members for ministry does not mean developing a support system for the pastoral staff nor ensuring that there are enough people to fill church committees. Neither does it imply developing members to be faithful and committed to shoring up and perpetuating the congregational institutional organization. A ministry of empowering the laity is about helping the members of a church discover their own call to ministry as disciples and to make a vocational response to that call. When this happens, members create and shape their own ministry—most of which will be outside the walls of the church and of the congregation's organizational structure. Leaders who are committed to empowering the members for ministry will create the structures and processes that will help the members respond to God's call and acquire the necessary ministry skills to actualize their spiritual gifts.

The theological vision of empowering members for ministry will require a fundamental shift in the church's educational enterprises and in
the structures of the congregation. This means that churches will need
to stop engaging in "pretend learning" and commit to providing the kind
of training that actually helps people learn to *do* ministry as opposed to
merely learn *about* ministry. The frustrating reality in most congregations is that the educational enterprises—their approaches, methods,
and programming—and the structures of the church seem to be designed
to actually inhibit members from learning how to do ministry and pre-
vent them from being able to engage in ministry and missions. Unless a
congregation changes these ineffective structures and puts in place those
that are consistent with the vision of empowering and training members
for ministry, the vision will merely be wishful thinking. The danger is that
eventually the hidden life of the church culture will communicate effectively to the members that while we preach one thing about Christian discipleship and commitment, we practice another thing—namely a way of
doing church that actually prevents people from answering the call of God.

Focus on Process

Effective congregational leaders know the difference between content
and process—and they focus on process rather than content. Content
has to do with what people say, while process has to do with how people
function. Beliefs, doctrines, mission statements, organizational plans,
and program agendas are content. Relationships, the hidden life dynamics, vision, leading from the self, and staying connected have to do with
process. A focus on process will examine the way a congregation works,
how it solves its problems, gathers information, makes decisions, com-
municates among its members, and so on. Learning how to distinguish
content from process is difficult, especially during times when the hidden life force of Systemic Anxiety is at play and leaders become prone to
be seduced by the content—precisely the time when they most need to
focus on process in order to know how to respond.

Goleman cites a study of leadership among star performers that identified the unique strengths among that elite group. The study identified
four competencies: the drive to achieve results, the ability to take initiative, skills in collaboration and teamwork, and the ability to lead teams.
But here is the challenge to prevailing notions of leadership as expertise: Not a single technical or cognitive competency was identified as a
unique strength among these effective leaders.[13] This finding helps to
highlight that effective leadership is not about expertise or technique—

it is about the ability to influence emotional process. This requires a good level of what I call "with-it-ness." With-it-ness refers to the level of awareness that a leader has about the emotional process at work in the hidden lives of congregations. With-it-ness, however, begins with the leader's own self-awareness—being in touch with what one is feeling, whether one is reacting or responding (a distinction that is not always easy to make), and with what is going on inside one's head. Unless congregational leaders can observe and assess their own feelings, biases, perceptual distortions, and impulses, they cannot tell whether their interventions are based on perceptions or reality, or determine what would be the most helpful response in a situation. Without with-it-ness, leaders cannot assess how the hidden life forces of the congregation are being played out and, therefore, they will not be able to distinguish content from process.

With-it-ness includes what Goleman calls resonance, which is akin to empathy. Resonance means being attuned to how others feel in the moment. Only in this way can leaders influence process by saying and doing what is appropriate for emotional process—whether it be to calm anxiety or raise it, confront anger, or respond with humor.[14] Being attuned to the emotional process enables the leader to sense how the shared cultural values and priorities of the congregation are influencing the members. A leader who lacks with-it-ness will not be able to influence the emotional process of his or her congregation because he or she will tend to be out of sync with what is really going on in the group. With-it-ness enables leaders to stay connected emotionally, which facilitates listening and taking other people's perspectives—to see things from the vantage point of their place in the system. This in turn allows leaders to tune into the emotional channels between people that create emotional resonance. Only when there is emotional resonance between the congregational leader and the congregation are the members able to hear and respond to the challenges of vision. Emotional resonance is what makes it possible for people to hear each other, regardless of the words that are used and regardless of whether the message is comfortable— like a prophetic challenge or in times when brutal honesty and speaking the truth in love are necessary.

Focus on Coaching and Consulting

Focusing on process requires that the congregational leadership take a supportive, coaching approach and a democratic style. When leadership focuses on process, it is more effective to take a consultant or coaching stance as a helping posture. These approaches help the church leadership and the members better understand and act on the emotional process of the hidden life forces that take place in the congregation's environment and culture. The traditional formal authority granted to pastors provides a great temptation—accompanied by implied expectations—to fall into the role of the resident expert. This is especially prevalent in congregations that have been used to taking a dependent, passive posture in terms of their discipleship involvement in the life of the congregation. But if the congregational leaders are committed to empowering the members in their Christian discipleship, then giving up the "expert" (and often overfunctioning) role and adopting the coaching and consulting roles is preferable.

Effective leaders have a broad repertoire of approaches from which to draw and need to know when to use one over the other. During times of crisis or in eras of transition, leaders can choose to take a more directive stance in the congregation. But when the crisis is over or homeostasis has been reclaimed after a transition, they will step back into a more democratic stance to allow the congregation to take on more of the processes. They will delegate leadership responsibilities, as appropriate, to people who are competent in the task assigned or who have the capacity to respond to challenge and grow into the position of responsibility. In this way, they safeguard the congregation's health while not giving opportunity for membership to become dependent for their destiny on the position or the person in charge.

Leaders who act out of the consulting stance focus on emotional process. They ask questions, help the congregation clarify its vision, help people discover their calling and mission, and interpret the culture for those too steeped in it to see how the hidden life of the congregation affects the members. In the role of consultants, leaders challenge members to take responsibility for their own spirituality and for the well-being of their congregation. The congregational leader who wishes to be effective needs to discern the difference between being helpful by giving advice and helping churches develop ways to figure out their own solutions. The trap, and the seduction, that most pastors fall into is the tendency to assume that they "know" the solution to what the congregation needs, or the answer to the questions the members are asking.

Sitting in the leader position can feel like a vulnerable spot—after all, it is the chief focus of Systemic Anxiety. Taking on the self-assigned role of resident expert, change agent, go-to guy or gal, or problem solver can provide the insecure leader with a sense of being indispensable to the congregation. And indeed, he or she may succeed in convincing some members that this is the case. But the ones who will be convinced will not be the most mature in the congregation—rather, it will be the ones who are most dependent, passive, insecure, and easily seduced. Pastoral leaders who constantly engage in advice giving are basically willful and exhibit an inability to really listen to what the other person is saying. Advice giving usually solicits two responses. The first is from people who lack a sense of self and are willing to give up personal or corporate autonomy and follow advice they are given rather than to think on their own. The second group are those who will ask for advice and then resist, point out how the leader has missed the point, then play a game of "Yes, but…" and invent reasons why the advice the leader gave did not or will not work. The most effective way to empower congregational members to take responsibility for the work of the ministry is not to make them dependent on the leader for answers and solutions, nor to focus on the most dependent and needy individuals in the system, but rather to focus on helping the congregation as a whole—the system— work at changing its own culture and to understand the hidden life of the congregation.

The effective congregational leader knows when to choose the right function for the right means. If the pastor and lay leaders are to be influential and genuinely helpful, they must learn when and how to be in the role of expert advice-giver and when to be in the role of facilitator and catalyst, whether to take control of a situation or to allow the congregation to deal with anxiety and pain and find its own solution. In fact, those congregational leaders with a long-range vision for their church will develop a high tolerance for other people's pain and will intentionally structure situations for the lay leaders in which they can learn to solve problems for themselves.[15]

Congregational leaders who take a consulting role will need to resist diagnosis. Diagnosis is a helpful and necessary tool for the medical intern at a hospital, but not an effective one for a pastor and lay leaders who take a relationship system perspective to congregational leadership. Diagnosis tends not to work for several basic reasons. First, diagnosis leads to prescriptions, which, in the congregational setting, basically is advice giving. Second, this approach assumes that the diagnosis process itself is helpful, but, in truth, it is difficult to separate diagnosis from willful intervention. The diagnostic approach too readily assumes that the person or group assumed to be "sick" (the "identified patient" or symptom-bearer) is actually the problem, which is rarely the case. Third, the leader will need to assume that a person or the group who is the focus of anxiety and the identified patient will have enough self-awareness and insight into the hidden life dynamics that affect them to be able to provide the information needed for the leader to make a valid diagnosis.

A correct diagnosis depends on getting all of the facts, the right kind of information, and knowing enough about the symptom to prescribe a solution. But it is almost impossible for a congregational leader to have that kind of data at his or her disposal, which means that the leader's diagnosis of the problem is most probably wrong to some unknown degree because of the nature of the hidden lives of congregations. Fourth, even if the leaders can make the right diagnosis, the members of the congregation will likely not accept the diagnosis and will resist any prescription or advice. Additionally, it may be possible that the solution prescribed may be beyond the capacity of the congregation to achieve, as is often the case with a congregation in its Prime stage of development. Finally, even if the congregational members accept the diagnosis, both the leaders and the congregation have failed in empowering the congregational system to acquire the ability to be self-aware of their problem or condition; they have not learned, which will leave them vulnerable to the same problems again and again. Congregational leaders who take a consulting approach will work to ensure that the members share in the process of assessing what may be wrong and to see the problem for themselves. In this way they empower the members to take ultimate responsibility for deciding what to do.

An empowering congregational leadership that views a church primarily as a system of relationships (and only secondarily as an institutional organization) starts with very different assumptions about the nature of leadership than that of management or of a medical model involving diagnosis and prescription. One central assumption is that it is the congregation who owns the problem, and will continue to own it throughout the tenure of any congregational leader. This is one of the hardest things for both pastors and church members to accept: that it is not the job of the congregational leader to solve the congregation's problems. Edgar Schein points out that this insight cannot be emphasized strongly enough because, when someone asks for help, all of the forces are pulling in the direction of the helper to take responsibility and relieve the pain and anxiety the system feels.[16] Relationship systems that are dependent and immature work hard at seducing leaders to take care of them by asking for care and getting the leader to comply rather than to take an enabling stance that says, "It's your problem, but I'll help you find a way to deal with it."

Most of the hidden life forces and conditions that lead to conflict and institutional deficits in the congregation do not fit a management, or what Schein describes as a "doctor-patient," model of leadership. The major difference in the leadership approach that focuses on emotional process and takes a consulting stance lies in, as Schein points out, how the consultant-leader structures the relationship, not in what the client does.[17] Leaders who take a consultant stance can find some relief from performance anxiety or from the myth of competence[18] by accepting that, as a consultant, they may or may not be an expert in solving a congregation's particular problems. But that level of omniscient expertise is less relevant to the life of a congregation than are the skills of empowering members in self-awareness and helping them learn to assess and solve their own problems honestly. What the consultant leadership must be an expert in is systemic emotional process and in staying connected to the members in order to affect a regulating influence on the system.

Focus on the Most Mature and Most Motivated

Congregational leaders that focus on emotional process understand that the primary responsibility of leadership is to the entire system first, and only secondarily to the individuals that make up the system. This is another counterintuitive and challenging shift in understanding the nature of congregational leadership that is difficult for many ministers to make. Most clergy training emphasizes pastoral-care skills that focus on the needs of individuals. This is appropriate, since caring for the needy, the troubled, and "bearing each other's burdens" is a high Christian value. Being cared for spiritually and emotionally is one of the reasons people join a congregation in the first place—so much so that finding a "caring and warm" church is on the top of the shopping list when people seek a new church to join.

But a more appropriate understanding of congregational leadership accepts that the care of church members is primarily the responsibility of the *church*, and not exclusively of the pastor. This understanding of congregational leadership is evident in the early formation of the churches in the book of Acts. As congregations began to form and to grow in size and move through the Formation and Formatting stage of the lifespan, the care of the members was given over to the lay leaders specifically in order to free the pastoral leaders to focus on the whole church (Acts 6:1-6). Coaches and leaders who are committed to empowering the congregational members for ministry value and practice the delegation of authority, leadership functions, and pastoral ministries.

The fact of the matter is that, as discussed in chapter six, as an emotional relationship system, congregations tend to attract, if not foster, a dependent and passive style of faith among members. Often the very values and hidden life dynamics that make a church a warm and caring place perpetuate a focus on the needy members. These emotionally fragile and often immature members can hold a lot of influence in the church. This is because of the hidden life force of Systemic Anxiety that often tends to settle on the most dependent in the system. The challenge for the pastoral leader often is to give up trying to meet the needs of the perpetually needy individuals in the congregation by delegating it to the church so that he or she can concentrate on investing in the most mature and motivated in the congregation. Leaders committed to emotional process and empowering need to incorporate the insight into their thinking and functioning that the way to bring about visionary and fundamental change in the congregation's culture is by investing in the most mature members in the system rather than in the most needy and dependent ones.

Edwin Friedman pointed out that, from a systems point of view, the greatest change comes about not by focusing on the individual persons in the system, but by changing the emotional process of the system itself.[19] Investing in the needy and unmotivated does not work, because, as Friedman put it, "The unmotivated are notoriously invulnerable to insight."[20] That is, the unmotivated have incapacity to learn, and learning involves change and being changed. It comes as no surprise, then, that coaching works best with those lay leaders and members who show initiative, are motivated about their own personal growth, and want to grow in their Christian discipleship. Coaching will always fail when it is invested in those who lack motivation or require excessive personal direction, constant oversight, and an inordinate amount of emotional investment.

Focus on the Vision

Effective congregational leaders understand the need to keep their focus on the vision. Staying focused on the vision toward which the congregation is heading provides a constant reminder that there is a qualitative difference between a view of church and ministry whose measure of success is in numbers, and a view of ministry where the spiritual formation and growth of all the people of God is the criterion for effective pastoral leadership.[21] Congregational leaders who focus on the vision and are able to lead out of the self can articulate the church's vision of where the group is going, but will not take primary responsibility for how it will get there. Instead, empowering leaders will give the lay leaders and members permission to exercise courage by taking calculated risks and exercising faith in working toward the vision. Keeping a focus on the vision allows the members to understand the big picture so they can then figure out how a given ministry or a sacrificial decision fits in with the overall goals of the congregation. Furthermore, by focusing on the vision, leaders can help the congregation exercise a theology of call and challenge members to respond to the vision that God has for the congregation. When this happens, members use their spiritual gifts, talents, and resources and find immediate application in the ministries and mission in which they participate in response to the vision. "Visionary leaders help people to see how their work fits into the big picture, lending people a clear sense not just that what they do matters, but also why,"[22] says Goleman.

Focus on Challenge and Cultural Change

Managers solve problems by providing answers and finding solutions; leaders bring about fundamental change through emotional process. Congregations need leaders, not managers. Congregational leaders, therefore, need to deal with issues related to a church's culture as an emotional system and with a view as to how the hidden lives of congregations affect that system. In order to help bring about cultural change, congregational leaders ask a different set of questions than those managers face. Congregational leaders empower others in asking: How do we encourage meaning and commitment to our values and vision? How do we deal with loss and change as we move toward our vision? How can we shape symbols that convey the essence of our identity and ministry enterprises to insiders and outsiders? Furthermore, mature pastoral leaders who focus on congregational development and process give staff and members challenging assignments that stretch them, rather than tasks that simply get the job done. They can tolerate a short-term failure, understanding that, if handled right and accompanied with an ability to learn from the experience, it is not a reflection of weak leadership. Deep cultural change often comes through failures more than happens through following "safe" procedures or ten recommended steps to success borrowed from an outside source.

According to Schein, all groups face at least five basic survival problems.[23] These basic survival needs appear clearly in the hidden lives of congregations. Congregational leaders who want to focus on challenge and cultural change will need to be aware of these basic survival needs and provide effective leadership for the congregation in meeting them. First, *congregations need to define the fundamental mission that justifies its existence*—its primary task. This requires a clear theology of the nature of the Church, one that informs the leaders and members of the mission of the congregation. Second, *congregations need to set specific goals derived from the mission.* These goals both inform and are derived from the vision that congregational leaders offer the members. These goals also inform how the structural elements like written goal statements, formal planning procedures and their outcomes, and defining for the congregation targets and deadlines for accomplishing the goals facilitate the realization of the vision.

Third, *congregations need to decide what means they will use to accomplish the goals.* The structures for accomplishing the congregation's goals are the defined formal organization (its polity), the assigned tasks and roles of clergy, leaders, and other members, and the task of putting in place procedures for solving problems and making decisions. The fourth survival need involves *measuring and monitoring whether or not goals are being accomplished*—an element that many congregations fail to deal with. This includes tapping into the Controlling hidden life force and putting in place formal information and control systems, managerial planning, budgeting, and review processes. Finally, congregations need to put in place *ways of getting back on course by fixing problems once they are identified,* like when the congregation discovers it is off target or not accomplishing its ministry goals, or when the leaders see that the declining forces are affecting the vitality of a life stage. A congregation needs effective processes for remedying situations, fixing problems, and getting itself back on track.

A focus on cultural change and challenge helps congregational leaders to work on emotional process rather than react to or focus on content. This focus on the influence of culture, with the underlying hidden life forces, helps remind congregational leaders that there are only three ways that cultural relationship systems change. The first is when a congregation experiences survival panic. This is when a congregation realizes it has given in to the degenerating hidden life forces to such an extent that, unless it changes the church's culture and system, it will die. Understanding the dynamics of the lifespan will help leaders understand that a congregation may get to this point only after a long period of denial. The second way that relationship systems change is through the influence of a strong, self-defined, visionary leader who is willing to pay the price and commit to the tenure necessary to realize systemic change. This kind of leader knows that he or she cannot bring about change in the congregation alone, and will practice sharing the leadership functions as appropriate by empowering the other congregational leaders. The third way that congregations change in their culture and in the relationship system is in response to the call of God and the movement of the Spirit. Like congregational leaders, God also works through influence and not coercion. Like them, God also seeks to call out the members of the Church to engage in ministry and empower them through the Spirit. Like them, God works primarily through relationships, and only secondarily through institutional organizational systems. Like them, God also trumpets a vision and lays out the mission and mandate the Church is to fulfill.

Conclusion

Clergy and lay congregational leaders who want to be effective in the Church need to acquire a theological and cultural understanding of the nature of faith communities. Effective congregational leaders work at understanding the hidden lives of congregations and on the appropriate and necessary leadership functions that only they can provide for the congregation. They take responsibility for providing these functions, and are able to give away responsibility for other leadership functions and ministries that rightly belong to the church members. Effective congregational leaders know that their greatest impact on the congregation will be through their influence, and will not come as a result of their expertise, skills, or competence—as important as those qualities are. They maintain the vision that they are called to build the congregation as an expression of the Body of Christ by empowering the members and by building structures and processes that facilitate its redemptive presence in the world for the benefit of both the members and of the community at large.

Effective congregational leaders stay focused on the things that will enable them to function best in their capacity as leaders, including the creation of a supportive, enabling environment. They cultivate and communicate clear attainable goals that are consistent with their vision for the church and practice being an influential presence who can effectively break the homeostasis that is holding the congregation back. Effective leaders use a systematic, planned process that is open and subject to alteration; welcome the involvement of the community as an active partner and participant in any major change; assert the presence of effective leadership with vision, a sense of mission, the practice of courage, and staying emotionally connected with the members; and value a commitment to renewal that disallows compromising for lesser goals but instead always challenges the congregation to higher levels of relevance.

Appendix A

Hidden Life Church Profile Summary

DIRECTIONS: Take your best informed guess and choose the profile element that best fits your congregation. Determine how this profile element influences your church.

Profile		*Influence*
Life Stage	❐ Establishing Stage ❐ Formation and Formatting Stage ❐ Adolescence Stage ❐ Prime Stage ❐ Maturity Stage ❐ Aristocracy Stage ❐ Bureaucracy Stage ❐ Dissolution Stage	
Church Size	❐ Family (< 50) ❐ Shepherding (50–150) ❐ Programmed (150–350) ❐ Corporation (350 >) ❐ Mega (1000 >) ❐ Size-independent	
Socioeconomic	❐ Lower-income ❐ Middle-income ❐ Upper-income ❐ Affluent	
Staff	❐ Single-staffed ❐ Multistaffed ❐ Specialized staff	
Staff Tenure	❐ Long pastoral tenures ❐ Short pastoral tenures ❐ Long staff tenures ❐ Short staff tenures	

Profile		*Influence*
Membership Tenure	❑ Stable membership tenures ❑ Short-term membership tenures	
Financial Giving	❑ Generous ❑ Adequate for development ❑ Adequate for maintenance ❑ Challenged	
Rate of Growth	❑ Rapid Growth ❑ Steady Growth ❑ Maintenance Growth ❑ Decline	
Type of Growth (predominant)	❑ Biological ❑ New converts ❑ Transfer of membership ❑ Transitional membership	
Organization	❑ Organizational maintenance organization ❑ Program maintenance organization ❑ Needs-based organization ❑ Mission-focused organization ❑ Gifts-based organization ❑ "Teams" organization	
Processes in the Congregation	❑ Facilitate the formation of values and vision ❑ Inhibit the formation of values and vision	

Appendix B

The Hidden Life of Congregational Identity

DIRECTIONS: Use this worksheet to help you identify your congregation's identity. Remember that your congregation's identity is arrived at by the way in which it faces and uses its corporate experiences in relation to its spirituality, stance, and style.

Key components of identity...

Spirituality Churches adopt or emphasize a preferred spirituality. This often is influenced by faith tradition, the personality of the pastor, or by culture.	❐ Cognitive (head) spirituality ❐ Affective (heart) spirituality ❐ Pilgrim (feet) spirituality ❐ Mystic (soul) spirituality ❐ Servant (hands) spirituality ❐ Crusader spirituality
Stance Your church's stance has to do with how it views its mission and ministry. Often a congregation's stance is determined by its immediate context, sometimes it is determined by a doctrinal or a mission task emphasis.	❐ Urban Ministry Church ❐ University Church ❐ Country Club Church ❐ Community Church ❐ Mission Church ❐ Pillar Church ❐ Shepherd Church ❐ Outreach Church ❐ Crusader Church
Style Style has to do with the outward corporate expression of the spirituality that your church embraces. These styles can be plotted on a spectrum.	Open..Closed Inward-focused.........................Outward-focused Inviting..Excluding Culturally Conservative.............................Liberal Professional.....................................*Laissez-faire* Conventional...Pioneering

Appendix C

The Hidden Life of Congregational Theology

DIRECTIONS: You can use this worksheet to think about your congregation's theology.

Metaphors for the Church...

Major Major metaphors of the Church tend to emphasize the corporate nature of the Church and a connection with the Old Testament understanding of God's relationship with God's people.	❏ Body of Christ ❏ Fellowship of the Saints ❏ The People of God ❏ Community of Faith ❏ Kingdom ❏ The New Creation ❏ The New Israel ❏ A Mystery
Minor Minor metaphors of the Church tend to focus on illustrating God's relationship with the Church and the Church's relationship to the world.	❏ Salt of the Earth ❏ Table of the Lord ❏ The Boat ❏ The Altar ❏ The Ark ❏ The Cup of the Lord ❏ Fish and Fish Net ❏ Wine ❏ Unleavened Bread ❏ Branches of the Vine ❏ Vineyard ❏ God's Planting ❏ Fig Tree ❏ God's Vineyard ❏ Olive Tree ❏ God's Building ❏ Bride of Christ ❏ Building on the Rock ❏ The Elect Lady ❏ Wearers of the White ❏ Citizens Robes ❏ Exiles ❏ The Poor
Emphases Understanding the nature of the Church through metaphors tends to highlight the following points:	❏ The nature of the church is more corporate than individual ❏ The Church has a vertical relationship with God, who is the source of the Church's being ❏ The Church has a horizontal relationship to the world that is in keeping with God's purpose for the Church ❏ Any one metaphor is inadequate to contain a full understanding of the *nature* of the Church ❏ Any single expression of the Church—in terms of form and polity or congregational model—cannot fully be equated with the Church.

Some Major Theological Issues....

Theology	Practice
In this column, articulate your response as to what theology your congregation adheres to:	*In this column give evidence that your congregation holds that theology by the way it engages in its practice(s):*
What primary metaphor of Church informs our congregation?	
What is our theology of Christian calling?	
What is our theology of worship?	
What is our theology of Christian discipleship?	
What is our theology of what constitutes membership in our church?	
What is our theology of how the Church engages in and with the world?	

Appendix D

The Hidden Life of Congregational Vision

DIRECTIONS: Your congregation's vision is what you will choose to be based on who you have been and what you are called to be. Use the following as a tool to help you begin to articulate your congregation's vision.

The process of vision...

Clarity of values	You know what you value by what you practice and who you follow. What are those things that we value most?
Clarity of identity	Write out your statement of identity: "We are . . . "
The courage to choose	What decisions does your congregation need to make about... ❏ Its ministry ❏ Its direction ❏ Its mission ❏ Its practices To what do we need to commit? What will it cost? (either way)

Appendix E

The Hidden Life of Congregational Leadership

The primary functions of leadership are:
- ❏ to provide vision
- ❏ to challenge toward integrity of vision
- ❏ to facilitate mature emotional process
- ❏ to influence through authentic relationship

If you are needing to make changes in your congregation to address issues related to the hidden life dynamics consider the following leadership actions as they relate to the hidden life of your congregation:

1. Clarify and articulate your theology of Church

2. Clarify your vision

3. Work to remove obstacles to growth and health

4. Establish structures and processes that enable the realization of your vision

5. Support innovative, entrepreneurial ministry efforts and programs

6. Redesign and personalize ministry programs

7. Emphasize ministry relevance and discipleship

8. Invest in your congregational resources: committed and mature members

9. Build strategic and complementary networks (denominational, local organizations, like-minded churches)

10. Incorporate systems thinking into strategic thinking

11. Critically assess program quality, congruence, and relevance

12. Clarify and exploit your unique congregational advantages

Work at making essential changes (rather than managerial or cosmetic) to bureaucracy, culture, and assumptions to match your vision. Start with your strengths, but don't neglect to address your deficits.

Notes

Introduction

1. Carl S. Dudley, Jackson W. Carroll, and James P. Wind, eds., *Carriers of Faith: Lessons from Congregational Studies* (Louisville: Westminster John Knox Press, 1991), p. 9.

2. C. Ellis Nelson, ed., *Congregations: Their Power to Form and Transform* (Atlanta: John Knox Press, 1988), p. 5.

Part One: Understanding the Congregation

1. Edwin H. Friedman, *Generation to Generation: Family Process in Church and Synagogue* (New York: Guilford Press, 1985).

Chapter 1

1. Penny Edgell Becker, *Congregations in Conflict: Cultural Models of Local Religious Life* (Cambridge, England: Cambridge University Press, 1999), p. 8.

2. Bruce C. Birch, "Memory in Congregational Life," in C. Ellis Nelson, ed., *Congregations: Their Power to Form and Transform* (Atlanta: John Knox Press, 1988), p. 26.

3. Barna Research Online Website, http://www.barna.org.

4. Generous Giving Website, "Statistics," http://www.generousgiving.org/page.asp?sec=4&page=311. See also John L. Ronsvalle and Sylvia Ronsvalle, *The State of Church Giving through 2000* (Champaign, Ill.: Empty Tomb, 2002), p. 40.

5. David C. Leege, "The Changing Context of Parish Leadership," in Carl S. Dudley, Jackson W. Carroll, and James P. Wind, eds., *Carriers of Faith: Lessons from Congregational Studies* (Louisville: Westminster John Knox Press, 1991), p. 44.

6. Edward H. Hammett, *Making the Church Work: Converting the Church for the 21st Century* (Macon, Ga.: Smyth & Helwys, 1997), p. 32.

7. Barna Research Online Website, http://www.barna.org.

8. See Israel Galindo, "The Myth of Competence," *Congregations* 29, no. 1 (Winter 2003): pp. 17–19.

9. C. John Miller, *Outgrowing the Ingrown Church*, Ministry Resources Library series (Grand Rapids, Mich.: Zondervan, 1986), p. 34.

Chapter 2

1. Jackson W. Carroll, "The Congregation as Chameleon: How the Present Interprets the Past," in C. Ellis Nelson, ed., *Congregations: Their Power to Form and Transform* (Atlanta: John Knox Press, 1988), p. 46.

2. Penny Edgell Becker, *Congregations in Conflict: Cultural Models of Local Religious Life* (Cambridge, England: Cambridge University Press, 1999), p. 181.

3. Nancy Tatom Ammerman, *Congregation & Community* (New Brunswick, N.J.: Rutgers University Press, 1997), p. 337.

4. Carl S. Dudley and Earle Hilgert, *New Testament Tensions and the Contemporary Church* (Philadelphia: Fortress Press, 1987), p. 14.

5. Ibid.

6. Bruce C. Birch, "Memory in Congregational Life," in Nelson, ed., *Congregations*, p. 28.

7. Cf. Johannes Quasten et al., *Epistles of St. Clement of Rome and Ignatius of Antioch* (New York: Paulist Press, 1946); First Epistle of Clement to the Corinthians 42:X; Ignatius to the Ephesians 4:1; Ignatius to the Philadelphians 1:1-2 and Salutation.

8. Becker, *Congregations in Conflict*, p. 211; referencing Phillip Hammond, "Religion and the Persistence of Identity," *Journal for the Scientific Study of Religion* 27 (I): 1–11.

9. Ibid.

10. Donald Livingstone, "Communitarians, Liberals, and Other Enemies of Community and Liberty," *Chronicles* (July 2002), p. 23.

11. Dudley and Hilgert, *New Testament Tensions,* p. 33.

12. James F. Hopewell, *Congregation: Stories and Structures* (Philadelphia: Fortress Press, 1987). See also Dan P. McAdams, *The Stories We Live By: Personal Myths and the Making of the Self* (New York: William Morrow & Co., 1993), and C. Ellis Nelson, *Where Faith Begins* (Atlanta: John Knox Press, 1984).

Chapter 3

1. C. John Miller, *Outgrowing the Ingrown Church*, Ministry Resources Library series (Grand Rapids, Mich.: Zondervan, 1986), p. 20.

2. Paul S. Minear, *Images of the Church in the New Testament* (Philadelphia: Westminster, 1960).

3. Bruce C. Birch, "Memory in Congregational Life," in C. Ellis Nelson, ed., *Congregations: Their Power to Form and Transform* (Atlanta: John Knox Press, 1988), p. 23.

4. Penny Edgell Becker, *Congregations in Conflict: Cultural Models of Local Religious Life* (Cambridge, England: Cambridge University Press, 1999), p. 12.

5. H. Richard Niebuhr, *Christ and Culture* (New York: Harper & Row, 1951).

6. H. Barry Evans and Bruce Reed, "The Success and Failure of a Religious Club," in Carl S. Dudley, ed., *Building Effective Ministry: Theory and Practice in the Local Church* (San Francisco: Harper & Row, Publishers, 1983), p. 39.

7. James Desmond Anderson, "Crisis, Communication, and Courage: A Ministry Development Approach," in Dudley, ed., *Building Effective Ministry*, p. 193.

8. Becker, *Congregations in Conflict*, p. 30.

9. Ibid., p. 14.

Part Two: Understanding the Hidden Lives of Congregations

1. Martin F. Saarinen, *The Life Cycle of a Congregation* (Bethesda, Md.: Alban Institute, 1986), identifies all but Systemic Anxiety as listed here but refers to these as the congregation's "gene structures." He includes four dynamics and calls them energy, program, administration, and inclusion. The use of the term *dynamic* in this study is used as an attempt to describe more accurately the hidden life forces at play. The gene metaphor is popular, as is, increasingly, the use of "DNA" as a metaphor. But genes and DNA do not work the way they are described when typically used as metaphor, which means that, ultimately, those metaphors are not helpful in understanding whatever is under consideration.

2. Donald Eugene Miller, "Centers of Vision and Energy," in C. Ellis Nelson, ed., *Congregations: Their Power to Form and Transform* (Atlanta: John Knox Press, 1988), p. 116.

3. Margaret J. Wheatley and Myron Kellnor-Rogers, *A Simpler Way* (San Francisco: Berrett-Koehler Publishers, 1996), p. 28. See also Wheatley's book *Leadership and the New Science: Discovering Order in a Chaotic World*, 2nd ed. (San Francisco: Berrett-Koehler Publishers, 1999), for an excellent treatment on self-organizing systems.

4. Newton Malony, "A Framework for Understanding and Helping the Church: Organization Development," in Carl S. Dudley, ed., *Building Effective Ministry: Theory and Practice in the Local Church* (San Francisco: Harper & Row, Publishers, 1983), p. 176.

5. Ibid., p. 179.

Chapter 4

1. Ichak Adizes, "Organizational Passages—Diagnosing and Treating Life Cycle Problems of Organizations," *Organizational Dynamics* 8, no. 1 (Summer 1979); Martin F. Saarinen, *The Life Cycle of a Congregation* (Bethesda, Md.: Alban Institute, 1986).

2. William Shakespeare, *As You Like It,* act 2, scene VII (Cambridge, England: Cambridge University Press, 1948), pp. 38–39.

3. Edwin H. Friedman, lecture notes, 1992.

4. Sue Mallory, *The Equipping Church: Serving Together to Transform Lives* (Grand Rapids, Mich.: Zondervan, 2001); Peter Senge, *The Fifth Discipline* (New York: Currency, 1990).

5. Saarinen, "The Life Cycle of a Congregation."

6. See Gil Rendle, *The Multigenerational Congregation: Meeting the Leadership Challenge* (Bethesda, Md.: Alban Institute, 2001).

7. Edwin H. Friedman, "Bowen Theory and Therapy," in A. S. Gurman and D. P. Kniskern, *Handbook of Family Therapy*, Vol. II (New York: Brunner/Maze, 1991), p. 140.

8. Ernest Becker, *The Denial of Death* (New York: Free Press, 1997).

9. Nancy Tatom Ammerman, *Congregation & Community* (New Brunswick, N.J.: Rutgers University Press, 1997), p. 328.

Chapter 5

1. James Desmond Anderson, "Crisis, Communication, and Courage: A Ministry Development Approach," in Carl S. Dudley, ed., *Building Effective Ministry: Theory and Practice in the Local Church* (San Francisco: Harper & Row, 1983), p. 195.

2. Janet F. Fishburn, "Leading: *Paideia* in a New Key," in C. Ellis Nelson, ed., *Congregations: Their Power to Form and Transform* (Atlanta: John Knox Press, 1988), p. 209.

3. Alice Mann, *The In-Between Church: Navigating Size Transitions in Congregations* (Bethesda, Md.: Alban Institute, 1998); Loren B. Mead, *More Than Numbers: The Way Churches Grow* (Bethesda, Md.: Alban Institute, 1993); Beth Ann Gaede, ed., *Size Transitions in Congregations*, Harvesting the Learnings series (Bethesda, Md.: Alban Institute, 2001); Arlin J. Rothauge, *Sizing Up a Congregation for New Member Ministry*, available for download from http://www.ecusa.anglican.org/congdev_4579_ENG_HTM.htm.

4. Cynthia Woolever and Deborah Bruce, *A Field Guide to U.S. Congregations: Who's Going Where and Why* (Louisville: Westminster John Knox Press, 2002), p. 18. Woolever and Bruce report that, in terms of people who "regularly participate," the average (median) size is 110. In terms of the average attendance in worship, the average among all congregations is 90 people.

5. Malcolm Gladwell, *The Tipping Point: How Little Things Can Make A Big Difference* (New York: Little, Brown, 2000). The concept of the "tipping point" comes from the field of epidemiology. The concept states that small changes will have little or no effect on a system until a critical mass is reached. Then a further small change "tips" the system and a large effect is observed. Gladwell applies the concept of the tipping point to sociological, educational, business, and relational contexts.

6. Penny Edgell Becker, *Congregations in Conflict: Cultural Models of Local Religious Life* (Cambridge, England: Cambridge University Press, 1999), p. 12.

7. Ibid., p. 14.

8. James W. Fowler, *Becoming Adult, Becoming Christian: Adult Development and Christian Faith* (San Francisco: Harper & Row, 1984), p. 50.

9. James W. Fowler and Sam Keen, *Life Maps: Conversations on the Journey of Faith*, ed. Jerome Berryman (Waco: Word Books, 1978), p. 18.

Chapter 6

1. Israel Galindo, *The Craft of Christian Teaching* (Valley Forge, Pa.: Judson Press, 1998), pp. 34–37.

2. See Benjamin S. Bloom et al., *Taxonomy of Educational Objectives: Hand-book II: Affective Domain* (New York: David McKay Co., 1964).

3. James W. Fowler, *Stages of Faith: The Psychology of Human Development and the Quest for Meaning* (New York: Harper & Row, 1981).

4. James W. Fowler, *Becoming Adult, Becoming Christian: Adult Development and Christian Faith* (San Francisco: Harper & Row, 1984), p. 38.

5. Fowler, *Stages of Faith*, p. 184.

6. Jackson W. Carroll, "The Congregation as Chameleon: How the Present Interprets the Past," in C. Ellis Nelson, ed., *Congregations: Their Power to Form and Transform* (Atlanta: John Knox Press, 1988), p. 53.

7. Corinne Ware, *Discover Your Spiritual Type: A Guide to Individual and Con-gregational Growth* (Bethesda, Md.: Alban Institute, 1995), provides four styles based on the work of Urban Holmes: the spirituality of the head, the heart, mystic spirituality, and kingdom spirituality. See Urban T. Holmes, *Spirituality for Ministry,* The Library of Episcopalian Classics (Harrisburg, Pa.: Morehouse, 2002) and *A History of Christian Spirituality: An Analytical Introduction*, The Library of Episco-palian Classics (Harrisburg, Pa.: Morehouse, 2002).

8. Ibid.

9. Peter L. Benson and Carolyn H. Elkin, *Effective Christian Education: A Na-tional Study of Protestant Congregations: A Summary Report on Faith, Loyalty, and Congregational Life* (Minneapolis: Search Institute, 1990), p. 2.

10. Jonathan Edwards, *The Works of Jonathan Edwards*, Edward Hickman, ed. (Edinburgh, Scotland: Banner of Truth Trust, 1995), vol. 3, sect. III, p. 159.

Chapter 7

1. See Jackson W. Carroll, "Preserving Christian Identity: The Task of Leader-ship in the Congregation," in Carl S. Dudley, Jackson W. Carroll, and James P. Wind, eds., *Carriers of Faith: Lessons from Congregational Studies* (Louisville: Westminster John Knox Press, 1991), p. 125.

2. Jackson W. Carroll, "The Congregation as Chameleon: How the Present Interprets the Past," in C. Ellis Nelson, ed., *Congregations: Their Power to Form and Transform* (Atlanta: John Knox Press, 1988), p. 62.

3. Carl S. Dudley and Earle Hilgert, *New Testament Tensions and the Contem-porary Church* (Philadelphia: Fortress Press, 1987), p. 114.

4. Carroll, "The Congregation as Chameleon," p. 67.

5. Carl S. Dudley, "Using Church Images for Commitment, Conflict, and Re-newal," in Nelson, ed., *Congregations*, p. 93.

6. Nancy Tatom Ammerman, *Congregation & Community* (New Brunswick, N.J.: Rutgers University Press, 1997), p. 324.

7. See Carl S. Dudley and Sally A. Johnson, "Congregational Self-Images for Social Ministry," in Dudley et al., eds., *Carriers of Faith*, pp. 104–21, for their de-scription of five self-image types, some not included here, and their relationship to the church's response to mission and ministry.

8. Thomas Groome, *Christian Religious Education: Sharing Our Story and Vision* (San Francisco: Jossey-Bass, 1999).

9. Bruce C. Birch, "Memory in Congregational Life," in Nelson, ed., *Congregations,* p. 29.

10. Max Weber, *The Sociology of Religion*, trans. Ephraim Fischoff (New York: Free Press of Glencoe, 1964), p. 107.

11. Carroll, "The Congregation as Chameleon," p. 62.

Chapter 8

1. Edwin H. Friedman, *A Failure of Nerve: Leadership in the Age of the Quick Fix*, ed. Edward W. Beal and Margaret M. Treadwell (Bethesda, Md.: The Edwin H. Friedman Estate, 1999), p. 29.

2. Dietrich Bonhoeffer, *No Rusty Swords: Letters, Lectures, and Notes 1928–1936* in *The Collected Works of Dietrich Bonhoeffer*, ed. Edwin H. Robinson and John Bowden (New York: Harper & Row, 1965), p. 196.

3. H. Paul Douglas and Edmund deS. Brunner, *The Protestant Church as a Social Institution* (New York: Russell and Russell, 1935), cited in Jackson W. Carroll, "The Congregation as Chameleon," in C. Ellis Nelson, ed., *Congregations: Their Power to Form and Transform* (Atlanta: John Knox Press, 1988), p. 67.

4. Jay P. Dolan, "Patterns of Leadership in the Congregation," in James P. Wind and James W. Lewis, eds., *American Congregations, Vol. 2: New Perspectives in the Study of Congregations* (Chicago: The University of Chicago Press, 1994), p. 225.

5. E. P. Hollander, "Conformity, Status and Idiosyncrasy Credit," *Psychological Review* 65 (1958): pp. 117–27.

6. David C. Leege, "The Changing Context of Parish Leadership," in Carl S. Dudley, Jackson W. Carroll, and James P. Wind, eds., *Carriers of Faith: Lessons from Congregational Studies* (Louisville: Westminster John Knox Press, 1991), pp. 47–48.

7. Nancy Tatom Ammerman, *Congregation & Community* (New Brunswick, N.J.: Rutgers University Press, 1997), p. 344.

8. Daniel Goleman, Richard Boyatzis, and Annie McKee, *Primal Leadership: Realizing the Power of Emotional Intelligence* (Boston: Harvard Business School Press, 2002), p. 58.

9. George Barna, *The Power of Vision* (Ventura, Calif.: Regal Books, 1992), p. 109.

10. Ibid., p. 29.

11. Israel Galindo, "Staying Put," *Congregations* 30, no. 1 (Winter 2004): pp. 34–37.

12. Carroll, "The Congregation as Chameleon," in Nelson, ed., *Congregations*, pp. 62–63.

13. Jackson Carroll, Carl S. Dudley, and William McKinney, *Handbook for Congregational Studies* (Nashville: Abingdon Press, 1986), p. 12.

14. Carl S. Dudley, "Using Church Images for Commitment, Conflict, and Renewal," in Nelson, ed., *Congregations*, p. 90.

15. Goleman et al., *Primal Leadership*, p. 42.

16. Ibid., p. 43.

17. Carl S. Dudley and Earle Hilgert, *New Testament Tensions and the Contemporary Church* (Philadelphia: Fortress Press, 1987), p. 117.

18. C. John Miller, *Outgrowing the Ingrown Church*, Ministry Resources Library series (Grand Rapids, Mich.: Zondervan, 1986), p. 19.

19. R. Paul Stevens and Phil Collins, *The Equipping Pastor: A Systems Approach to Congregational Leadership* (Bethesda, Md.: Alban Institute, 1993), p. 73.

20. Jackson W. Carroll, "Preserving Christian Identity: The Task of Leadership in the Congregation," in Dudley et al., eds., *Carriers of Faith*, p. 130.

21. James Desmond Anderson, "Crisis, Communication, and Courage: A Ministry Development Approach," in Carl S. Dudley, ed., *Building Effective Ministry: Theory and Practice in the Local Church* (San Francisco: Harper & Row, 1983), p. 204.

22. Don Browning, "Integrating the Approaches: A Practical Theology," in Dudley, ed., *Building Effective Ministry*, p. 220.

23. Carroll, "Preserving Christian Identity," p. 126.

24. Bruce C. Birch, "Memory in Congregational Life," in Nelson, ed., *Congregations,* p. 25.

25. Donald Eugene Miller, "Centers of Vision and Energy," in Nelson, ed., *Congregations,* p. 121.

26. James F. Hopewell, "The Jovial Church: Narrative in Local Church Life," in Dudley, ed., *Building Effective Ministry*, p. 80.

27. Birch, "Memory in Congregational Life," p. 26.

28. Miller, "Centers of Vision and Energy," p. 131.

29. Janet F. Fishburn, "Leading: *Paideia* in a New Key," in Nelson, ed., *Congregations,* pp. 209–10.

30. Stevens and Collins, *The Equipping Pastor*, p. 76.

31. Dudley and Hilgert, *New Testament Tensions*, p. 66.

32. Anderson, "Crisis, Communication, and Courage," p. 194.

33. Goleman et al., *Primal Leadership*, p. 51.

34. Stevens and Collins, *The Equipping Pastor*, p. 109.

35. Birch, "Memory in Congregational Life," p. 116.

Chapter 9

1. Daniel Goleman, Richard Boyatzis, and Annie McKee, *Primal Leadership: Realizing the Power of Emotional Intelligence* (Boston: Harvard Business School Press, 2002), p. 42.

2. Ibid., p. 38.

3. Donald Eugene Miller, "Centers of Vision and Energy," in C. Ellis Nelson, *Congregations: Their Power to Form and Transform* (Atlanta: John Knox Press, 1988), p. 118.

4. R. Paul Stevens and Phil Collins, *The Equipping Pastor: A Systems Approach to Congregational Leadership* (Bethesda, Md.: Alban Institute, 1993), p. xviii.

5. Israel Galindo, "The Myth of Competence," *Congregations* 29, no. 4 (Winter 2002): p. 17.

6. In case you're wondering, the three other classic books, in this author's opinion, are: (1) *The Prince*, by Nicolo Machiavelli (various editions available). He

was the first to conceive of the group (the city/state) as a system and to define leadership according to function rather than primarily by station, status, personality, or power; (2) *Think and Grow Rich*, by Napoleon Hill (various editions available), one of the first books to popularize and propagate the singularly powerful idea that if you can conceptualize it (envision it), you can make it a reality—a concept that speaks to the power of vision on the part of the leader; and (3) *The Leadership Challenge*, by James Kouzes and Barry Posner (San Francisco: Jossey-Bass Publishers, 1995), a timeless book on leadership that says almost everything that needs to be said about the topic. Three emerging classics that will soon prove their perennial worth, in my opinion, are: *Leadership without Easy Answers*, by Ronald A. Heifetz (Cambridge: The Belknap Press of Harvard University Press, 1994), and two books by Edwin H. Friedman, *Generation to Generation: Family Process in Church and Synagogue* (New York: Guilford Press, 1985), and *A Failure of Nerve: Leadership in the Age of the Quick Fix,* ed. Edward W. Beal and Margaret M. Treadwell (Bethesda, Md.: The Edwin H. Friedman Estate, 1999).

7. Stevens and Collins, *The Equipping Pastor*, p. 120.

8. Ibid., p. 3.

9. James W. Fowler, *Becoming Adult, Becoming Christian: Adult Development and Christian Faith* (San Francisco: Harper & Row, 1984), p. 92.

10. Goleman et al., *Primal Leadership*, p. 46.

11. Ibid.

12. Friedman, *Generation to Generation*.

13. Goleman et al., *Primal Leadership*, p. 93. Goleman cites a study that suggests that the more responsible the leader becomes in the organization, the greater the risk of CEO disease. He states that top executives typically get the least reliable information about how they are doing and cites an analysis of 177 separate studies that assessed more than 28,000 managers, which found that feedback on performance became less consistent the higher the manager's position or the more complex the manager's role.

14. Nancy Tatom Ammerman, *Congregation & Community* (New Brunswick, N.J.: Rutgers University Press, 1997), p. 327.

15. Friedman, *A Failure of Nerve*, p. 19.

Chapter 10

1. R. Paul Stevens and Phil Collins, *The Equipping Pastor: A Systems Approach to Congregational Leadership* (Bethesda, Md.: Alban Institute, 1993), p. 88.

2. Janet F. Fishburn, "Leading: *Paideia* in a New Key," in C. Ellis Nelson, ed., *Congregations: Their Power to Form and Transform* (Atlanta: John Knox Press, 1988), p. 209.

3. Jay P. Dolan, "Patterns of Leadership in the Congregation," in James P. Wind and James W. Lewis, eds., *American Congregations, Vol. 2: New Perspectives in the Study of Congregations* (Chicago: The University of Chicago Press, 1994), p. 225.

4. Edgar H. Schein, *Organizational Culture and Leadership* (San Francisco: Jossey-Bass Publishers, 1985), p. xi.

5. Ibid., p. 43.

6. Stevens and Collins, *The Equipping Pastor,* p. 109.

7. Daniel Goleman, Richard Boyatzis, and Annie McKee, *Primal Leadership: Realizing the Power of Emotional Intelligence* (Boston: Harvard Business School Press, 2002), p. 219.

8. Ibid.

9. Ibid., p. 82.

10. Nancy Tatom Ammerman, *Congregation & Community* (New Brunswick, N.J.: Rutgers University Press, 1997), p. 330.

11. Fishburn, "Leading," p. 208.

12. Ammerman, *Congregation & Community*, p. 327.

13. Goleman et al., *Primal Leadership*, p. 36.

14. Ibid., p. 49.

15. Edgar H. Schein, *Process Consultation: Lessons for Managers and Consultants*, vol. II (Reading, Mass.: Addison-Wesley, 1987), p. 21.

16. Ibid., p. 29.

17. Ibid.

18. Israel Galindo, "The Myth of Competence," *Congregations* 29, no. 4 (Winter 2002): pp. 17–19.

19. Edwin H. Friedman, *Generation to Generation: Family Process in Church and Synagogue* (New York: Guilford Press, 1985), p. 22.

20. Edwin H. Friedman, *A Failure of Nerve: Leadership in the Age of the Quick Fix*, ed. Edward W. Beal and Margaret M. Treadwell (Bethesda, Md.: The Edwin H. Friedman Estate, 1999), p. 257.

21. Fishburn, "Leading," p. 209.

22. Goleman et al., *Primal Leadership*, p. 57.

23. Schein, *Process Consultation*, p. 44.

Bibliography

Ackerman, John. *Spiritual Awakening: A Guide to Spiritual Life in Congregations*. Bethesda, Md.: Alban Institute, 1994.

Adizes, Ichak. "Organizational Passages—Diagnosing and Treating Life Cycle Problems of Organizations." *Organizational Dynamics* 8, no. 1 (Summer 1979): pp. 3–25.

Ahlen, J. Timothy, and J. V. Thomas, *One Church, Many Congregations: The Key Church Strategy*. Ministry for the Third Millennium series, ed. Lyle E. Schaller. Nashville: Abingdon Press, 1999.

Ammerman, Nancy Tatom. *Congregation & Community*. New Brunswick, N.J.: Rutgers University Press, 1997.

Anderson, James Desmond. "Crisis, Communication, and Courage: A Ministry Development Approach." In *Building Effective Ministry: Theory and Practice in the Local Church*, ed. Carl S. Dudley, pp. 192–207. San Francisco: Harper & Row, 1983.

Armour, Michael C., and Don Browning. *Systems Sensitive Leadership: Empowering Diversity without Polarizing the Church*. Joplin, Mo.: College Press Publishing Company, 2000.

Avery, William O. *Revitalizing Congregations: Focusing and Healing through Transitions*. Bethesda, Md.: The Alban Institute, 2002.

Barna, George. *The Power of Vision*. Ventura, Calif.: Regal Books, 1992.

Becker, Ernest. *The Denial of Death*. New York: Free Press, 1997.

Becker, Penny Edgell. *Congregations in Conflict: Cultural Models of Local Religious Life*. Cambridge, England: Cambridge University Press, 1999.

Benson, Peter L., and Carolyn H. Elkin. *Effective Christian Education: A National Study of Protestant Congregations: A Summary Report on Faith, Loyalty, and Congregational Life*. Minneapolis: Search Institute, 1990.

Birch, Bruce C. "Memory in Congregational Life." In *Congregations: Their Power to Form and Transform*, ed. C. Ellis Nelson, pp. 20–42. Atlanta: John Knox Press, 1988.

Bloom, Benjamin S., et al. *Taxonomy of Educational Objectives: Handbook II: Affective Domain*. New York: David McKay Co., 1964.

Bonhoeffer, Dietrich. *No Rusty Swords: Letters, Lectures, and Notes 1928–1936.* In *The Collected Works of Dietrich Bonhoeffer,* ed. Edwin H. Robinson and John Bowden. New York: Harper & Row, 1965.

Brown, Wilena G. *Faithstyles in Congregations: Living Together in a Christian Community.* Toronto, Ontario: United Church Publishing House, 1994.

Browning, Don. "Integrating the Approaches: A Practical Theology." In *Building Effective Ministry: Theory and Practice in the Local Church,* ed. Carl S. Dudley, pp. 220–37. San Francisco: Harper & Row, 1983.

Carroll, Jackson W., "The Congregation as Chameleon: How the Present Interprets the Past." In *Congregations: Their Power to Form and Transform,* ed. C. Ellis Nelson, pp. 43–69. Atlanta: John Knox Press, 1988.

———. "Preserving Christian Identity: The Task of Leadership in the Congregation." In *Carriers of Faith: Lessons from Congregational Studies,* ed. Carl S. Dudley, Jackson W. Carroll, James P. Wind, pp. 125–40. Louisville: Westminster John Knox Press, 1991.

———, Carl S. Dudley, and William McKinney. *Handbook for Congregational Studies.* Nashville: Abingdon Press, 1986.

Dawn, Marva J. *Truly The Community: Romans 12 and How to Be the Church.* Grand Rapids, Mich.: Wm. B. Eerdmans, 1992.

Dolan, Jay P. "Patterns of Leadership in the Congregation." In *American Congregations. Vol. 2: New Perspectives in the Study of Congregations,* ed. James P. Wind and James W. Lewis, pp. 225–56. Chicago: University of Chicago Press, 1994.

Douglas, H. Paul, and Edmund deS Brunner. *The Protestant Church as a Social Institution.* New York: Russell and Russell, 1935.

Dudley, Carl S. "Using Church Images for Commitment, Conflict, and Renewal." In *Congregations: Their Power to Form and Transform,* ed. C. Ellis Nelson, pp. 89–113. Atlanta: John Knox Press, 1988.

———, and Sally A. Johnson. "Congregational Self-Images for Social Ministry." In *Carriers of Faith: Lessons from Congregational Studies,* ed. Carl S. Dudley, Jackson W. Carroll, and James P. Wind, pp. 104–21. Louisville: Westminster John Knox Press, 1991.

———, and Nancy T. Ammerman. *Congregations in Transition: A Guide for Analyzing, Assessing, and Adapting in Changing Communities.* San Francisco: Jossey-Bass, 2002.

———, and Earle Hilgert. *New Testament Tensions and the Contemporary Church.* Philadelphia: Fortress Press, 1987.

———, Jackson W Carroll, James P. Wind, eds. *Carriers of Faith: Lessons from Congregational Studies.* Louisville: Westminster John Knox Press, 1991.

———, ed. *Building Effective Ministry: Theory and Practice in the Local Church.* San Francisco: Harper & Row, 1983.

Edwards, Jonathan. *The Works of Jonathan Edwards*. Vol. 3, ed. Edward Hickman. Edinburgh, Scotland: Banner of Truth Trust, 1995.

Evans, H. Barry, and Bruce Reed. "The Success and Failure of a Religious Club." In *Building Effective Ministry: Theory and Practice in the Local Church*, ed. Carl S. Dudley, pp. 38–54. San Francisco: Harper & Row, 1983.

Fishburn, Janet F. "Leading: *Paideia* in a New Key." In *Congregations: Their Power to Form and Transform*, ed. C. Ellis Nelson, pp. 193–217. Atlanta: John Knox Press, 1988.

Fowler, James W. *Becoming Adult, Becoming Christian: Adult Development and Christian Faith*. San Francisco: HarperCollins, 1984. Second edition, San Francisco: Jossey-Bass, 1999.

———, and Sam Keen. *Life Maps: Conversations on the Journey of Faith*, ed. Jerome Berryman. Waco: Word Books, 1978.

———. *Stages of Faith: The Psychology of Human Development*. New York: Harper & Row, 1981.

Friedman, Edwin H. "Bowen Theory and Therapy." In *Handbook of Family Therapy*. Vol. II, ed. A. S. Gurman and D. P. Kniskern, pp. 134–70. New York: Brunner/Maze, 1991.

———. *A Failure of Nerve: Leadership in the Age of the Quick Fix*. Ed. Edward W. Beal and Margaret M. Treadwell. Bethesda, Md.: The Edwin H. Friedman Estate, 1999.

———. *Generation to Generation: Family Process in Church and Synagogue*. New York: Guilford Press, 1985.

Gaede, Beth Ann, ed. *Ending With Hope: A Resource for Closing Congregations*. Bethesda, Md.: Alban Institute, 2002.

———, ed. *Size Transitions in Congregations*. Bethesda, Md.: Alban Institute, 2001.

Galindo, Israel. *The Craft of Christian Teaching*. Valley Forge, Pa.: Judson Press, 1998.

———. "Staying Put." *Congregations* 30, no. 1 (Winter 2004): pp. 34–37.

———. "The Myth of Competence." *Congregations* 29, no. 1 (Winter 2003): pp. 17–19.

Gladwell, Malcolm. *The Tipping Point: How Little Things Can Make a Big Difference*. New York: Little, Brown, 2000.

Goleman, Daniel, Richard Boyatzis, and Annie McKee. *Primal Leadership: Realizing the Power of Emotional Intelligence*. Boston: Harvard Business School Press, 2002.

Goldberg, Michael J. *The 9 Ways of Working*. New York: Marlow & Company, 1999.

Groome, Thomas. *Christian Religious Education: Sharing Our Story and Vision*. San Francisco: Jossey-Bass, 1999.

Gurman, A. S., and D. P. Kniskern, eds. *Handbook of Family Therapy.* Vol. II. New York: Brunner/Maze, 1991.

Hammett, Edward H. *Making the Church Work: Converting the Church for the 21st Century.* Macon, Ga.: Smyth & Helwys, 1997.

Hawkins, Thomas R. *The Learning Congregation: A New Vision of Leadership.* Louisville: Westminster John Knox Press, 1997.

Hollander, E. P. "Conformity, Status and Idiosyncrasy Credit." *Psychological Review* 65 (1958): pp. 117–27.

Holmes, Urban T. *Spirituality for Ministry.* The Library of Episcopalian Classics. Harrisburg, Pa.: Morehouse, 2002.

———. *A History of Christian Spirituality: An Analytical Introduction.* The Library of Episcopalian Classics. Harrisburg, Pa: Morehouse, 2002.

Hopewell, James F. "The Jovial Church: Narrative in Local Church Life." In *Building Effective Ministry: Theory and Practice in the Local Church,* ed. Carl S. Dudley, pp. 68–83. San Francisco: Harper & Row, 1983.

———. *Congregation: Stories and Structures.* Philadelphia: Fortress Press, 1987.

Leege, David C. "The Changing Context of Parish Leadership." In *Carriers of Faith: Lessons from Congregational Studies,* ed. Carl S. Dudley, Jackson W. Carroll, and James P. Wind, pp. 31–48. Louisville: Westminster John Knox Press, 1991.

Livingstone, Donald. "Communitarians, Liberals, and Other Enemies of Community and Liberty." *Chronicles* (July 2002): pp. 22–23.

Malony, Newton. "A Framework for Understanding and Helping the Church: Organization Development." In *Building Effective Ministry: Theory and Practice in the Local Church,* ed. Carl S. Dudley, pp. 175–91. San Francisco: Harper & Row, 1983.

Mallory, Sue. *The Equipping Church.* Grand Rapids, Mich.: Zondervan, 2001.

Mann, Alice. *The In-Between Church: Navigating Size Transitions in Congregations.* Bethesda, Md.: Alban Institute, 1998.

McAdams, Dan P. *The Stories We Live By: Personal Myths and the Making of the Self.* New York: William Morrow & Co., 1993.

McIntosh, Gary L. *One Size Doesn't Fit All: Bringing Out the Best in Any Size Church.* Grand Rapids, Mich.: Revell, 1999.

Mead, Loren B. *More Than Numbers: The Way Churches Grow.* Bethesda, Md.: Alban Institute, 1993.

Miller, C. John. *Outgrowing the Ingrown Church.* Ministry Resources Library series. Grand Rapids, Mich.: Zondervan, 1986.

Miller, Donald Eugene. "Centers of Vision and Energy." In *Congregations: Their Power to Form and Transform,* ed. C. Ellis Nelson, pp. 114–40. Atlanta: John Knox Press, 1988.

Minear, Paul S. *Images of the Church in the New Testament.* Philadelphia: Westminster, 1960.

Nelson, C. Ellis. *Where Faith Begins*. Atlanta: John Knox Press, 1984.

———, ed. *Congregations: Their Power to Form and Transform*. Atlanta: John Knox Press, 1988.

Niebuhr, H. Richard. *Christ and Culture*. New York: Harper & Row, 1951.

Palmer, Helen. *The Enneagram in Love and Work*. San Francisco: HarperSanFrancisco, 1996.

Phillips, Roy D. *Letting Go: Transforming Congregations for Ministry*. Bethesda, Md.: Alban Institute, 1999.

Quasten, Johannes, et al. *Epistles of St. Clement of Rome and Ignatius of Antioch*. New York: Paulist Press, 1946.

Rendle, Gil. *Behavioral Covenants in the Congregation: A Handbook for Honoring Differences*. Bethesda, Md.: Alban Institute, 1999.

———. *Leading Change in the Congregation: Spiritual and Organizational Tools for Leaders*. Bethesda, Md.: Alban Institute, 1998.

———. *The Multigenerational Congregation: Meeting the Leadership Challenge*. Bethesda, Md.: Alban Institute, 2001.

Richardson, Ronald W. *Becoming a Healthier Pastor: Family Systems Theory and the Pastor's Own Family*. Creative Pastoral Care and Counseling. Minneapolis: Fortress Press, 2004.

———. *Creating a Healthier Church: Family Systems Theory, Leadership, and Congregational Life*. Creative Pastoral Care and Counseling. Minneapolis: Fortress Press, 1996.

Ronsvalle, John L., and Sylvia Ronsvalle. *The State of Church Giving through 2000*. Champaign, Ill.: empty tomb, 2002.

Rothauge, Arlin J. *Sizing Up a Congregation for New Member Ministry*. Available for download from http://www.ecusa.anglican.org/congdev_4579_ENG_HTM.htm

Saarinen, Martin F. "The Life Cycle of a Congregation." Bethesda, Md.: Alban Institute, 1986. Available for download at http://www.alban.org/BookDetails.asp?ID=862

Schein, Edgar H. *Organizational Culture and Leadership*. San Francisco: Jossey-Bass, 1985.

———. *Process Consultation: Lessons for Managers and Consultants*. Vol. II. Reading, Mass.: Addison-Wesley, 1987.

Senge, Peter. *The Fifth Discipline*. New York: Currency Books, 1990.

Shive, Linda T., and Marian B. Schoenheit. *Leadership: Examining the Elusive*. 1987 Yearbook of the Association for Supervision and Curriculum Development. n.c. ASCD, 1987.

Southern, Richard, and Robert Norton. *Cracking Your Congregation's Code: Mapping Your Spiritual DNA to Create Your Future*. San Francisco: Jossey-Bass, 2001.

Steinke, Peter L. *Healthy Congregations: A Systems Approach.* Bethesda, Md.: Alban Institute, 1996.

——. *How Your Church Family Works: Understanding Congregations as Emotional Systems.* Bethesda, Md.: Alban Institute, 1993.

Stevens, R. Paul, and Phil Collins. *The Equipping Pastor: A Systems Approach to Congregational Leadership.* Bethesda, Md.: Alban Institute, 1993.

Tamney, Joseph B. *The Resilience of Conservative Religion: The Case of Popular, Conservative Protestant Congregations.* Cambridge, England: Cambridge University Press, 2002.

Ware, Corinne. *Discover Your Spiritual Type: A Guide to Individual and Congregational Growth.* Bethesda, Md.: Alban Institute, 1995.

Weber, Max. *The Sociology of Religion.* Trans. Ephraim Fischoff. New York: Free Press of Glencoe, 1964.

Wheatley, Margaret J. *Leadership and the New Science: Discovering Order in a Chaotic World.* Second edition. San Francisco: Berrett-Koehler Publishers, 1999.

——, and Myron Kellnor-Rogers. *A Simpler Way.* San Francisco: Berrett-Koehler Publishers, 1996.

Wilson, Robert L. *Shaping the Congregation.* Into Our Third Century series, ed. Ezra Earl Jones. Nashville: Abingdon Press, 1981.

Wind, James P., and James W. Lewis. *American Congregations. Vol. 2: New Perspectives in the Study of Congregations.* Chicago: University of Chicago Press, 1994.

Woolever, Cynthia, and Deborah Bruce. *A Field Guide to U.S. Congregations: Who's Going Where and Why.* Louisville: Westminster John Knox, 2002.